CHANGE IN THE SMALL COMMUNITY

CHANGE

in the

SMALL COMMUNITY

An Interdisciplinary Survey

Edited by

WILLIAM J. GORE

LEROY C. HODAPP

FRIENDSHIP PRESS
New York

LIBRARY OF CONGRESS CATALOG CARD NUMBER: 67-26279

PRINTED IN THE UNITED STATES OF AMERICA

FOR KATHLEEN JOANNA,
AND FOR ANNE LYNN AND NANCY ELLEN
AND THEIR MOTHERS

CONTENTS

FOREWORD

This book is commended to the use of church administrators who appreciate the need for more objective study of the small community context for their parish planning and to the social scientists who appreciate the institutional role of the church in the small community collective. Its writing is the cooperative endeavor of a group of churchmen and a group of social scientists, whose mutual respect led to an initial consultation—or "dialogue," as popular terminology would have it. They hope to continue the process in the form of periodical symposia on research in the small community setting.

In Chicago on October 24-25, 1966, six social scientists and seven church administrators met in a Symposium on Research in the Small Community at the invitation of the Department of Town and Country Work of the National Division, Board of Missions of The Methodist Church. Participants were: as social scientists—Roger and Mrs. Barker, Social Psychology and Child Psychology, University of Kansas; Karl Fox, Department of Economics, State University of Iowa; William Gore, Department of Government, Indiana University; Arthur Gallaher, Department of Anthropology, University of Kentucky; Sheldon Lowry, Department of Rural Sociology, Michigan State University; John Mitchell, Department of Rural Sociology, Ohio State University; Bert Swanson, Institute of Community Studies, Sarah Lawrence College; and as church administrators—William Burton, Administrative Assistant to Bishop's office, Indiana Area; James H. Davis, Executive Secretary for Research and Survey, National Division; Leroy Hodapp, District Superintendent of Bloomington District, Indiana Conference; Harold S. Huff, Executive Secretary for Town and Country Work, National Division; William Smith, Graduate Student and Assistant to District Superintendent for Town Project; B. J. Stiles, Editor, *motive magazine*; and Colin Williams, Associate Secretary, Division of Christian Life and Mission, National Council of Churches.

The papers that were read and discussed appear as chapters 2 to 8 in this book. Professor William Gore, formerly in the Department of Government, Indiana University and currently in the Department of Political Science, University of Washington, was the initiating, organizing, and guiding person for the Symposium and has further served as chief editor to complete this book. He has been assisted in the editorial work by the Rev. Leroy Hodapp, District Superintendent of Bloomington District, Indiana Conference of The Methodist Church.

A bit of developmental history will presumably be of interest to the reader. During the three-year period 1964-1966, two streams of experience have converged to bring forth this book. A hitherto unrelated group of people have given common attention to some of our small communities in our changing society and have discovered that they share concerns as churchmen and as social scientists for what is happening to these communities—or more pointedly, for what is happening to people in these communities.

One of these converging streams runs through Clay County, Indiana. Church administrators from The Methodist Church and the Evangelical United Brethren Church, facing the problems of long-range parish planning for small communities, were forced to admit a need for better knowledge of the present and future results of the dynamics of change within and impinging upon these communities. The church cannot be an isolated institution but must be related to the processes of change, and church administrators had to admit they were unprepared to cope with the responsibilities of relatedness. They lacked the knowledge, the concepts, and the models to deal with community change.

Fortunately, the churchmen discovered that Indiana University's social scientists, Professor William Gore and his colleagues, had also selected Clay County as a field site for research into the dynamics of changing small communities. A project of research and planning developed from mutual concerns for more precise understanding of the phenomena of small community change and especially the roles of agents of change (either the institutional functionaries coming to the communities or the resident-agents as indigenous leaders).

As the joint project of The Methodist Church and Indiana University developed, becoming known as "The Town Project," the perhaps unusual partnership of theologically oriented church administrators with social scientists was itself an object of some examination. One of the results of such examination was an attempt to develop a rationale for the apparently satisfying experience. The question quite naturally arose: "If theologians can enter into dialogue with *some* social scientists, why cannot social scientists communicate among the specific disciplines and why could not the theologians and the several social scientists greatly benefit from a symposium on current research on small community life?" Professor William Gore acted as the initiator and agent to bring together the five social science disciplines with a theologian and a selected group of church administrators.

The second stream was also moving, but in a separate channel of experience. Another group of church administrators—an interdenominational group of national executives responsible for planning more effective mission in nonmetropolitan communities—had become concerned with the need to bring church institutional structures into more productive involvement in the process of community change. They were especially interested in small communities where the churches seem to be more a part of community problems than of any creative solutions. They believed that a *process* of confrontation and consultation is needed among "decision-making people" on all levels, from local community residents to national leaders, to deal with issues in community life. To bring this consultation process into being, a National Consultation on the Church in Community Life met on the Ohio State University Campus, September 5–8, 1967.

A crucial consideration was soon formulated in the question: "What do we mean by saying, 'to deal with issues in community life'?" Approximately the same response was reached as in Clay County. We need objectively sound knowledge with guiding concept formulation and models of interaction systems germane to the small community context, to provide a more adequate grounding for the administrative consultation process in planning.

The two streams converged when the working papers from the

small community research symposium were gathered together into a resource volume for the National Consultation on the Church in Community Life. This book is that resource piece.

As a church administrator who has assumed, with more boldness than knowledge or ability would justify, some responsibility for experimentation in Clay County and the subsequent small community research symposium, and also as chairman of the Steering Committee for the National Consultation, I would call attention with great appreciation to the personal contributions of the participants in the symposium. In addition, with great appreciation, I acknowledge the contribution of each of the denominational representatives from the sixteen denominations and church bodies participating on the steering committee of the National Consultation.

Harold S. Huff

CHAPTER 1

AN OVERVIEW OF SOCIAL SCIENCE PERSPECTIVES TOWARD THE SMALL COMMUNITY

WILLIAM J. GORE

The small community holds a dramatic place in the history of man's attempts to order and stabilize his affairs through the creation of civilization. It must have been through the elementary forms of collective activity made possible by the family that primitive man came to appreciate the economies he could realize by channeling interpersonal relations through the structure of a social institution. The fact that social structures were advantageous because they regularized activities, reduced conflict and provided a basis for many kinds of ad hoc cooperation was probably sensed for some time before primitive man found ways of devising these structures.

There is reason to suspect that the emergence of the first communities was dependent on the invention of a kind of social relationship qualitatively different from those based on kinship. Unfortunately recorded history does not stretch back far enough to provide a reliable account of how this extrafamilial relationship came into existence. We cannot reconstruct the circumstances under which the conception of relationships based on mutually accepted obligation evolved from the more elemental, emotionally loaded relationship grounded in an all-encompassing filial loyalty. It is difficult to imagine how the primitives came to conceive of a relation-

William J. Gore is a Professor of Political Science, University of Washington. He was recently associated with the University of Indiana, where he and the Reverend Mr. Hodapp were collaborators in the Clay County Project.

ship founded, not upon total mutual reciprocity, but upon a concrete and situationally limited transaction based on a bond that was primarily cerebral rather than affective.

Some students of primitive peoples feel that the family was probably a quite satisfactory device for providing creature comforts in a hostile environment where hunting was the primary means of securing food. Not until the appearance of techniques for cultivating crops and domesticating animals was there any need for the bedouin-like primitives to devise a larger collective—one that would connect extended families into a superordinate grouping. The assertion that the first revolutionary development in human affairs was the creation of an agricultural technology some 50,000 years ago is exciting; but it fails to explain satisfactorily how nomadic bands of primitives created communities of families sometime in the following 20,000 or 30,000 years.

Even so, there is widespread agreement that the germ of civilization was contained in the creation of the extrafamilial relationships that probably manifested themselves in a circle of crude thatched huts on the northern shores of the Mediterranean about 20,000 years ago.

Interestingly enough, the appearance of these early communities did not lead to the proliferation of other, more complicated social mechanisms. The evidence we have indicates that thousands of years passed before these three basic collectives—family, tribe (extended family), and community—were expanded.

It is not difficult to imagine widely separated small societies of simple men, whose basic object was to obtain the necessities that sustain life, slowly developing herds to make available both milk and meat, as well as the cereals and other dry foods that could be preserved for long periods after they were harvested.

The availability of these staples, which served as the core of a readily available source of food, must have provided a spectacular advance over the daily scramble for food that the bedouin existence had imposed. Over time, these elementary food-producing technologies must have been woven into social mechanisms that would sustain a simple life style, based on a set of collective enterprises sufficiently powerful to sustain life in the face of an unsympathetic environment. As these social structures matured there must have come a point at which the balance between what the individual had to do through and by his own efforts and what the family, tribe, or community could do for him shifted. Sometime roughly 30,000 years ago the individual discovered that he was no longer dependent on his own efforts to sustain life. The collectives in which he involved himself accumulated the effort expended during one season. What was stored in the larder could be drawn on during other seasons, regardless of either an individual's circumstances or the availability of game.

At some point, that is, primitive man found that the family, the tribe and the community were so linked that they not only facilitated life but also became life-sustaining.

The capacity to sustain life through a network of social interrelationships is the hallmark of civilization. And though there were a succession of civilizations before the emergence of what we know as Western civilization, it is from these very social structures—and from the community above all—that our civilization was constituted.

During the period antedating Western civilization, the obligational relationship was differentiated into an increasing number of forms, many of which became the prototypes of structures which, in contrast to the community, were highly specialized. Warriors organized themselves into bands of fighting men capable of providing for the security of the community. Traders, who first linked the community to growing networks providing access into other communities and thereby extended their village's life-sustaining capacity, eventually formed themselves into companies of merchants. In what must have been similar processes the shaman probably established the idolatrous church, and the tribal leaders some form of early polity.

Over time the community evolved into a secondary structure, ordering the relationships *between* these differentiated forms—the polity, the merchant companies, the tribes, and the families. Somewhere along the way the point of balance between the individual and the collective shifted dramatically. The individual no longer partook of the collective as an external facility for sustaining life; the collective, having become the receptacle for highly stylized ways of behaving, *imposed a life style on him*. The primitive, having created the rudiments of society—surely without any intention of so doing—found that his creation was socializing and civilizing him. The community now not only sustained life; it had come to define how man should live. And when instrumentalities of social control were added to those of socialization, human affairs took on a pattern. Continuity gave birth to history, and history became a social larder from which generations of men have drawn sustenance.

This early life style was sufficiently persistent to survive—at least in some of its essentials—and we know it today as the rural way of life. That it is no longer the dominant life style of our society will be one of our central assumptions in what follows. In this, however, we are exceptions, for the rural life style comprehends such civilization as most of the people sharing this earth with us know.

SOME PERSPECTIVE-SETTING ASSUMPTIONS

Unraveling some of the origins of the small community seems a tortuous way to introduce the familiar idea that the small community is the social receptacle of the rural style of life. Yet this truism needs to be declared if we are to recognize the role of the community as the original engine of civilization. Possibly some of our difficulties in understanding the strains of our highly urbanized society can be overcome by contrasting urban forms with their forerunners in the rural setting.

The history of contemporary civilization is in some important respects synonymous with the history of urbanization and urbanism. Most of us have some sense of how what started with Sparta culminated in Los Angeles. Our own experiences with the still-evolving urban forms of our society give us some sense of the series of evolutionary mutations through which the small community was succeeded by the town which was transcended by the city which was displaced by the great city. And today that fifth-generation urban form, the metropolis, provides the structure for our life style.

The next five of the following chapters, by the representatives of five social science disciplines, are designed to assemble in one place some of our knowledge about the small community. Some assumptions articulated by the urbanist are listed here, to provide a meaningful perspective on what will be said about the small community.

1. Our society provides a range of choices in ways of living—from the rustic, rural life in the upper reaches of Appalachia to the life of a super-sophisticated Manhattan Island urbanite.

2. Urban life styles are almost everywhere preferred to rural life styles; though there is a considerable, if not complete, tolerance of and respect for diverse life styles.

3. There are real as well as latent tensions between the receptacles of alternative life styles, reflected in a low-grade competition between town and country areas and the major metropolitan centers.

INTERPENETRATION OF LIFE STYLES

Each of the metropolitan centers around which our society is currently organized encompasses a wide range of life styles. And each of these life styles contains an admixture of activities and attitudes, some of which are distinctly rural in quality. Likewise even the most provincial rural resident combines some distinctly urban elements with his way of life.

One of the underlying themes in our society is that the rural and urban life styles have interpenetrated each other until in only isolated instances do Americans practice one to the exclusion of the other.

Because different ways of living are not entirely complementary, a consequence of interpenetration is strain—strain within the individual who embraces incompatible activities and attitudes, between individuals who accept competing beliefs as to what the basis of collective behavior should be, between groups committed to one life style to the exclusion of others.

This heterogeneity of life styles is the hallmark of our society.

ASCENDANCE OF URBAN LIFE STYLE

The virtual dominance—economic, cultural, and more recently political—of the urban over the rural centers reflects the ascendant position of urban life styles in our society. Until only recently most Americans have looked on the continued ascendance of urban patterns with a benign casualness that often reflected an expectation that rural life styles would gradually suffer eclipse.

The urbanite who is an in-migrant from a small town where his parents still maintain the family home illustrates this situation. While he has no intention of perpetuating either the parental home or his parents' community, he may be warmly nostalgic toward both. Intent on better schools for his own children than the small town or community provided for him, he might regret that state intervention into local school affairs distressed his parents while wholeheartedly agreeing with the state's goal of abolishing the obsolete little school.

As long as our view of the future presupposed the superiority of the urban standard of living and life style to the rural, we could anticipate that the rural community would become unnecessary and wither away. But an unpleasant factor has intruded on the scene. All urban places are suffering increasingly from social disorganization (and its consequence, social disintegration); apparently the larger the urban complex, the more intense and pervasive the social pathologies enveloping them. Though to most of us disasters such as Watts and Cicero and Harlem are something new and unexpected (and hence intimidating, as evidenced by backlash voting), students of urbanism have long warned us of the existence of these social pathologies. They have also suggested a multiplicity of remedies (public housing, family planning, vocational rehabilitation), and they have predicted that violence will be compounded by more violence unless the situation is effectively ameliorated.

Because we are now confronting at least the possibility that urban pathology will run wild before we can understand and control it, our traditionally benign attitude toward the urban center as the appropriate receptacle for our civilization is coming under scrutiny, at least in some quarters.

Scrutiny may not be the best word, however, for our recent difficulties have shown us the ineffectiveness of experience and familiarity and common sense in combatting urban problems. Even the numerous programs of the War on Poverty may not be sufficient, for it is possible that we do not know enough about urban centers as social mechanisms to put right the increasing number of things that are going wrong with them.

In any event, as this volume appears it is not difficult to imagine a time when, because of our many efforts or because of an elemental instability within the urban center, the problems will have substantially changed.

THE CONTEXT OF THESE PERSPECTIVES

Raising the possibility of far-reaching changes in the dominant institution of our society may be a somewhat overly dramatic or misleading way of introducing this volume. Yet our current posture of toleration toward the nonurbanized portion of our society may require an initial overdramatization and oversimplification if we are to push our perspectives through the parochial barriers that restrain them. Should the history of this period of tremendous turmoil in American society show that it is a prelude to a series of traumatic changes through which some of society's institutional superstructure will be reconstituted, it will also certainly show that some of these changes recast our conception of the urban center in new molds. Because most of those who will read these pages will be looking for an attempt to justify the revitalization and refurbishment of a grand old American institution, we will devote a few paragraphs here to some larger implications of the analyses of the small community that follow.

The small community, that closely knit, folksy, little society of neighbors, is no more. It did not die, it was displaced. We outgrew it—as we did our childhood, or the apartment that served well "before the children came," or that first family automobile, or whatever it was we did before the "new math" came along. Today's farm wife feels no more sense of loss over the boarded-up general store than she feels for the wood-burning stove. She cooks on gas and frequents a super market, usually in a fine family automobile. Her husband's pickup truck could negotiate the muddy, rutted road his father traveled with a team, but a county road commissioner misguided enough to suggest that he do so would receive short shrift. Any discussion that even implicitly entertains the injunction that the rural farm community ought to be restored is irrelevant and irresponsible.

This book focuses on the multitude of changes that have disrupted for all time the collective activities of the traditional rural community as many of us knew or heard about it. Its primary function is to inventory some of the more basic changes that have taken place and then attempt to place them against a meaningful perspective. We cannot come to grips with the portion of our society comprehended by these communities without a reliable understanding of its current condition.

INDETERMINACY OF FINDINGS

Such a reliable understanding is difficult to achieve, however. Change has been proceeding more rapidly than we can study it. At the moment, we have only enough evidence to indicate that things are not what we thought they were, but not enough to establish precisely what they are. And so we find ourselves in a no-man's-land of uncertainty.

Change in the Small Community

What we know indicates that mutational-level change has occurred in the community. At the moment, we are in the position of a newspaper reporter attempting to write an account of some event no one witnessed; we must painstakingly reconstruct what must have occurred from any evidence we can obtain after the fact. Because there is so much left that is familiar (and meaningful to us), we tend to cling to the reassuring belief that things have not really changed much. One of the secondary purposes of this volume is to assemble enough evidence of change to do away with this misleading belief.

The conviction that some of these changes are utterly profound is widely held, and it leads almost immediately to a sense of caution and a desire to look more carefully at what we do know.

NECESSITY FOR RELIABLE KNOWLEDGE

The scientist is deeply committed to the principle that things are not always what they seem to be. As a corollary, he insists on the use of formal concepts and what the nonscientist often views as elaborate and not entirely self-explanatory operations for processing and organizing facts.

In essence, the scientist is carefully checking and testing his explanations until it can be demonstrated that they comprehend the dynamic of the small community. There being various levels of proof (the current term is substantiation), some of what follows is very tentative. Much of it will undoubtedly be substantiated through further research, and some of it has already been substantiated beyond any reasonable doubt.

The importance of reliable knowledge as a prerequisite to responsible attempts to work out community problems can be seen by considering some of our attempts at problem solving in the urban setting. Unquestionably, some of the projects we have undertaken to ameliorate urban problems have precipitated other equally disruptive problems. The great expressways, for example, have resulted in relief from traffic-clogged streets, but only at the cost of nearly insoluble central business district parking problems.

The urban centers, we have discovered, must be viewed as pieces of social machinery; that is, their component parts are so linked together that changes in one of them must be made in the light of the implications for others. Parking and parks both take immense amounts of open space. To the extent that there are not unlimited amounts of unbuilt land, these uses become competitive both with each other and with the marketplaces that dominate our city centers.

Probes into the small community suggest that changes there have probably resulted in the emergence of important new linkages between traditional institutional components. If these social mechanisms now operate in terms of new principles, it becomes important to create reliable conceptions of what these are.

What are the changes in the roles and the interrelationships resulting from school consolidation? What has the diminution of the local business center, brought on by the rise of the new shopping center down the fine new highway, done to the local power structure? If changes were to be made in the local church, what consequences would they have for the family? And is the rural family under the same level of pressure, and is it subject to the same quality of disintegration, boring in on the urban family?

Because answering questions such as these depends on the existence of reliable, substantiated models or theories, much of what follows has some of the quality of a tour de force, for we cannot at this time talk directly to such questions. Scientists have not yet designed the scaffolding they will require to put the carefully fitted layers of fact into a theory.

One of the reasons for this unfortunate state of affairs is that we have been preoccupied with other domestic and overseas problems and the necessary resources have not been made available. Even if they were available, there would be difficulties internal to science to be surmounted.

DISCIPLINARY FRAGMENTATION AMONG SCIENCES

Science—in the sense of a corporate body of investigators linked together within a comprehensive web of relationships connecting one set of researchers to all others—simply does not exist. We have a multiplicity of scientific disciplines, each with its own myopic set of interests and its own traditional identifying concerns. One who wishes to find out what scientists have discovered must know enough about the scope and focus of each discipline to be able to identify which ones contain something germane to his interests. And he must, in turn, know enough about each of these disciplines to find which of its discoveries is relevant for him.

Because this is an all but impossible undertaking for anyone outside a given discipline, the chapters that follow seek to inventory and mobilize what we have found out about the changes that have taken place in the small community. Each chapter will focus on one of five individual disciplines. The remainder of this introductory chapter will be devoted to the commonalities and points of contact among them.

CHANGE IN THE SMALL COMMUNITY: AN OVERVIEW

A point of congruence for the findings of the scientist and the perceptions of the nonscientist provides a convenient place to begin a survey of some of the substantive findings of later chapters. The contrast between the small community as the receptacle of rural society and the great metropolitan centers where urban society is inherent is such a point.

One of the first contrasts that comes to mind is that of the noise and fast pace of urban living in comparison with the quiet and even solitude of the more casual pace of rural living. Most of us have enough experience with small communities so that our thoughts proceed easily to less stereotyped, more meaningful, and frequently more personal contrasts. To one, the closeness of family ties stands out in a time when the urban family is disintegrating. To another, the direct contact with nature that is intrinsic to rural living is appealing. To a third, the possibility of knowing and being known by everyone, the potentiality of existing as a person instead of being swallowed up by urban anonymity, is most meaningful.

Whatever the particulars of our awareness of these contrasting life styles, there is likely to be an element common to most of our perceptions—with only a modest number of exceptions we evaluate the rural life style somewhat more positively than that of the urban center. This is interesting, especially since most of those who hold such an opinion have chosen to make their home in the urban setting.

This fact raises the interesting question of why people who seem to idealize rural living do not implement their sentiments by leaving the cities. Are our cities filled with people who find them so abrasive that they are already vicariously moving back to the countryside? Or perhaps our idealization of rural life is only a residue of the migration into the city earlier in this century—a pang of conscience, but only a vestige that will eventually erode away.

A third suggestion, which comprehends parts of both others, may penetrate nearer to root causes. The modern American city is a tangle of contradictions, which tear away at the coherence of personality. Most urbanites live under unremitting pressure from a social system which is in some important respects inhospitable. Urban living is irritating at best; at worst, it is destructive of our very humanity. Yet with all its annoyances, urban living offers some advantages that most of us are loath to forego to regain the coherence that the rural resident once knew.

Table 1 of Chapter 2 develops the contrast between these two life styles in some detail. Inherent in the rural ethos is a presumption that once an individual "puts his roots down" he takes on an obligation in the community and is expected to keep his home there as a prerequisite to fulfilling his obligations. "Greener pastures" is a symbol that rural residents value negatively, for they are inclined to deny that an individual can improve his circumstances by relocating. To the urbanite, on the other hand, not only physical but occupational and social mobility are salient facts of life. He has largely put aside the responsibilities that form the core of the values underlying rural living. One of the findings of the researcher has relevance here. Urban centers use large bureaucratic agencies to accomplish what the residents of the small community often do for themselves with only the most casual organizational arrangements. As a result, the urbanite *has much done* for him that the rural resident does for himself.

This is easily seen in the case of local leadership. The very survival of a small community may hinge on the children of a prominent rural leader taking up his mantle, but few urban centers are deeply dependent on one family. The importance of old families is everywhere on the decline in the cities as the responsibility for urban leadership comes to rest more and more completely on those who have achieved position. Where family, occupation, and similar factors are traditional determinants of ascribed position in rural social systems, the ability and willingness "to get the job done" have come to be the most important determinants of social power and position in urban centers. The urbanite is not only free to move, he is expected to try his luck in another city if he cannot make good where he is.

These contrasting expectations are symptomatic of a crucial difference between urban and rural social systems. The urban life style presumes an individual who is self-sufficient and self-directing. He is expected to participate where he feels he can benefit; he is inclined to involve himself only where he can benefit himself the most. So long as he observes norms that guard against his trespassing on the rights and opportunities of others, he is free to take and partake as he chooses. So deeply honored is achievement in most urban centers that a supplementary set of norms exists, which provides for disproportionate rewards for those who are willing to make a larger investment of their energies.

That things are very much different in the rural setting may explain why few people choose to live there. There is a closedness about the small community, which the individual is expected to recognize. The community's boundaries are the limits of the social world maintained for the express purpose of reinforcing the individual as what he is. Social rewards are carefully rationed to stabilize the community; competing for more than one's share is frowned on. Without denying that there is another world "out there," without even denying the individual access to some of its opportunities (specialized medical treatment, for example), the rural social system presumes that the individual has cast his lot with an older, more stable, and more secure kind of collective.

If freedom is the dominant value of the urban life style, perhaps security is the dominant value of the rural life style. But here we use security in a much larger sense, for it is not the economic security so prized by the urbanite but the security of the person, his sense of being, that is provided for in the social system of the small community. Identity is not the terrible, often nearly impossible, problem for the rural resident that it is for most urbanites. The community serves as a primary as well as a direct referent group. The structural properties of the small community are constituted not only to protect the individual from identity crises but to affirm and at least indirectly impose an identity on him. The urbanite, on the other hand, can involve himself in a multitude of organizations, which compete not only for his time but for his loyalty. It is commonplace for urbanites to undergo wrenching stresses when, for example, their union presses them toward one political commitment and their family toward another, while their employer frowns on any overt manifestation of political involvement. The *community* protects its residents from just these kinds of strain in the rural setting, for the union leader, the head of the family, and the employer are linked in a closed net of power relations.

Furthermore, because the small community has an ultimate kind of autonomy, because the rural social system is so firmly rooted in the individuality and the humanness of local families, it is possible for the rural resident to protect himself from the intrusion of external forces by increasing his identification and involvement with persons who embody the local ethos.

Chapter 2 contrasts urban and rural settings on several other levels. Primary groups, the molecular units from which the social system of the small community is constituted, provide a great deal more identity reinforcement to the individual than the secondary groups that serve as the cells from which the urban corpus is constituted. And the referent function of these primary groups is greatly facilitated by the existence of a more homogeneous structure of social values. The almost overwhelming spectrum of opportunities in the urban center leads many urbanites into a pattern of activities dominated by the violent tensions among the incompatible roles they select. As Chapter 6 suggests, the urbanite is casually involved in a relatively large number of unrelated or secondary associations, while his rural counterpart is deeply committed to a smaller set of primary associations, which are in large measure compatible because of the coherence the community infuses into them.

As if further to insure the security of the individual's person, power and influence in the small community are likely to be concentrated in the hands of a well-knit, like-thinking local elite. Chapter 5 deals with this in some detail. Because informality is traditional, these elites are seldom as clearly seen as the publicly visible power holders in the great cities, but as the findings of Swanson suggest, power figures in the small communities may exercise a much more conclusive kind of influence on local affairs than their urban counterparts. People can, if they care to or dare to, dominate rural institutions. At least some of the institutions of urban society have taken on a dynamic which is important far beyond the grasp of individual leaders. The social mechanisms man created to serve him soon civilized him; they come now to possess him—which is almost tantamount to destroying him.

Perhaps the most pervasive force operating to secure the identity of the resident of the small community is the basis on which permissible and legitimate behavior is distinguished from that which is deviant and subject to social controls.

In the urban center, when there is conflict over what should be done the issue is likely to be decided in very pragmatic terms. Does what is done serve someone's interests well? Does it injure others? Especially, does it do violence to what others would like to do? The ideological query, "Is it consistent with what ought to be done?" which is the dominant basis for legitimating actions in the small community, is not really relevant in the urban center with its multiplicity of fragmentary ideologies.

On this point the urbanite's tolerance for his rural counterpart may break down. Though he might be willing to admit that he is less secure in his knowledge of who and what he is, and though he may admit this is a critical factor in the higher incidence of identity crises, he is, he might maintain, free to draw on a repertoire of attractive role-taking opportunities vastly larger than those available to a person living in a small community. If he can never be sure just who he is and if he must live without much of the referent group ratification of his being and person that the rural resident knows, neither does he have to bear the frustration of being frozen into a configuration of roles that may all but eliminate spontaneity and experimentation. If we can talk of such an illusive thing as creative self-determination, the rural resident may have the opportunity for relatively little of it in comparison with his urban nephews and nieces.

There are those who maintain that spontaneity and experimentation (in the sense of trial and error learning) are essential to the full flowering of the humanity in man, and thus some people charge that the rural life style has a fatal flaw. This kind of charge could be more easily sustained before urban social mechanisms began crumbling in the face of the violence of those whose lack of a functional identity left them all but unable to enter freely into stable, productive collective involvements. To be freed from the responsibility to have an identity has something in common with being freed from membership in the human race.

Perhaps we have arrived at a point where it seems possible to maintain that neither rural nor urban mechanisms are adequate to nurture the full man. It is at least possible that we shall come to believe that the small community (whether a neighborhood in a core city, a suburb, or a country town) promotes the capacity for investing oneself in others, which can only be acquired in the bosom of a family. That is to say, in our effort to perfect the urban center as a productive mechanism we may have overlooked the place of an appropriate set of smaller-scale collectives required for the conduct of social relations between people as people rather than as role-takers. It seems possible that in our attempt to develop a social mechanism through which we could replace our traditional rural life style with a way of life offering freedom from the constraints of ascribed roles, we have underestimated the need for authoritatively ascribed role elements in human affairs. We may need to find some way of nesting the mutated community that is now ours within the context of great urban centers so designed that they simultaneously loosen some of the most onerous restraints of the traditional life style and provide a floor of known and knowable behavior directives.

This is precisely what most urban land-use planners have sought. The disintegration of urban society is a disheartening commentary on their inability to accomplish their ends. If we were to publicly espouse the need for nested micro-units as the primary components of the urban macro-systems, if we should come to a national commitment to closed social systems as the basic units of our society, one would expect that a considerable interest would develop around the design and development of communities.

SOME CONTRASTS BETWEEN PRESENT AND PAST

The point that it is not the traditional community being discussed here could not be overemphasized. The traditional, self-sufficient, and essentially autonomous rural market center, that sturdy tool with which we successfully pushed our frontier from the Alleghenys to the Pacific, is in eclipse. Gallaher points out in Chapter 4 one of the reasons for this: the urban center has intruded itself deep into the rural ethos, displacing one after another of the rural structural components.

But in Chapter 3, Fox points up another potent reason for the disappearance of the traditional community. The rural resident adopted much of the technology of our industrialized society; the changes that he thereby introduced into his own productive activities have been a major source of change in the small community. As is the case in so many places in our society, the adoption of the automobile dramatically illustrates this process.

The size of the small community at the turn of this century was heavily influenced by the concept of a team-haul day—the distance a farmer could cover on his Saturday visit to town and be home in time to take care of his stock that evening. The substitution of a vehicle that could travel 50 miles an hour for one that averaged 5 miles an hour led, over a period of several decades, to a tenfold increase in the distance across a community and to an increase of its area by one-hundred fold. (See Figures 1-5 in Chapter 3.)

The technological revolution in agriculture, which has led to literally fantastic increases in farm production, has generated a second set of changes in the local environment. The first of these was a substantial increase in the amount of disposable income available to the farmer. His ability to pay for additional services has increased steadily.

Secondly, increases in the size of the community expanded its tax base. When this was added to the increase in disposable income, the stage was set for the mutation of the economy of the traditional community.

Larger numbers of customers with more disposable income led to a demand for specialized stores and services, and this pressure displaced the general store.

Expanding tax bases also made possible significant increases in governmental services, which were minimal in the traditional community. Volunteer fire departments secured additional trucks and up-to-date equipment; the backyard well was displaced by a professionally engineered water system and indoor plumbing; streets were paved and sometimes, even more importantly, they were maintained; zoning was considered and sometimes grudgingly accepted; and law enforcement took on some of the firmness of its urban counterpart.

But the truly significant—and often traumatic—expansion of public services concerned not the town or township government but the school district. School boards could and did tap the expanding tax base. Educators presented them with a steady stream of suggestions for new facilities and programs. And a rural population which had traditionally honored only basic intellectual skills began extending its interests and its educational commitments at the insistence of the educational bureaucracy. Accepting the superintendent's repeated demands that the school board impose the necessary tax levies became a habit.

Education, once only a passive enterprise, became one of the most vital local institutions. In many communities the school system has been a source of an uninterrupted series of innovations. Not the least of these has been the conditioning of many members of the community to acceptance of the fact that the future, unlike the past, would bring an ever-expanding stream of changes in rural life.

While it probably cannot be demonstrated that these changes in the small community became self-regenerating, they may have led to its becoming vastly more open to the mounting stream of changes formed in the urban centers.

Gallaher in Chapter 4 makes the point that the consequences of the changes taking place in the small community are far-reaching indeed, for the community is the immediate link between the individual and the larger institutions of his society. Communities serve to connect and relate the individual to the mass society we have erected with the urban center as its base. If the structural cleavages appearing in small communities rip or tear completely across the fabric of traditional human relationships supporting personality development, the inhabitants could come to be isolated from the culture on which they are dependent (and which is ultimately dependent on their assimilation into it). Isolation could have some of the same socially pathological consequences for the resident of the small community that it has had for so many in megalopolis. Isolation breeds alienation; alienation results in a generally decreasing rate of participation in local affairs. There follows in turn a falling-off of need reductions and then (a) loss of mass support for local institutions and (b) rapidly rising, widespread frustration. There being no other creditable, apparently viable collective vehicle for reducing the anxieties that are a normal consequence of deprivation, they are converted into a cycle of frustration, hostility, aggression—and then violence, which sets off the whole destructive cycle once again.

Yet, though there are broad tears, which probably reflect discontinuities, in the fabric of face-to-face relationships that constitute the small community, as well as great changes in its institutional structure, it is not (in the view of Gallaher and Swanson) disintegrating so much as mutating. So far, at any rate, communities that have been researched have shown a substantial resiliency. Small communities have assimilated many of the artifacts of urbanization through the simple device of structural discontinuity, that is, by absorbing elements of social structure and social mechanisms that are not only incompatible with, but opposite to, those that exist.

Gallaher holds that the idea that the "little community has become a combination of opposites," in the words of Redfield, has been documented. That what has come into being works can be illustrated through an example from current local law enforcement activities.

The local resident has available a remarkably broad choice of law enforcement officials. When the difficulty appears to involve someone from the community, the sheriff's office will be called, and a friendly deputy, who knows all the parties and is implicitly committed to avoiding any unpleasantness in the courts, will undertake a series of diplomatic visits among the persons involved. When some outsider has trespassed the boundaries of the community, the efficient professionals of the state patrol are called, in the knowledge that they will attempt to grind out a conviction as a natural consequence of their professional commitments.

A similar kind of social ambidexterity can be found in other program areas. Someone in ill health may be ministered to by his friends and neighbors, with or without benefit of a physician; or he may choose to become a nameless face in one of the wards of an urban hospital. And while there are those who seek out the services of a county welfare worker, there are almost always friends willing to help if one seeks to avoid entangling himself with "outsiders."

Perhaps it is the rituals associated with death that reflect the admixture of opposites most dramatically. Here the full range of the mortician's technology in the preparation of the deceased and the housing of his remains is employed; but in place of the social processes through which the urbanite effectively denies the existence of death as an event having anything more than private significance to the deceased and his family, the quality as well as some of the forms of the traditional rituals of the countryside are preserved. Death continues to be embraced as a simple eventuality of life. "No one who loved life and lived fully objects to death" is a theme which is developed in many of the steps of the rituals culminating at graveside.

It is as if the mutating community may be evolving in terms of a structural principle dramatically different from those found in some Wisconsin communities in a classic study around the turn of the century. As Fox demonstrates in Chapter 3, *social stability* based on structural complementarity was the hallmark of the rural community at the turn of the century. Recent studies of modern communities (cited by Gallaher, Fox and Swanson) all indicate it is structural tension, structural lesion, that is everywhere present.

Opposites delicately balanced with each other would seem to be the portent for the future. Not that a steady balance, an equilibrium, has been accomplished, for study after study documents the crazy gyrations of structural elements that are terribly out of balance. Still we have enough evidence of opposites in equipoise to sense the presence of an alternative, even though we do not have sufficient data to demonstrate that it is this principle that comprehends the trend in the changes that are everywhere in process in the small community.

What the social scientist has found indicates that there are some things we can assert:

First, the stability of the closed system that was the traditional rural community no longer exists.

Second, there is an almost universal ambivalence toward change on the part of the residents of small communities; they have benefited as well as suffered from what has transpired during the past fifty years.

Third, there is an expectation that pressures for change will continue to impinge on the community and that this will result in an increasing dependence on bureaucratic arrangements.

Fourth, there is little question but that the rate of urban-rural interpenetration will increase in the future. There seems to be every reason to expect that on this point the past has in fact been prologue to the future.

RESPONSES TO PRESSURES FOR CHANGE

Having surveyed some of what the following chapters suggest about the modification of the traditional structure of community and its implications, it might be worthwhile to sample the dynamics through which communities have responded to change in the past and hence might be expected to respond in the future.

The rising tide of urbanization has forever changed the environment of the small community from one that is benignly passive to one that is aggressive—sometimes predatory—toward local institutions.

Change in the Small Community

Lowry and Mitchell point up changes taking place in the structure of community power relationships. Swanson provides a new and powerful analytic construct for understanding these. Fox identifies some of the dramatic changes in the size and complexity of the economy of the community as a trade area, showing how the economy of the community has become increasingly interdependent with that of the nation. And Gallaher shows how urbanization has substantially penetrated the small community.

The small community has lost its position as the receptacle for the dominant life style in our society. In some respects it has become a refuge for those who choose to maintain a style of life no longer generally preferred in our society (even though it is widely regarded with a sentimental nostalgia).

Given this kind of environmental relationship, we must expect that the rate of urban penetration will probably increase. The rate of mutation (some would say capitulation) of local institutions will surely increase, even if only modestly. The immediate result will be increased difficulty in maintaining enough of a balance between the urban and rural components of community social structure so that its basic functions can be maintained. The mutations taking place in small communities often jeopardize their capacity to fulfill traditional functions, with the result that these are displaced to some external agency.

These chapters do not, however, provide a basis for forecasting the disappearance of the small community. Rather, those who are researching the small community foresee a complete mutation in its structure and processes, as we now understand them. The small community, engulfed by the successive waves of urbanization that have swept through our society, is being further assimilated into the urban centers with each new "big city" practice that its residents accept. The consistent pattern indicating an increasing rate of urban interpenetration leads one to expect small communities to become integral elements of vast, sprawling urban complexes.

Given Fox's analysis of the dramatic changes in the area comprehended by small communities, demonstrating how it has increased one hundred times in this century, it is easy to assume the assimilation of these trade areas into the hinterland of the great metropolitan centers as they expand and assimilate the surrounding countryside in increasingly more comprehensive infrastructures.

And if one takes only one more step, that of projecting the emergence of a completely urbanized society, it becomes almost illogical not to forecast the ultimate substitution of the urban for our traditional rural life style. This appears to be a path most Americans have followed, if only vicariously. But for the most part they have done so without knowledge of an emerging body of research findings indicating that there are serious, probably malignant, and conceivably fatal social pathologies not in some but in all urban centers.

It is not that some are healthy and some are socially diseased—as we have assumed until recently—but that social disease is present in all our urban places. It is not out of control in all of them at this time; the social psychologist would say pathology has not yet reached epidemic proportions in all of them.

This is not the place to attempt a prognosis of the urban malaise. The evidence of social pathology, and its concomitants, is so conclusive that there is a reasonable doubt of the viability of the city as a social mechanism for the maintenance of a healthy, functional, and desirable life style.

To put the matter succinctly, to project the demise of the small community or at least its assimilation into and subsequent subordination to an urban center without regard to the quality of this urban environment would amount to something less than fully responsible scholarship.

In like manner, for community influentials to suggest that the root problem of their constituents is to accept the necessity of accommodating to further and more disruptive urban penetration may amount to something less than enlightened leadership.

The difficulty with an appraisal which asserts (a) that the traditional community is even now succumbing to the dominance of urbanism and (b) that urban places may no longer be viable mechanisms for nurturing productive and meaningful personalities is that it leaves us with a problem for which there is no available solution.

Presumably our civilization embodies a style of life which is not only facilitated by but dependent on the existence of appropriate and viable social instrumentalities—the city and the small community as well as the family and a multitude of referent groups. To the extent that civilized life depends on the availability of appropriate collective devices, it is jeopardized by social pathologies which threaten the social mechanisms that bring it into being.

Change in the Small Community

In the absence of reliable ways of diagnosing the extent, kind, and probable course of urban pathologies, there is no scientific basis for forecasting their demise. We do not know enough to know whether or not their infections are, in the physician's words, likely to be terminal.

Though theirs are not the voices to which we presently respond, some people hold that the great urban center does not facilitate the development of man's full range of potentialities. In this view, the materialism that grips urban man may be partly accounted for by the fact that our great cities are serviceable primarily as mechanisms for the production of goods and services. They may be, the evidence begins to indicate, inadequate devices for such rudimentary social functions as the complete socialization of a healthy personality; and they may be quite inhospitable environments for such rudimentary socializing agents as the family. Perhaps it is worth emphasizing once more that these are what the scientist labels speculations—hunches derived from the fragmentary findings we have available. They are not intended to do more than illustrate the quality of our problems with the urban center.

If, however, there is reason to question the desirability of the apparently inexorable drift from rural toward urban life styles through the progressive displacement of the community by the city, we are faced with a policy problem of different dimensions than the one we have, until now, articulated.

Is it not our assumption, for example, that the War on Poverty means that once the impoverished have the wherewithal to enter the middle classes, the strains the poor and the disadvantaged create in the urban setting will be reduced to a level where the city will function once more as a framework for social commerce? Likewise, may we not infer that proposals for elaborate mass transit systems assume that rapid transit will allow us to surmount the gross dysfunctions the automobile has introduced into the urban complex? Ever-expanding educational activities represent, among other things, an attempt to provide a viable substitute for the disintegrating family.

To repeat, if we have taken as our ultimate policy premise the position that the urban center is the most appropriate host for the culture (civilization) of our society, and if this has led us to a problem-solving strategy designed to save the city through various urban renewal activities, then the assertion that there may be some ineradicable defects in the urban mechanism, that the city is subject to pressures seeking release through mutational changes of the same quality that are remaking the small community, holds some bold implications which we have succeeded in avoiding with our current policies.

Bluntly put, there is at least some reason for considering an alternative policy premise: The small community was a reasonably appropriate vehicle for the life style we accepted in the eighteenth and nineteenth centuries; the metropolis has been a reasonably practicable instrumentality for fostering the life style we have evolved in the first two-thirds of the twentieth century; it is possible that history will show that it was our lot to develop a new form of collective, one appropriate to making and sustaining a new style of living.

In the initial stage of our attempts to develop the post-urban collective, perhaps we shall come to a mixed form, such as the low-density or decentralized city. We cannot anticipate at this time what the product of experimentation with nested hierarchies of communities, regional trade areas, cities, metropolitan districts and administrative regions might be. That there will even be the invention of some essentially new form to displace the urban center cannot be forecast with any certainty. But this is not necessary, nor is it completely pertinent to a full appreciation of research on the small community.

That the small community will not serve the economic requirements of a nationally integrated production-distribution system may not mean that reliable knowledge about this traditional device for the socialization of personality, the sustaining and maintaining of the family, and the linking together of the activities of the church, the school, and the local lodge groups has only historical interest. If the ultimate strategy for the solution of all social problems is to plot a course of change to an unknown point in the future by drawing a line through two known points, the past and the present, then reliable knowledge about the community as the anchor point for such a line is essential. And the importance of fixing the position of this base point increases in rough proportion to the extent one questions the premise that we need only renew the urban center. If one approaches urban pathology with the intent of reconstituting the city instead of renewing it, the importance of understanding change in the small community becomes clear.

What is the small community today? What happened to the traditional rural trade center? What is happening in the small community? How has this affected the way people live?

These are the kinds of questions to which this book is addressed. Clearly any responsible answer must be prefaced with the disclaimer that we do not really know. In part the fragmentation of science has thrown what we do know into half a dozen different disciplinary repositories. In part we have been preoccupied with other, seemingly more pressing, concerns. Above all, however, our ignorance is an implicit assertion that we have not felt that understanding communities is vitally important.

RESOURCE PAPERS FOR A POLICY DIALOGUE

This book is, among other things, an affirmation that effectively comprehending the role and status of the small community represents an important resource in coming to terms with some of the larger problems we shall confront during the remainder of the twentieth century.

Quite obviously the responsibility for the perspectives and value preferences of the social scientists whose papers constitute the bulk of this volume must rest with their individual authors. As Williams notes in his interpretive response to the papers of the scientists, the fact of overriding importance is not the existence of strains between the perspectives of various scientists or between the theologian and the scientist, but the complementarity between them *when we address ourselves to the proper questions.*

We do violence to both science and theology to hold that one provides us with tools for establishing what is while the other provides us with ways of establishing what ought to be. What we require is a mating of two complementary, and in some senses alternative though not entirely compatible, ways of knowing.

If one of the products of this encounter is the possibility that the depth and extent of what someone has labeled "the unnoticed crisis in the American way of life" is a little more fully seen, these chapters will have served a useful purpose. For if this unnoticed crisis poses a latent threat to many of our social institutions, it is imperative that the quality of our policy response be modified so that the scope of what we are doing to ameliorate our problems is increased to comprehend their true extent.

If man's Christian inheritance includes the freedom to create the objects through which his quest for a self and his strivings toward fulfilling his aspirations can be consummated, he must accept the responsibility for dealing with the difficulties entailed by some of the objects created by his forebears. Their honest exercise of this freedom requires of us a response of similar quality.

The small community, which served our predecessors as an instrumentality through which they "made good" on the goals they set for themselves, has mutated. Some are prepared to discard it, claiming it is really a parasitical element in our society. Likewise, the urban centers that once facilitated and sustained our communities are viewed by some as having taken a predatory role toward them.

This displacement of facilitative, reinforcive, sustaining relationships by parasitical and predatory ones is one of the visible symptoms of the unnoticed crisis. If effectively disposing of such symptoms requires major surgery instead of merely a course of pills, the quality of our response may deserve scrutiny.

But reconstituting some of the institutional superstructure of our society is not our purpose. One suspects that the difference between renewing and reconstituting is the difference between inconvenience and discomfort or even injury. If, for example, we undertook instead of a War on Poverty (which has as its goal the rehabilitation of the impoverished and impotent minority at the base of our socio-economic hierarchy) a War on Alienation or a War on Escape, or Irresponsibility or Debilitating Anxiety or Prejudice, our renewal enterprises might be differently appraised.

Perhaps the quality of our response is a product of a problem-solving strategy that we have seldom articulated but persistently followed. It may have originated in our deeply rooted public commitments to pragmatism, which result in a problem-solving strategy recently given the label Incrementalism—a series of relatively inexpensive, often irritating, but seldom painful changes which accumulate and at some time culminate in a major innovation. Conceivably, our capacity to institute major changes in society has atrophied, so complete is our adherence to incrementalism. Before we try to decide whether innovation rather than adaptation is needed to re-establish the functionality of such collective mechanisms as the community and the city, there are prior questions: What do we confront? What is the full extent of our difficulties?

Because answers to questions of this nature indicate the quality of response these chapters are seeking, and because the premise of the remainder of this volume is that we are not at all certain we know how to ask these questions, let alone answer them, two chapters which have not yet been mentioned deserve brief consideration.

While the Barker and Hodapp chapters do not provide a procedure for raising and answering such questions, between them they give some profoundly useful guidelines.

Hodapp's chapter implicitly rejects the classical process of what is technically known as dialectical analysis—abstract speculation about our affairs in general and our problems in particular. Instead he seeks to explicate a basis on which the scientist and the nonscientist can collaborate in using the elaborate, cumbersome, and costly regimes science provides for assessing "the real world" in that world beyond and behind those social-psychological constructs that are the product of dialectic speculation.

In answering the rhetorical question, what does the Christian layman bring to such an undertaking, Hodapp specifies a basis for collaboration which, when perfected, might well provide a method for asking and answering the questions in which inhere changes with a redemptive quality.

Because the Barker chapter is an almost classical example of research reporting, it offers the nonscientist an unusual opportunity to become familiar with the raw product of science—findings. It reports some of the findings from a comparison of two small communities, one located in America's Midwest, the other in England's Midlands; and it manifests much that the scientist brings to a consultation with theologians.

Certainly one of the things the scientist brings to a collaborative effort is a concern with definition, which is really only indicative of his larger concern with exact communication. This care with definition is familiar to all nonscientists, for it manifests itself in awkward formulations couched in what is usually an unfamiliar jargon (not infrequently reduced to mathematical symbols). The immediate purpose of this subtechnology is to facilitate ever more sensitive and accurate definition. Its larger function, however, is to allow scientists to take ideas and problems that are beyond the capacity of any one individual and subdivide them into components, each of which can serve as the assignment for an individual researcher. Ultimately much of the analytic power of social science stems directly from the fact that this definitional technology provides the basis from which corporate research enterprises can be organized.

But it is from a different aspect of the scientist's concern with defining that another, and in some senses more profound, capacity of science is derived. What the nonscientist knows as measuring and taking measurements has been elaborated into a process of describing real world phenomena through well-articulated quantifications. Thus Barker takes the familiar processes of the community church and, instead of the casual description that the nonscientist might provide, he derives several simple (the scientific term is parsimonious) measures through which what happens in the sanctuary, in the church school, in the choir are described. In the process of describing *each* of the component settings of the church through the *same* set of measures (actually measurement operations), the scientist works a subtle transformation in the quality of descriptive facts, and in the process he enables himself to take advantage of the great analytical tool of his profession—comparison.

That is, because he has created a set of measures comprehending the essentials of a large number of church activities, he is able to make exacting comparisons of, for example, the church choir and a Sunday school picnic. And while there may be little that can be learned from this particular comparison, the history of science shows us that it is precisely this capacity—the capability of making meaningful comparisons between previously uncomparable entities or events—that allows the construction of the laws which serve as the foundation of our knowledge.

Another component of scientific technology need not be elaborated here. Most nonscientists are increasingly familiar with the electronic marvels by means of which the scientist executes complicated calculations, which once would have taken years, in seconds. By using the language of mathematics he is able to extend his explanatory capacity still further.

Yet though technology is synonymous with science, science is more than a series of techniques, mysterious or otherwise. Ultimately—penultimately is perhaps the better word—science is a highly refined guessing game. The fact that those who developed a theory to explain poker playing (Game Theory) found they could apply it to science reveals this seldom-seen face of an austere profession. Ultimately what the scientist does amounts to saying "it is my guess that A is the cause of B under conditions P, Q, and R." He then translates this into a hypothesis that specifies the circumstances and conditions under which he expects A to be followed by B. He proceeds to examine carefully as many instances as possible comprehended by his hypothesis, keeping a careful score of the accuracy of his prediction. Like a football forecaster, if he finds his guesses are not generating good predictions, he begins changing the basis on which he makes his forecasts, that is, he reformulates his hypothesis.

Any scientist is free to use whatever predictive scheme he chooses, and other scientists judge his success by the predictive power of his forecasting system. This fact points up another kind of contribution of science to any collaborative relationship. Science is above all the interplay of free intellects within the discipline provided by the acceptance of a shared regime for knowing. While there are many instances where this freedom is abused, scientists have, by and large, behaved responsibly. The interplay of their creative efforts has been purposeful. Yet it has—again with some unfortunate exceptions—not been fettered by dogma, by the imposition of one point of view at the expense of another.

As a result science—and perhaps this is the quality of science that a security-oriented society regards with apprehension—is not a repository of eternal verities. Practically nothing we thought we knew about the world 2,000 years ago is accepted today. Perhaps half of what we accepted at the turn of the century is substantiated by what we know today. And the so-called half-life of what we are finding out now is contracting at a precipitous rate.

If it aggrandizes the scientist, still it tells us something important about him to suggest that he brings to any collaborative relationship a regimen for knowing where learning (and consequently change) are given a prominent place. Some of the fruits of this knowledge-generating regimen as it relates to the small community are set forth in the chapters that follow.

CHAPTER 2

DISTRIBUTION OF SOCIAL POWER IN SMALL COMMUNITIES

SHELDON G. LOWRY AND JOHN B. MITCHELL

The basic purpose of this chapter is to summarize the major research findings on community power structure primarily, though not only, in small communities. We will review several alternative methods for the analysis of community power. Critical reviews of research in this area are available, and the reader who would like to delve into them will find them included in the reading references, which appear at the end of the chapter.

COMMUNITY CHANGE—AN OVERVIEW

Only a short generation ago, the family was the major producing and consuming unit, particularly in the more rural and isolated communities. Each family was an almost entirely self-contained unit, producing and consuming virtually all the goods and services required for its existence.

The rural community was characterized by C. J. Galpin as the "team haul" community, which implies that the community boundaries extended no farther in any given direction than a horse and wagon could travel and return the same day.[1] Thus, the day-to-day

---

Sheldon G. Lowry is Professor of Sociology and Associate Chairman of the Department at Michigan State University, East Lansing. John B. Mitchell is Professor of Rural Sociology in the College of Agriculture, The Ohio State University, Columbus.

[1] C. J. Galpin, *The Social Anatomy of An Agricultural Community*. Madison: Wisconsin Agricultural Experiment Station, Research Bulletin No. 34, May, 1915.

interaction patterns of those who lived in the rural community were limited by transportation and communication to a very narrow range of individuals.

American communities—large and small, rural and urban—have always been in flux. In recent years, however, particularly since World War II, change has been more rapid and widespread. Malcolm Knowles said recently that a child born today will live through a complete change in culture in his lifetime. Change has not only encompassed the physical world in which we live but is also challenging our way of life, including our basic values, in such a fundamental way that it is almost impossible to predict what the culture of tomorrow will be like.

Powerful social, economic, and technical forces are making and remaking American communities. Among the more important are:[2] growth of science and technology; industrialization, specialization, and automation; mechanization and specialization of agriculture; developments in transportation, communication, and sources of power; urbanization, suburbanization, and interurbanization; growth of the economy; increases and shifts in population; and rising levels of living and public service demands.

These forces have produced increasingly complex and highly specialized communities, which are intricately interdependent with one another and with the larger society. Some of the consequences of these forces are the following new dimensions of small communities: high mobility; few stable groups; development of special interests and specialized social subsystems (as contrasted with general interest systems); intensive competition between subsystems for membership, leadership, loyalty, and support; increasingly important role for large-scale, centralized, formal social systems based outside the community; widespread feelings of powerlessness and remoteness from centers of influence and decision making; relationships among people tending to become segmented and impersonal; substantial changes in traditional patterns of social status (for example, labor, new resi-

---

[2] Sheldon G. Lowry and Edward O. Moe, "The Community in Transition," *Adult Leadership*, Vol. 11 (September, 1962), pp. 72 ff.; Robin M. Williams, Jr., *American Society* (2nd ed.). New York: Alfred A. Knopf, 1960, Ch. XII, pp. 471 ff.

dents, managers, new economic power, general upgrading of unskilled jobs).

Thus, with the growing body of scientific knowledge and rapidly expanding technology, there followed not only a specialization in industry and the economic segment of our lives but also a specialization of all other institutional services. About all that has remained for the family is the reproduction of new members and care of the young. A host of health and welfare organizations and agencies have been developed to provide for proper biological functioning. The socialization of new members has been taken over by a variety of public and private educational institutions and mass media at an increasingly early age. A complicated set of economic institutions has developed to provide goods and services. A large, complex political and governmental system has been organized to maintain order and to render many other services once provided by the family. Finally, the church has increasingly taken over most of the activities related to the questions of where we come from, why we are here, and where we are going. Religion, by comparison with former days, is largely gone from the home.

Change has been so dramatic and so far-reaching that the traditional differences between rural and urban communities have virtually disappeared. In fact, Jessie Bernard has pointed out that: "There are so many kinds of rural communities and so many kinds of urban communities that one generalization can scarcely cover them all."[3] Bernard goes on to indicate that to lump together into a category called "rural" a prosperous Iowa farm, a cotton plantation, and a factory farm in California is rather meaningless. Differences between urban centers are equally great: for example, consider the cities of Glendale, California; Winnetka, Illinois; Gary, Indiana; and Omaha, Nebraska. The obvious conclusion to be drawn, therefore, is that "most generalizations about rural-urban differences have circumscribed validity."[4]

Despite the obvious difficulties in drawing such generalizations,

---

[3] Jessie Bernard, *American Community Behavior* (rev. ed.). New York: Holt, Rinehart and Winston, 1962, p. 21.

[4] *Ibid.*

there do seem to be some patterns emerging for community power structure.[5] The power structure in the old "team haul" community described by Galpin was dominated by the male head of the household, usually the father or the grandfather. Matters of community-wide concern were usually decided by the male heads of one or more of the prominent families. This type of community is usually regarded as having a monolithic power structure which, in its extreme form, is represented by a community dominated by a single family or a one-industry town.

With the ever-increasing complexity of our society, there has been a tendency to shift from the monolithic to a pluralistic type of power structure. As a consequence, there are communities all along the continuum between these two extremes, with some rather distinct identifiable points that can serve as "types."

If one were to try to characterize these two extremes, the resulting picture would look essentially like the one summarized in Table 1. To be sure, some of the factors do overlap with others to some degree, but such a descriptive characterization may still be useful as a means of outlining the gross differences between the two basic types of community power structures which have been identified.

---

[5] While there are variations in the specific definitions of power among various researchers, there is general overall agreement as to the nature of power. Professor Joe M. Bohlen and his associates at Iowa State University have competently reviewed and synthesized the major conceptions of social power into what they have called a "social power model." While their model takes into account the work of other researchers, it draws largely from the work of Charles P. Loomis at Michigan State University, who sees social power as one of the major elements of a social system. For a discussion of the social systems model, see: Charles P. Loomis, *Social Systems: Essays on Their Persistence and Change*. New York: D. Van Nostrand Company, 1960; and Charles P. Loomis and J. Allan Beegle, *Rural Sociology: The Strategy of Change*, Englewood Cliffs, N. J.: Prentice-Hall, 1957. For a presentation of the power model and research based on this model, see: Joe M. Bohlen, George M. Beal, Gerald E. Klonglan, and John L. Tait, *Community Power Structure and Civil Defense*. Ames, Iowa: Iowa Agricultural and Home Economics Experiment Station, 1964; Ronald C. Powers, "Social Power in a Rural Community," unpublished Ph.D. dissertation, Iowa State University, 1963; John L. Tait, "Social Power in a Rural Social System," unpublished Masters thesis, Iowa State University, 1964; Joe M. Bohlen, John L. Tait, George M. Beal, and Gerald E. Klonglan, "An Analysis of Influence and Authority As Components of Social Power in Five Iowa Communities," Iowa Agricultural and Home Economics Experiment Station, Journal Paper No. J-5458, August, 1966 (mimeographed).

TABLE 1

SOME GENERAL CHARACTERISTICS OF COMMUNITIES WITH MONOLITHIC AND PLURALISTIC TYPES OF POWER STRUCTURES

Monolithic	Pluralistic
Rural, isolated communities	Urban
Homogeneous population	Heterogeneous population
Marked vertical differences in segments of the population	Differences more horizontal than vertical
Little communication between segments	Few major blocks to communication
Primary-type relationships	Secondary-type relationships
Gemeinschaft like	Gesellschaft like
Affective relationships	Contractual relationships
Few organized groups	Proliferation of groups
Lack of specialization	Intense specialization
General farm organizations	Specialized farm organizations
Emphasis on traditional values	Emphasis on rationality
High value on ascribed characteristics	High value on achieved characteristics
Slow rate of social change	Rapid social change
Little mobility (vertical or horizontal)	Marked mobility
Power structure and social class tending to coincide	Power structure and social class related but not coterminous

METHODS OF DETERMINING COMMUNITY POWER STRUCTURES

Although leadership and power are related, they are not identical. A vast literature is available on "leadership." Most of it is not based on well-designed research, but tends to be the product of "common sense knowledge" or "principles based on experience." Because of the heterogeneity as well as the incomplete coverage of research on leadership we do not, at this time, have the conceptual raw materials to fashion an authoritative concept of leadership. Therefore, this discussion will be concerned with the concept of power rather than leadership.

METHODS OF LEADERSHIP ANALYSIS

In their rather extensive review of the literature dealing with public leadership, Bell, Hill, and Wright outlined five approaches to the study of leadership:[6]

[6] Wendell Bell, Richard J. Hill, Charles R. Wright, *Public Leadership*. San Francisco: Chandler Publishing Company, 1961, Ch. 2.

The Positional or Formal Leadership Approach. This approach simply selects out those persons who occupy important organizational positions. The researcher is left to judge which organizations and which positions within a given organization are to be designated as "important." In such studies some of the more frequently listed individuals are identified as political leaders, higher civil servants and political appointees, business leaders, military leaders, and office holders in voluntary associations.

The Reputational Approach. Here members of the community who are referred to as "community knowledgeables" are asked to identify those persons they regard as the leaders in the community. The researcher may refer to specific community issues, or he may ask about leadership in the community in general. This approach, which has a number of variations, will be outlined in greater detail in the discussion of power analysis in the next section of this chapter.

The Social Participation Approach. A substantial amount of literature has accumulated on various aspects of social participation. One of the more common approaches, originated by Chapin in 1937, is the social participation scale. This scale calls for detailed information from community leaders about their membership, attendance, contributions, offices held, and committee service in various formal and voluntary organizations. From this information an index or scale of social participation is computed and members of the community are ranked, with those receiving the highest scores being designated as community influentials.

The Personal Influence or Opinion Leadership Approach. This procedure is designed to identify those to whom others turn for information or advice about some topic, or those who have influenced some specific decision or opinion of the respondent or others. Opinion leaders are not necessarily individuals in formal positions in the community. They may be friends, relatives, neighbors, or others.

The Decision-Making or Event Analysis Approach. This approach involves tracing the history of a particular community decision through which some problem was engaged, confronted, and resolved. The research usually focuses on the course the decision-making process follows from inception to completion. One of the primary aims is to identify which leaders served as decision makers at each stage of the process.

Other Approaches to Leadership. Other approaches, which are not covered by the preceding five categories, are included in studies of social stratification, analysis of newspaper stories, published listings of individuals in such references as *Who's Who* and the *Social Register*. In addition there is considerable literature on leadership in small groups. Although the small group literature contains much information pertinent to social power, it is less relevant than other studies for the purpose at hand.[7]

MAJOR METHODS OF POWER ANALYSIS

Several methodological approaches have been used in the study of social power in the community. Because of differences in the definition of concepts and in the intent and objectives of various studies, it is often difficult to equate the findings of one study with those of another. Furthermore, the literature on social power often confuses sources of information with methods of determining who the power actors are.

There are two broad methods: the decision-making approach, that is, determining who makes decisions of consequence for the community (or who blocks decisions or actions); and the reputational technique, that is, determining who the individuals are who are reputed to have power by other community members. These two methods will be outlined in greater detail below. The major sources of information, regardless of the method used, are: personal observation; organizational charts of selected organizations; news media or other published materials; judges, highly informed observers of the local scene; and personal interviews. Some studies make use of both techniques; in fact, to get at the full scope of community power it is likely that both approaches must be combined.

The Decision-making Approach. This approach is based on the assumption that those individuals with the greatest social power will play instrumental roles in the decision-making process of the community. It begins with the identification of what are considered to be some of the major community issues, for example, the establishment of a United Fund, a general hospital, a public health service, or some other undertaking. Because research suggests that the structure of community power varies from one issue or decision to

---

[7] For a brief discussion of these approaches and a list of references dealing with them, see *Ibid.*, pp. 30-31.

another, to determine the entire power structure of a community it would be necessary to analyze more than one community decision.

This approach involves tracing the history of a community decision from its inception to its completion and identifying the decision makers at each stage of development. It has a number of limitations. The researcher must go through the time-consuming process of either analyzing a community issue as it occurs or reconstructing the process after it has taken place. Such research involves extensive commitment of resources—time, money, and personnel. Furthermore, the expenditure must be multiplied by the number of issues deemed necessary to be studied for a complete analysis of social power in the community. This method has the further limitation that it assumes that community influentials actually do something visible, while in reality they may not take "visible" actions.[8]

The Reputational Approach. In this approach the researcher seeks to identify individuals with social power through the opinions or judgments of other members of the community. There are several major steps:[9]

1. To identify major issue areas of current concern in the community. These may be essentially the same ones that were discussed in the section on decision making. They generally include such broad community areas as education, agriculture, industrial development, health, social and economic development, rural development, and urban redevelopment. In addition, information is sought on persons who are perceived to have generalized power in community affairs.

2. To select a small number of individuals in the community who are most likely to be knowledgeable about key influentials in community affairs. Such "knowledgeables" would likely include editors of newspapers, bankers, officials in the Chamber of Commerce, local government officials, officers in key community organizations, and others. Normally, these knowledgeables would be selected from different sectors of the community such as business, government, education, religion, and politics. The number selected would depend on the size of the community.

---

[8] Ronald C. Powers, *Identifying The Community Power Structure*. Iowa State University, Cooperative Extension Service, North Central Regional Extension Publication No. 19, November, 1965, p. 8.

[9] For a more extensive discussion of this approach, see *Ibid.*, pp. 8 ff.

3. To interview the knowledgeables with the prime objective of determining whom they see as the key individuals in power positions with regard to the issue areas under consideration. The frequent overlap between knowledgeables and community influentials is recognized by the researchers, and therefore the knowledgeable being interviewed is always asked whether or not he considers himself to be a member of the group he names.

4. To sort through all the names he has been given, retaining the names of those who are mentioned a given number of times for each issue under consideration. The researcher goes on the assumption that the individuals with the most "mentions" in each issue area are the top influentials in the community for that area. The top influentials for all issues under consideration are regarded as the individuals constituting the power structure of the community.

5. To check the reliability of the list of names derived through the first four steps. One of the primary methods of checking reliability is to interview either the entire group or a sample of the community influentials named thus far and ask them essentially the same questions that were asked of the knowledgeables.

The discussion here is not a critical analysis, but it seems appropriate to point out a few of the shortcomings of the reputational approach. One of its major limitations stems from the problem of validity—do those individuals with a reputation for power in a community indeed have power and exercise it? A person may be judged to have power when in reality he is merely held in high esteem. Likewise, an individual who is highly visible in a community because of an office he holds may be regarded as having power when he does not. Another individual may appear to have power when in reality he may simply be responding to the pressure of persons in power positions who in fact control him.

A growing difficulty with using such an approach in our increasingly mobile society is that of identifying influentials who are geographically or socially removed from the community. This problem is the reverse of the problem of visibility in the community. In many instances individuals behind the scenes may exert more power than individuals who are more visible.

Another difficulty is the time lag that often exists between the emergence of a new influential and the time he is reputed to be an influential. Individuals may be exercising a good deal of power long before they develop a reputation for power or influence in the community, and their reputations may continue for some time after they are no longer in a position to exercise power.

In view of the limitations of these two approaches to the study of power, it would seem that some combination of them would increase the validity of power studies.

TYPES OF POWER STRUCTURES

We have seen that the various types of power structures can be placed along a continuum from the most monolithic to the most pluralistic—recognizing, of course, that undoubtedly there are no pure types. Perhaps the "ideal type" of monolithic power structure can be represented by the single family dominating power positions in a community or by a company town where power is in the hands of corporate managers, whereas an ideal type of pluralistic community power structure can be depicted by what is often referred to as a "leadership pool."[10]

Monolithic power structures are more likely to be found in communities with a low degree of industrialization; small population; religious, ethical, and occupational homogeneity; weak local government; and limited unionization and organization of the working classes.[11]

ONE FAMILY AND/OR ONE INDUSTRY

This type of power structure is exemplified by a dominant family or industry,[12] which controls the major source of employment and the resources.

---

[10] David Rogers, "Community Political Systems: A Framework and Hypothesis for Comparative Studies," in Bert E. Swanson (ed.), *Current Trends in Comparative Community Studies*. Kansas City, Missouri: Community Studies, Inc., Public Affairs Monograph Series, No. 1, 1962, pp. 37 ff.

[11] *Ibid.*, p. 47.

[12] See William H. Form and Delbert C. Miller, *Industry, Labor, and Community*. New York: Harper and Row, 1960; W. Lloyd Warner, et al., *Democracy in Jonesville*. New York: Harper and Row, 1949; W. Lloyd Warner, *The Social System of the Modern Factory*. New Haven: Yale University Press, 1947; Robert A. Dahl, Unpublished research on New Haven politics; James McKee, "Status and Power in the Industrial Community," *American Journal of Sociology*, Vol. 58 (1953), pp. 364–370; Robert O. Schultze, "The Bifurcation of Power in a Satellite City," in Morris Janowitz (ed.), *Community Political Systems*. New York: The Free Press, 1961, pp. 19–81; Eugene V. Schneider, *Industrial Sociology*. New York: McGraw-Hill, 1957.

In the case of a family, positions of power in the community tend to be inherited and, therefore, held for many years. In the one-industry town, the power structure of the plant carries over into community affairs. The top officer of the company is a key influential in the community. If the company is locally owned it is often the father or the son of the dominant, perhaps the founding, family. In extreme cases of one-industry towns, the company owns the stores and places of residence, and everyone works for the company.

A well-known study, describing an extended family that dominated much of the economic life of a city, is the research of the Lynds of Middletown.[13] Several brothers had settled in this community at the turn of the century. Later, as their sons and daughters married, many of them remained in the town.

This family developed a prosperous industry and participated in many facets of the community's life. The family owned a bank; they were members of various boards of directors; and they took an interest in other community agencies. Very influential in the ongoing life of the community, this family had to be reckoned with in any major undertaking in the city.

Other kinds of monolithic power structures may be based on the domination of the community by education, such as a college town, or religion, such as Rimrock, New Mexico, where the Mormon Church plays an important role.[14]

In small communities one is more likely to find monolithic structures in which the whole range of major issues are dealt with by a single family, industry, or a small closely knit clique. There is little differentiation of function of influentials from one issue area to another. In addition, power and social class are likely to go hand in hand. There is a general fusing of the political, economic, and social status orders into a total unity, which may in local terminology be summed up in the terms "best families," or as expressed in *Plainville U.S.A.* by James West, the "upper crust."[15] In the more com-

---

[13] Robert S. Lynd and Helen Lynd, *Middletown in Transition*. New York: Harcourt, Brace, 1937.

[14] Evon Z. Vogt and Thomas F. O'Dea, "A Comparative Study of the Role of Values in Social Action in Two South-Western Communities," *American Sociological Review*, Vol. 18 (December, 1953), pp. 645–654.

[15] James West, *Plainville U.S.A.* New York: Columbia University Press, 1945.

plex industrialized and urbanized communities there is greater specialization of function by issue areas among influentials, and therefore a greater tendency toward a pluralistic power structure, as represented by the so-called "leadership pool." Status and power are likely to be specialized rather than diffused.

Given the present and anticipated trends in community structure, it is likely that one-family or one-industry dominance is on the wane. Increasing industrialization and urbanization and the increasing influence of forces from outside the local community will broaden the power base in most communities. Greater emphasis on organized labor, stronger farm organizations, and the unionization of teachers and other professionals must also be reckoned with in the years ahead.

CLIQUES OR COALITIONS

This type of community power structure is made up of a relatively small number of community influentials who "emerge" into an informal, though quite closely knit, clique group, which constitutes the primary policy-making structure of the community. These individuals come from the top levels of some of the dominant social systems in the community. The most frequently represented systems are business, industry, professionals, and occasionally representatives of local government. Except in communities in which a given church is dominant in the community, religion is seldom represented among the top influentials. The same holds true for education.

Even in rural areas, power is more likely to be vested primarily in the local town or village influentials from "main street" businesses and, in some instances, lawyers and newspaper editors or others who control mass media. An example of such a power structure is reported in *Small Town in Mass Society* by Vidich and Bensman.[16] In this community the "invisible government" was composed of the implement and feed dealer, a lawyer, and the newspaper editor. The leadership roles of these men appeared in virtually all important community issues. When farmers are represented in the power structures of such communities they are usually individuals

---

[16] Arthur J. Vidich and Joseph Bensman, *Small Town in Mass Society*. New York: Doubleday and Company, 1960.

who control large resources and are usually from the families with a past history of high social standing in the community.

While these influentials can and sometimes do act in concert on certain community issues, they are usually selective in their involvement. Some have more interest and, therefore, become more involved in certain issues than do others. These individuals have considerable power in their communities, however, and must be reckoned with in any major decision or project.

One of the best-known studies demonstrating the importance of cliques is Floyd Hunter's *Community Power Structure.*[17] He found that members of a policy-making clique had frequent contact and communication with one another and made decisions on a variety of projects.

Perhaps a more frequent grouping is that of coalitions or, as they are sometimes called, fluid coalitions. The basic notion portrayed here is that influentials from various loci of power form a temporary coalition with regard to certain key community issues in which they are interested. The membership of such coalitions varies from issue to issue, and once an issue is disposed of the coalition is dissolved.

Kent Jennings, in his study of community influentials in Atlanta, reported that the influentials in Atlanta's power structure consisted of several coalitions not dominated by economic notables.[18] He concluded that there was a moderate amount of overlapping membership among these coalitions.

Agger and Goldrich, in their study of Valley City and Boomtown, found a clique of top leaders in the former and a polynucleated set of leadership groups in the latter. Many small, short-lived cliques were found in this top leadership group.[19]

Miller and others, reporting on a study of Pacific City, observed two patterned groupings, a fluid coalition among influentials about

---

[17] Floyd Hunter, *Community Power Structure*. Chapel Hill: University of North Carolina Press, 1953.

[18] M. Kent Jennings, *Community Influentials*. New York: The Free Press, 1964.

[19] Robert E. Agger and Daniel Goldrich, "Community Power Structures and Partisanship," *American Sociological Review*, Vol. 23 (August, 1958), pp. 383–392.

most issues and clique relationships around a set of specific situations.[20]

These studies point up the prevalence of small groupings of influentials who have considerable power in their communities. The number of influentials that are concerned with multiple issues varies in these studies. In general, influentials are selective concerning their involvement in various issues, and the vast majority would not appear on lists of leaders in three or four projects.

LEADERSHIP POOL

The leadership pool is a pluralistic type of community power structure. It includes a sizable number of able people who address themselves to a particular issue; however, few of these individuals are involved in a large number of issues. In other words, a leader or influential in one area is not likely to be influential in another area. Where overlapping in leadership does occur from one issue to another, the persons are usually public officials, for example, a mayor who has broad community concerns. This type of power structure is more characteristic of modern urban industrial communities than of small rural communities.

Among the most prominent research efforts in this area is the work by Dahl and his associates who conducted an extensive study of New Haven.[21] Using the issue approach, they studied leadership patterns in three major issue areas: urban redevelopment, public education, and political nominations. Dahl concluded that an influential in one area is not likely to be influential in a second or third area.

Similar findings were reported by Wildavsky in his study of Oberlin.[22] He contends that no one person or group exerts leadership in all areas of community life. He found leadership to be a pluralistic phenomenon. Where an overlap in leadership occurred in Oberlin, Wildavsky found it among public officials such as the city manager, mayor, and members of the city council.

---

[20] Peter F. Drucker, Robert A. Dahl, and Delbert C. Miller, in *Power and Democracy in America*, William V. D'Antonio and Howard J. Ehrlich (eds.). Notre Dame, Ind.: University of Notre Dame Press, 1961, p. 56.

[21] Robert A. Dahl, *Who Governs?* New Haven: Yale University Press, 1961.

[22] Aaron Wildavsky, *Leadership in a Small Town*. Totowa, N. J.: The Bedminster Press, 1964.

ABSENTEE-OWNED CORPORATIONS

Much has been said in recent years about the influence of absentee owners. Officials of absentee-owned corporations can take a part in either a monolithic or polymorphic power structure. The literature reports instances of both these arrangements. In reviewing the literature, however, one gains the impression that the monolithic approach,[23] in which the corporation had considerable control, is giving way to more polymorphic arrangements, in which branch management becomes involved in issues where the parent corporation has some economic stake or where public relations programs are important.

Pellegrin and Coates, in their study of Bigtown, found that executives of absentee-owned corporations were discriminating in their choice of civic associations.[24] These executives did not belong to as many local organizations as the usual business or industrial people; but the research found that 60 percent of the executives belonged to both of the two most powerful organizations in the community. The two organizations played vital roles in charting the course of Bigtown's plans and projects via their policy and decision-making activities.[25] The executives were under-represented in the less powerful organizations.

Schulze, in his study of Cibola's power structure, found a different "situation."[26] The executives of the absentee-owned corporations maintained a "hands off" position and did not want to get involved. They felt that the hazards of possible alienation by such activities could not be offset by any advantages gained through playing roles in the local power structure.

LEVELS OF LEADERSHIP AND POWER

A wide range of studies points out that only a small percentage of a community's population is involved in the initiation, formulation, and even execution of many community projects. Dahl makes

---

[23] Rogers, *op. cit.*, p. 40.

[24] Roland J. Pellegrin and Charles S. Coates, "Absentee-Owned Corporations and Community Power Structure," *American Journal of Socoiology*, Vol. 61 (March, 1956).

[25] *Ibid.*, pp. 414–416.

[26] Robert O. Schulze, "Economic Dominants in Community Power Structure," *American Sociological Review*, Vol. 23 (February, 1958), pp. 3–9.

a distinction between the direct and indirect involvements of people. A large number of persons he identifies as constituents exert only indirect influence on decisions.

Various researchers have identified different levels in the leadership and power structure of communities, regardless of the type of power arrangements they discover. Although the terminology is not always the same, it denotes not only different levels of power but also different functions within each level.

Influentials. A term frequently used to denote individuals with the greatest amount of power is "influentials." This category is sometimes subdivided into the categories of "top influentials" and "key influentials,"[27] or essentially what Floyd Hunter called first-rate and second-rate influentials.[28] The essential distinction is one of degree, with the key influentials having more generalized power than top influentials. In sociometric terms, key influentials are those who are selected as leaders by other influentials. Key influentials are a kind of core of the community elite.

Persons occupying similar positions of power are referred to as "leaders" by Dahl in his study of New Haven.[29] In *Small Town in Mass Society*, Vidich and Bensman differentiate between general and specialized leaders.[30]

In general, influentials address themselves to top policy matters in the community. They may initiate policy, undertake the initiation, direction, or supervision of major community projects, and exert veto power in major projects and issues. They may also be active in the early planning and initiation stages of a community project.

Lieutenants. A second major echelon of community power may be labeled "lieutenants." This is the equivalent of "subleaders" as used by Dahl and "specialized leadership" as used by Vidich and Bensman. Lieutenants are not as likely to be evident in small communities as they are in larger communities. In smaller communities, their roles are often carried out by influentials.

In general, lieutenants are designated to carry through on the de-

---

[27] William H. Form and Delbert C. Miller, *Industry, Labor and Community.* New York: Harper and Row, 1960, pp. 444–448.

[28] Hunter, *op. cit.*

[29] Dahl, *op. cit.*

[30] Vidich and Bensman, *op. cit.*

tails of planning and implementing policy decisions of the influentials. Because of the high social visibility of lieutenants, the less knowledgeable persons in a community may identify them as influentials.

Doers. A third level of community power can properly be labeled "doers." These are the individuals who carry out the actions associated with the execution of a project or a decision. They may sometimes be referred to as "leg men." Doers are usually ministers, teachers, agency personnel, or other professional persons who serve on working committees, collect funds, carry petitions, formulate resolutions, and take care of the many details that are inevitably a part of actually accomplishing something.

Influentials are generally drawn from upper-level socio-economic groups and have long tenure in their positions. They are usually long-term residents, if not natives of their community.

CHARACTERISTICS OF INFLUENTIALS

Among the more salient characteristics of influentials is their prominent position in important social systems within the community. They usually own or control considerable resources. The vast majority are white males who have a higher than average education. Many have college degrees. In general, they are in the middle or upper income brackets, and are 45 years of age or older.[31]

Most of these individuals are from business and industry, primarily financial, commercial, and manufacturing. Professionals are also found among the influentials, particularly lawyers. Occasionally certain key local governmental positions are also represented. Only on rare occasions do farmers appear among the top influentials, and then primarily in highly rural areas. Some studies refer to the "economic dominants," businessmen or industrialists who are extremely influential in economic matters.

Research has shown that influentials belong to many organizations, but that their participation, as registered by frequency of attendance at meetings, is usually low.[32] Many influentials rarely attend

---

[31] For more details on leaders and subleaders see: Dahl, *op. cit.;* Wildavsky, *op. cit.;* and Vidich and Bensman, *op. cit.*

[32] William H. Form and Warren L. Sauer, *Community Influentials in a Middle-Sized City.* East Lansing: Michigan State University, The Institute for Community Development and Services, 1960, pp. 9 ff.

organizational meetings, and some are members in name only. In general, their highest level of participation was in past years. Their present participation consists primarily of advising and consulting with present officers, rather than attending meetings. In this capacity they can exert a major influence on community organizations and agencies.

Information on lieutenants and doers or leg men is not as extensively documented. They appear to be drawn heavily from the middle class. Occupationally most are from the white collar occupations, in general ministers, teachers, young lawyers, various agency personnel, middle management, and occasionally skilled labor.

A MODEL FOR COMMUNITY ACTION

Considerable attention has recently been given to the orderly development of communities through the creation of programs of planned change. These efforts have been given various names such as community development, community action, and resource development. They represent an important application to local problems of what we know about community structure, and should ultimately allow us to mobilize local resources much more effectively.

One of the elements of most attempts at programmed change is the division of effort into a series of overlapping stages. While these stages do not always occur in a well-defined sequence, they can be separated for purposes of this discussion into six stages.[33]

STAGE I CONVERGENCE OF INTEREST

As any system functions over time, various structural or functional problems emerge as people attempt to work toward their primary goals. Individuals and/or groups of people become interested in altering community structure and processes by introducing new structures, designing new programs, or taking action to make the system function more effectively. At this stage in the action process, there is a general sharing of ideas and an emergence and convergence of interests about what is needed, what might be considered, what could be done. People need not have identical motives behind their interest in the situation; convergence of their interests is the only requirement.

---

[33] This discussion is based primarily on Christopher Sower, John Holland, Kenneth Tiedke, and Walter Freeman, *Community Involvement*. New York: The Free Press, 1957.

STAGE II INITIATION OF ACTION

Through the convergence of interests, a group of individuals, usually influentials who represent groups, become interested in doing something about a particular problem. Gradually they move toward a position from which they might initiate some action. This typically happens as they begin to identify *specific* needs or problems, commit themselves to specific goals and objectives (at least in a preliminary way), and attempt to justify their action to the rest of the community. As needs are identified and approaches are outlined, an attempt is made to identify appropriate resources within and outside the local community. If these activities result in the proliferation of so many alternatives that some must be put aside, some preliminary priorities are set.

Some attempt may also be made at this stage to determine who in the power structure has the socially defined right to initiate action. Such a concern may anticipate the need to generate support for action and to overcome opposition that may form once concrete proposals are articulated.

STAGE III LEGITIMATION AND SPONSORSHIP

At this stage an attempt is made to gain approval from the individuals and groups in the power structure who are deemed most important to insure community-wide acceptance of program proposals. The right to initiate action must be legitimated if it is to be approved. In some instances, these rights may be contained within the sponsoring group because of its nature or composition. In many instances, however, access must be obtained to those groups or community influentials whose sponsorship or approval can insure acceptance. This must usually be secured before support can be gained from the remainder of the community, for people who are not directly involved in a program look to opinion leaders to guide them in their decision to give or withhold their support.

STAGE IV DEVELOPMENT OF AN OVERALL ACTION PLAN

Although much planning has taken place up to this point, planning activities are now passed into the hands of those who are empowered to cast them formally in the name of the community. Goals are defined; decision-making criteria are established; the necessary organizational machinery is projected; and an attempt is made to establish the kind of relationships across program areas that will assure effective operation over time. Self-study and research may be initiated, to secure the information needed to understand the community and its operations and to provide the information required to develop long-range plans.

STAGE V IMPLEMENTATION OF THE ACTION PLAN

After a comprehensive plan has been developed and been properly legitimated or approved by an appropriate configuration of community influentials, it is publicized in the community through public meetings or public hearings. A concerted attempt is made to gain public acceptance by providing it with necessary information.

Once it appears that public sanction will be obtained—if only eventually—some of those who will take responsibility for the day-to-day operation of the new activity begin the intricate process of mobilizing the men and materials they will require.

STAGE VI ASSESSMENT OR EVALUATION OF ACTION

An action program, once initiated, continues to be an integral element of a stable program of action. It may be highly successful; it may completely fail; or it may fall somewhat short of expectations but offer hope of allowing fulfillment of the goals initially associated with it. This stage involves attempts to assess the consequences of the decisions taken to implement community purposes. Evaluation involves the appraising of progress toward the goals, assessing the perceived costs and outlining appropriate modifications in the program.

This action framework is not a blueprint for community action. It is, however, a useful way to conceptualize what can become an immensely complex collective enterprise, one that is increasingly important to successful development of the planned changes through which we maintain communities.

SUGGESTIONS FOR FURTHER READING

Bell, Wendell, Richard J. Hill, and Charles R. Wright, *Public Leadership*. San Francisco: Chandler Publishing Company, 1961.

Dahl, Robert A., *Who Governs?* New Haven: Yale University Press, 1961.

D'Antonio, William V. and Howard J. Ehrlich (eds.), *Power and Democracy in America*. Notre Dame, Ind.: University of Notre Dame Press, 1961.

Form, William H. and Delbert C. Miller, *Industry, Labor, and Community*. New York: Harper and Row, 1960 (pp. 444-448).

Jennings, M. Kent, *Community Influentials*. New York: The Free Press, 1964.

Kimbrough, Ralph B., *Political Power and Educational Decision-Making*. Chicago: Rand McNally, 1964.

Pellegrin, Roland J. and Charles H. Coates, "Absentee-Owned Corporations and Community Power Structure," *The American Journal of Sociology* (Vol. 61, No. 5, March 1956), p. 413.

Powers, Ronald C., *Identifying the Community Power Structure*. North Central Regional Extension Publication No. 19, NCRS-5 Leadership Series No. 2. Ames, Iowa: Iowa State University, Cooperative Extentension Service, 1965.

Press, Charles, *Main Street Politics*. East Lansing: Michigan State University Press, 1962.

Presthus, Robert, *Men at the Top*. New York: Oxford University Press, 1964.

Swanson, Bert E. (ed.), *Current Trends in Comparative Community Studies*. Kansas City, Mo.: Community Studies, Inc., 1962.

Vidich, Arthur J. and Joseph Bensman, *Small Town in Mass Society*. New York: Doubleday and Company, 1960.

Walton, John, "Substance and Artifact: The Current Status of Research on Community Power Structure," *American Journal of Sociology* (Vol. 71, No. 4, January 1966), pp. 430-438.

Williams, Oliver P. and Charles Press, *Democracy in Urban America*. Chicago: Rand McNally, 1961.

CHAPTER 3

METAMORPHOSIS IN AMERICA:

A New Synthesis of Rural and Urban Society

KARL A. FOX

> *"What a man sees depends both upon what he looks at and also upon what his previous visual-conceptual experience has taught him to see."*
>
> —Thomas S. Kuhn[1]

In a small, isolated, primitive community—consisting essentially of an extended family and operating without the use of money—the processes we now think of as economic may have been merged in a simple flow of traditional and relatively undifferentiated activities.

Perhaps today the same kinds of activities are carried on through home and family, neighborhood and playmates, elementary school and church. Not only have the social processes of the small community been differentiated, but the fragmented and specialized processes have become linked to counterparts in other communities. The prospect of an integration of the small community into larger ones often arouses deep concern, for implicitly many rural residents value smallness, isolation, and self-sufficiency.

THE EMPHASIS OF MODERN ECONOMICS

In contrast, the economist takes it for granted that occupational specialization and interregional trade tend to increase because they enable us to produce more items that people want from a given

---

Karl Fox is head of the Department of Economics, Iowa State University. He has published extensively in the fields of urban and regional economics.

[1] Kuhn, Thomas S., *The Structure of Scientific Revolutions*. Chicago: University of Chicago Press, 1962, p. 112.

initial set of resources; because, that is, they allow for increased satisfaction of material values. Specialization is facilitated by the use of money; human skills are exchanged for money; money is exchanged for goods. The larger the circle becomes, the higher the level of value realization.

The money economy, particularly in the United States form of "cash and carry" with publicly displayed prices, saves a tremendous amount of time and energy, which in primitive societies was invested in less-efficient production processes. We make our choices and pay for them; our obligation to the storekeeper and his claim on us are canceled out at the cash register.

Money also provides the economist with a unit of account that reduces everything bought and sold to a common denominator. In one sense we cannot add apples and automobiles; but in another sense we can—we can add up the numbers of dollars we spend for them.

This fact has enabled modern economics to become, for the most part, a quantitative science. The money receipts and expenditures of a particular household can be organized into a set of household accounts. Similarly, the money receipts and expenditures of a business firm can be organized into a system of accounts. Government agencies and private nonprofit organizations also keep accounts of receipts and expenditures. Since the 1930's, all the receipts and expenditures mentioned have been aggregated and organized into a set of *national income and product accounts.* These accounts are published quarterly and provide a great deal of insight into the economy.

As a result, the economist can represent the sum of all economic values produced in the United States in any given year by a single number. In 1965, the Gross National Product (GNP) was estimated at $681.2 billion.[2] In 1958 the GNP was only $447.3 billion. But the price level in 1965 was 11 percent higher than in 1958. If all goods

[2] I do not mean to imply that economists have solved all the conceptual problems that lie behind this number. For example, the wages paid to a housekeeper are counted as part of the national income; the value of the same tasks when performed by a housewife is not. Such problems do not detract significantly from the power of the national income and product accounts to measure the performance of the market economy. Lack of such quantitative measures accounted for much of the tragic fumbling of economic policy in the United States and other countries during the 1920's and 1930's.

and services produced in 1965 were revalued at their 1958 prices, the 1965 GNP would be estimated at $614.4 billion (1958 dollars), or 37 percent larger than in 1958 in real terms. These economic concepts can also be applied to regions, states, counties, or towns. The economic values produced in a small community in 1965 can in principle be compared with those produced in 1958.

The fact that such figures exist tends to set economics apart from other social sciences. What was the value of all the activities of families in 1965? What value should be placed on church activities? How much greater was each of these sums in 1965 than in 1958, in total and as an average per person?

Economists have been able to provide answers, albeit crude and provisional ones, to such queries. The well-ordered income accounts, index numbers, and equation systems of modern economics started out from trade reports on market prices, from statistics collected as by-products of regulatory activities, and from other relatively haphazard sources of information that sprang up during the last century.

Since the early 1900's, the array of statistical time series on prices, production, employment, and income has been continually extended and refined. In the 1930's three brilliant economists lent a new sense of urgency and intellectual excitement to this endeavor and to the development of national income accounts. Let us look very briefly at the work of these three men—Keynes, Leontief, and Tinbergen—as background for the rest of the chapter.

Keynes demonstrated that, in principle, a national government could maintain high and relatively stable levels of employment, production, and income by means of a flexible countercyclical policy of taxation and expenditures.[3]

Leontief showed that the structure of a national economy as of a given year could be described by means of an input-output framework (matrix) showing the flows of primary factors of production (labor and capital) into each industry, the flows of intermediate goods from one industry to another (as coal to the steel industry and steel to the automobile industry), and the flows of finished goods and services into "final demand"—consumption by households, use by

[3] Keynes, J. M., *The General Theory of Employment, Interest and Money*. London: Harcourt, Brace, 1936.

government, or investment in plant and equipment by business firms.[4]

Tinbergen showed that time series data on employment, production, income, and other variables could be used to estimate a set of equations constituting a mathematical model of the national economy.[5] Such a model could be used (1) to predict short-run changes in economic activity and (2) to anticipate the probable consequences of specified economic policies.

Modern economics has built on the work of these men and others to produce a rapid cumulation of quantitative and empirical knowledge. For example, the Brookings Quarterly Econometric Model of the United States, published in 1965, represents the national economy as a set of about 150 mathematical equations.[6] The numerical coefficients of these equations are estimated on the basis of time series and other information. The national income accounts, an input-output production translator, and an input-output price translator are all imbedded in this equation system. The system as a whole constitutes a greatly improved and expanded model of the type pioneered by Tinbergen in the 1930's.

Tinbergen made a major contribution to the practical usefulness of such models in the 1950's with his theory of economic policy.[7] A recent synthesis and extension of work along these lines was published by Fox, Sengupta, and Thorbecke in 1966.[8]

The concepts we have been describing in relation to the national economy can be scaled to the level of the small community. We shall find that the processes of exchanging labor for money and money

---

[4] Leontief, Wassily W., *The Structure of American Economy, 1919–1929: An Empirical Application of Equilibrium Analysis*. Cambridge: Harvard University Press, 1941.

[5] Tinbergen, Jan, *Statistical Testing of Business Cycle Theories*, Vol. II: *Business Cycles in the United States of America, 1919–1932*. Geneva: League of Nations Economic Intelligence Service, 1939.

[6] Duesenberry, J. S., Gary Fromm, L. R. Klein, and Edwin Kuh (eds.), *The Brookings Quarterly Econometric Model of the United States*. Chicago: Rand McNally, 1965.

[7] Tinbergen, Jan, *Economic Policy: Principles and Design*. Amsterdam: North-Holland Publishing Company, 1956.

[8] Fox, Karl A., J. K. Sengupta and Erik Thorbecke, *The Theory of Quantitative Economic Policy: With Applications to Economic Growth and Stabilization*. Chicago: Rand McNally and Company, 1966.

for goods in an increasingly motorized society account for many of the perceived problems of the small community. These insights will also, I believe, point the way toward some creative resolutions of some of these problems.

Perhaps, before beginning, it will be helpful to assert that the result of the economist's efforts indicates that we must recognize and legitimate a revolution which on the economic level is a *fait accompli* and which has resulted in a new synthesis of rural and urban society.

GENESIS OF AGRICULTURAL COMMUNITIES IN THE MIDWEST

History casts long shadows. It is only 183 years since the American Revolution was successfully concluded. Only then did large numbers of people along the Atlantic seaboard find it safe to cross the Alleghenys, to settle western New York and Pennsylvania and, in due course, to clear the forests of Ohio, Indiana, Michigan, and Illinois.

The settlers who moved westward across the Allegheny Mountains were suffused with what Paul H. Johnstone called "the boomer psychology."[9]

> . . . Boomer psychology, although in a logical sense, merely an extension of the idea of progress, was much less the product of any intellectual vogue than of the everyday experience of a people feverishly colonizing the rich and unexploited continent in an age of unprecedented world-wide commercial expansion. . . ."[10]

Morris Birkbeck had been deeply impressed earlier by the sensational rises in land value in Eastern Ohio and by the way towns sprang up out of the wilderness:

> On entering the State of Ohio from Wheeling, we find a country beautiful and fertile, and affording to a plain, industrious and thriving population, all that nature has decreed for the comfort of man ***. It is also fully appropriated and thickly settled; and land is worth from twenty to

---

[9] Johnstone, Paul H., "Old Ideals Versus New Ideas in Farm Life," *An Historical Survey of American Agriculture*. Yearbook separate No. 1783, United States Department of Agriculture, Washington, D. C., 1941, pp. 129–130.

[10] Birkbeck, Morris, *Letters from Illinois*, Edition 3, London, 1818, p. 85, quoted in Johnstone, *op. cit.*, p. 130.

thirty dollars per acre. An advance of thousand percent, in about 10 years! *** looking forward for the interest of our families *** we must pass on, until we reach the country where good land is to be purchased at the Government price of two dollars per acre; and which, in return for a few temporary privations, increases in value in a similar ratio. . . .

On any spot where a few settlers cluster together *** some enterprising proprietor finds in his section what he deems a good scite (sic) for a town, he has it surveyed and laid out in lots, which he sells, or offers for sale by auction.

The new town then assumes the name of its founder:—a storekeeper builds a little framed store, and sends for a few cases of goods; and then a tavern starts up, which becomes the residence of a doctor and of a lawyer, and the boarding house of the storekeeper. . . . Soon follow a blacksmith and other handicraftsmen in useful succession: a schoolmaster, who is also the minister of religion, becomes an important accession to this rising community. Thus the town proceeds, if it proceeds at all, with accumulating force, until it becomes the metropolis of the neighborhood. Hundreds of these speculations may have failed, but hundreds prosper; and thus trade begins and thrives, as population grows around these lucky spots; imports and exports maintaining their just proportion. One year ago, the neighborhood of this very town of Princeton was clad in "buckskin"; now the men appear at church in good blue cloth, and the women in fine calicoes and straw bonnets.[11]

Here we see the process of agricultural settlement and the emergence of villages in an intimate pattern of social and economic interdependence with the farm people at its very beginning. Morris Birkbeck was describing a frontier community in Illinois in 1817.

It was almost one hundred years before the first systematic study of this process was undertaken, in Wisconsin, by a social scientist.

GALPIN'S "FUNDAMENTAL COMMUNITY," 1911–1913

In 1915 a University of Wisconsin sociologist published a bulletin on "The Social Anatomy of an Agricultural Community," which immediately became a classic.[12] C. J. Galpin made an intensive study of trade areas and other aspects of Walworth County, a 16-township county (24 miles on an edge, with a total area of 576 square miles) in southern Wisconsin. Galpin and his associates conducted

---

[11] *Ibid.*, p. 130.

[12] Galpin, C. J., *The Social Anatomy of an Agricultural Community*. Madison: Agricultural Experiment Station of the University of Wisconsin, Research Bulletin No. 34, May, 1915.

FIGURE 1

A MAP OF THE SCHOOL DISTRICTS OF WALWORTH COUNTY

The small zigzag areas on this map show the scale of the prevailing type of organized rural social life in Wisconsin. The village and city centers, however, suggest a changing scale commensurate with the coming economic rural order.

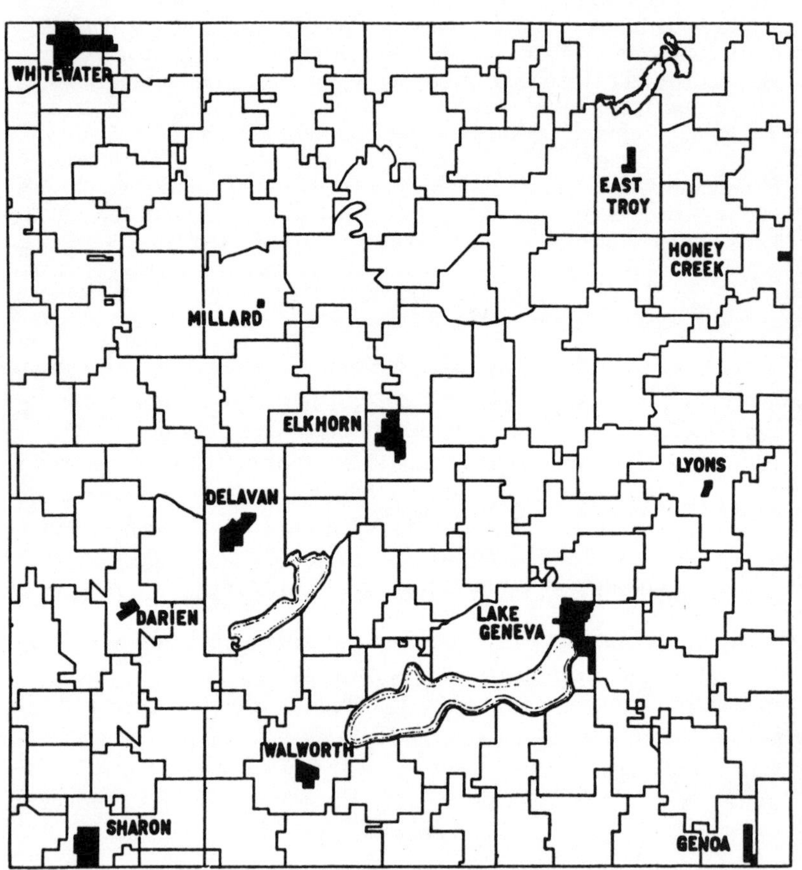

their survey between August 1911 and July 1913. The economy of Walworth County had had ample time (about three generations) to adjust itself to the horse and wagon pattern of local transportation. Walworth County was a mature economy, within the limitations of local travel by horse and wagon or on foot at perhaps 5 miles an hour, weather permitting.

For our purposes, the striking feature of the society described by Galpin was the small geographic scale on which its economic and social activities were organized.

Figure 1 (a reproduction of Galpin's Figure 11) is a map of the school districts of Walworth County in 1911. By casual inspection, there were approximately 100 school districts, covering an average area of about 6 square miles each. Most of these districts must have contained only the traditional one-room schools; few students would have lived more than one and one-half to two miles from such a school. The district boundaries, like other man-made boundaries, must have contained arbitrary and even capricious elements; the basic scale was designed for a pedestrian student body.

Figure 2 (a reproduction of Galpin's Figure 2) delineates 12 trade areas in Walworth County. On the average, each of the 12 trade centers served an area of perhaps 50 square miles. Within the black areas, a single town had a *de facto* monopoly; farm people living in the shaded areas traded at 2 or more of the 12 centers. Residents of the white areas near the borders of Walworth County traded at towns in adjoining counties.

Galpin made similar maps delineating 11 banking zones, 7 local newspaper zones, 12 village milk zones, 12 village church zones, 9 high school zones, and 4 village library zones.

As to the school districts, Galpin wrote:

> A study of the country school districts of the county shows the fact that the prevailing scale of organized farm life is that of the neighborhood. The schoolhouse, an open country church, and a creamery, may frequently be found together, among fifteen to thirty families, in a territory of from three to five square miles. A slight tendency to consolidate adjoining school districts exists, but it is only slight. There seems to be a greater tendency to enlarge the village or city districts by addition of farms. It will be seen that Delavan has a school district of thirteen square miles; Lake Geneva, ten; East Troy, seven; Lyons, six; and Elkhorn, four. This probably gives Delavan one million dollars more of taxable farm property for the maintenance of its schools than Elkhorn has, while it

FIGURE 2

TRADE COMMUNITIES

Twelve villages and small cities situated in the county serve as trade centers for the farm homes precisely as for the village and city homes and all the homes trading at the same center form a trade community. Township lines six miles apart indicate the distance.

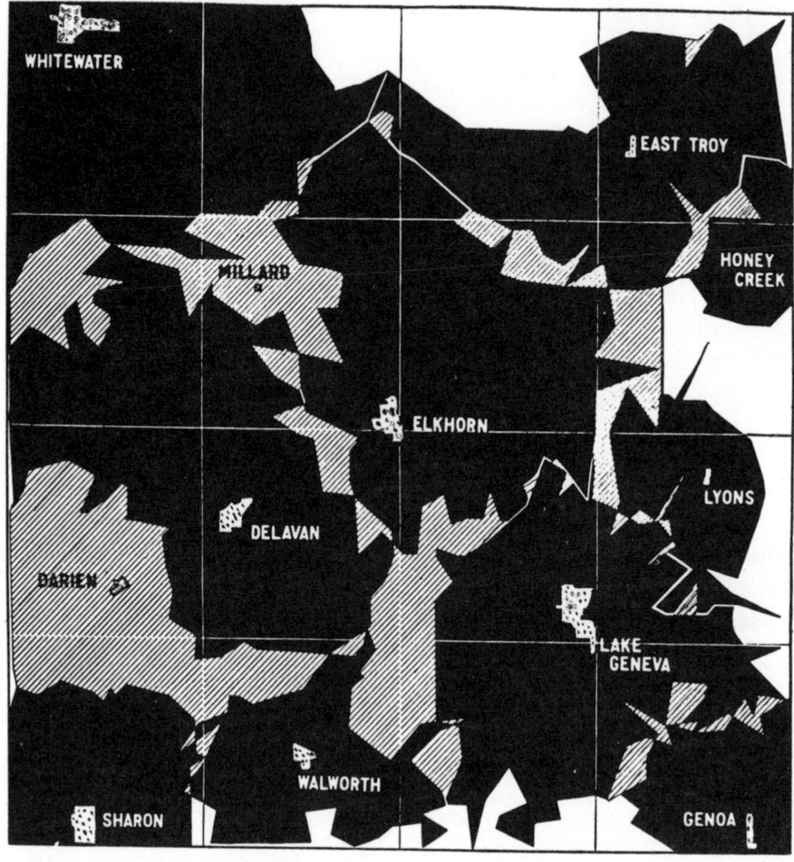

VILLAGE OR CITY CENTER — *TRADE AT ONE CENTER*

TRADE AT TWO OR MORE CENTERS — *TRADE OUTSIDE THE COUNTY*

gives to fifty farm families around Delavan the privilege of some control in their high school.[13]

Galpin also found 9 high school communities in Walworth County, similar to the trade communities but of smaller extent. Of particular and striking significance were the wide farmland areas that made no use of the high schools at all. Galpin's comments on the 9 high school zones are as follows:

With the exception of a few compactly grouped square miles in La Grange Township, and a scattered square mile here and there, no part of Walworth County is more than five miles distant from an existing high school. Practically every farm home in the county is easily within daily reach of some high school. Taking the county as a whole, less than fifteen percent of the farm homes are sending children to high schools.

The high school zones are not only much smaller than the trade or banking zones, but the proportion of farm homes within the zones using the high school is much smaller than that using the shop or bank. It will be noticed that the form of this zone follows the general lines of the trade zone. Instead of an overlapping of zone lines giving a belt of neutral territory, there appears surrounding every zone a belt of homes outside the influence of any high school.

With all the general deficiency apparent in the amount of farm use of these nine high schools, it is plain that a fair percentage of the farm families within two miles of each high school recognized its value. The character of the high school as an agent in idea-forming and association-making, play a wonderful part at the adolescent period of life in democratizing the children of the farm who attend and the children of the village. It would be difficult to overestimate its influence as a force for constructive cooperation, were each high school consciously controlled in adaptation of subjects and management of courses in the interest of those living upon the land as well as of those living in the small city.[14]

The society of 1911 was, of course, influenced by traditions and norms that the parents of 1911 teen-agers had absorbed during their own formative years in the 1870's and 1880's. At that time, crossroads stores, hamlets, and villages located before the railroad network was filled out provided an even simpler and smaller-scale frame for social life. A number of popular poems during this period and even later dealt with the situation in which a youth stays home and works on the farm while his childhood sweetheart is sent away

[13] Galpin, *op. cit.*, pp. 15–16.

[14] Galpin, *op. cit.*, pp. 14–15.

to school. The girl returns from school, after what we would now consider a very limited education, and starts correcting the young man's grammar. In the inevitable showdown, the masculine will predominates and the sweetheart drops back into the speech patterns of her masterful but semiliterate future husband.

It appears that for many adults and teen-agers in Walworth County as of 1911 the advantages of a high school education did not justify more than a 2-mile walk. Given the difficulties of transportation, an eighth grade education in one of the hundred independent school districts in the county was still the norm and a high school education the exception.

How did Galpin summarize his findings about the economy and society of Walworth County? He describes "the actual but unofficial community" in the following words:

> Eight of the twelve civic centers of Walworth County are incorporated; four as cities and four as villages. Officially, that is legally, the incorporated centers are treated as communities, each by and for itself. The foregoing analysis of the use of the leading institutions of each center by the farm population discloses the fact, however, that these institutions are agencies of social service over a comparatively determinable and fixed area of land surrounding each center; that this social service is precisely the same in character as is rendered to those people—whether artisans, employees, or professional persons—who happen to live within the corporate limits of the city or village; moreover, the plain inference is that the inhabitants of the center are more vitally concerned in reality with the development and upkeep of their particular farm land basis than with any other other equal area of land in the state.
>
> It is difficult, if not impossible, to avoid the conclusion that the trade zone about one of these rather complete agricultural civic centers forms the boundary of an actual, if not legal, community, within which the apparent entanglement of human life is resolved into a fairly unitary system of interrelatedness. The fundamental community is a composite of many expanding and contracting feature communities possessing the characteristic pulsating instability of all real life.[15]

The outlines of Galpin's trade communities look almost as irregular as the man-made boundaries of the elementary school districts. Galpin thought he discerned an underlying regularity, however. His trade centers performed similar economic functions and his trade areas were of roughly similar sizes.

---

[15] Galpin, *op. cit.*, pp. 16–19.

FIGURE 3

THE THEORETICAL FORM OF AN AGRICULTURAL COMMUNITY

If all the conditions relating to farm homes and the neighboring trade centers were conceived to be equal, then apparently the agricultural community would be in the form of a circle whose outer edge it would share more or less with neighboring communities.

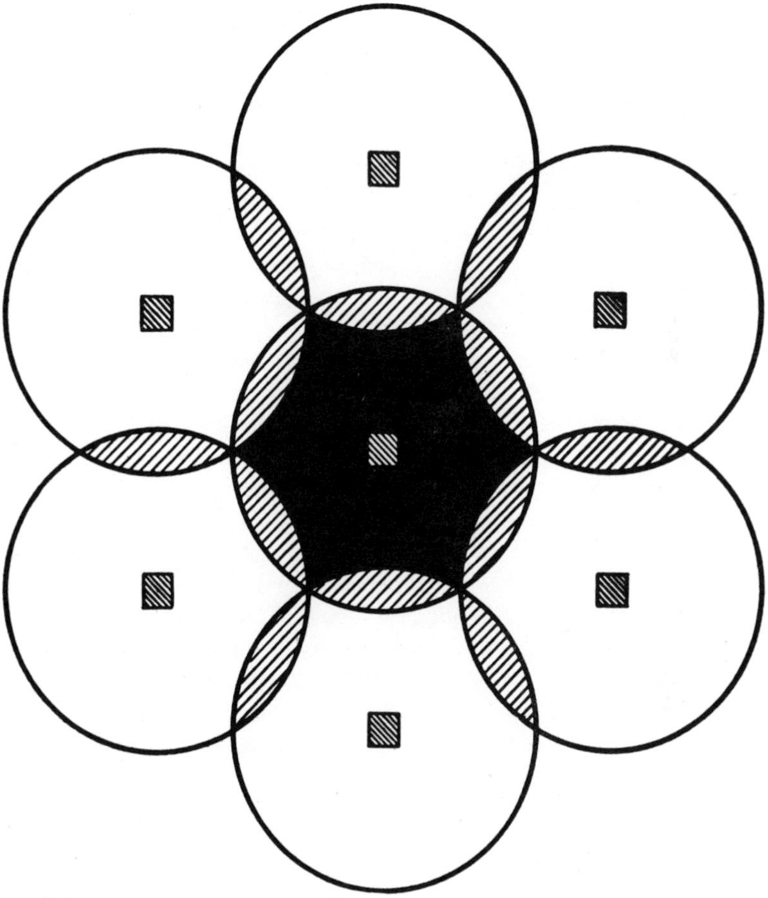

VILLAGE OR CITY CENTER

FARM HOMES USE INSTITUTIONS OF THE CENTER JUST AS DO RESIDENTS OF THE CENTER

FARM HOMES USE INSTITUTIONS OF MORE THAN ONE CENTER

Change in the Small Community

A conventionalized community form. It is possible to conventionalize the form and relationships of these twelve agricultural communities in the following way. Suppose the civic centers to be equal in size and population, equally complete institutionally, and equally distant from each other; suppose all farm homes to be connected with the centers by equally good roads at all seasons of the year, and also equally direct. Then apparently each community would be a circle, with the agricultural city as its center, having a radius somewhat longer than half the distance between any two centers. In order to include all the farm territory within some circle, and to have the least possible common area, we must impose the further condition that the centers be arranged so that only six centers are equally distant from any one center, as shown in Figure [3].[16]

If for administrative purposes it were necessary to draw clear-cut boundaries separating the various communities, a logical approach would be to draw a straight line dividing each shaded area equally between the two overlapping circles. The result would be a pattern of regular hexagons. The regular hexagon has one advantage, recognized by all tile setters—it can cover a large plane surface symmetrically and completely with no overlaps and no gaps.

Daniel Boone, alone in the wilderness with more territory than he can use, might be expected to hunt and gather food over a circular area around his dwelling. At least, this is what we would hypothesize, assuming that the hunting was just as good and the nuts and berries just as numerous in every direction. As other settlers came in and staked out their own hunting and gathering territories, these circular territories would begin to overlap and, to avoid trouble, the areas of overlap might be split fifty-fifty, with hexagons resulting. Lösch hypothesized that a set of towns or trade centers emerging in open country with uniformly distributed agricultural resources would tend to be arranged in a hexagonal pattern.

In practice there are enough variations in the topography of an area, and in the productivity of bottom land in contrast to hillside areas, that actual boundaries sometimes vary from what we might expect. Initial patterns of settlement will be disturbed by rivers, lakes, and fords. After people have settled a territory, the locations of their towns are influenced by the choices they make in laying out roads, railroads, and bridges. Galpin's detailed map of Walworth County, indicating the location of every farm home, shows three large lakes and several smaller ones and a number of winding

[16] Galpin, *op. cit.*, p. 19.

streams.[17] Here and there one can find sets of 2 or 3 contiguous sections in which there are no farm homes. There are some diagonal or winding roads in the county, but there is an underlying rectangular pattern of "section roads" giving access to the individual farm homes.

Thus the irregularity of natural features in Walworth County would have imposed some irregularities on the shapes of trade areas. Most of Galpin's maps, such as the one on trade communities, do the reader some disservice by omitting these natural features. A sizable area southwest of the town of Lake Geneva was inhabited exclusively by fish! A sizable fraction of the area extending westward from East Troy contained no human habitations.

The grid of farm-to-market roads most prominently influenced the shape of trade areas. In practice, horses and wagons followed the roads. If the road grid follows the section lines, as it does in many parts of the Midwest, there is no legal or practical way to generate hexagonal trade areas.

Figure 4 (by the author) shows the effects that the rectangular road grid would logically have had upon the shapes of trade areas in Walworth County. Like Galpin's circles, the rotated squares in Figure 4 ignore irregularities in the terrain, the existence of some diagonal or winding roads, and the possibility that some roads were faster than others (at least in bad weather).

Figure 4 assumes that horses and wagons could travel along any section of road at 5 miles per hour. If the boundaries of each trade area were approximately one hour's travel (5 miles) from the trade center, the boundaries of the trade areas would take the forms and locations shown. Starting from East Troy, a person could reach any corner of the square by traveling 5 miles along the road in the appropriate compass direction. If he lived along the northeast boundary of the square, however, his trip home from East Troy would involve some such pattern as 4 miles east and one mile north; 3 miles east and 2 miles north; 2 miles east and 3 miles north; or one mile east and 4 miles north.

Given the accidents of terrain and other factors, which determined the original locations of the trade centers, a set of rotated squares with boundaries at a distance of 5 road miles from the

[17] Galpin, *op. cit.*, Figure 1.

FIGURE 4

SCHEMATIC MAP OF COUNTY STUDIED BY C. J. GALPIN (1915)

This figure assumes a rectangular road grid and travel (pedestrian or horse and wagon) at 5 miles per hour.

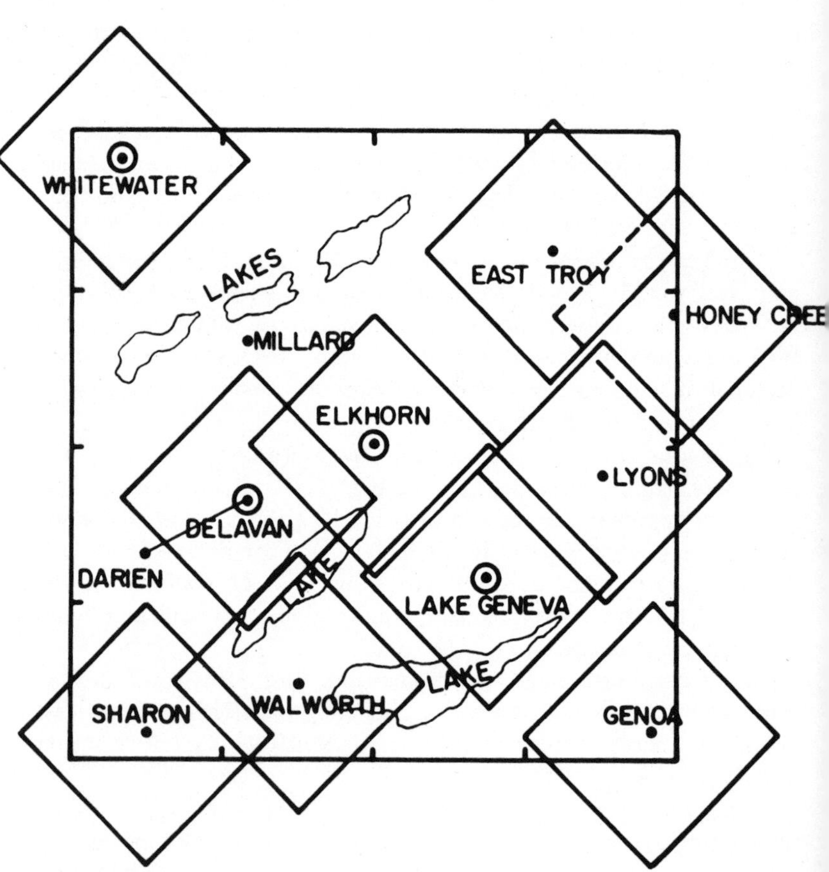

trade centers gives a reasonable approximation of the trade areas or "fundamental communities" found in Galpin's study. The great majority of the students actually attending the 9 high schools lived within the boundaries of such squares, that is, well within 5 miles of the towns in which the high schools were located.

Though the boundaries of Galpin's trade areas have been discussed in terms of distance, time is the determining variable here. The farmer required a service center where he could get in, shop, and get back to care for his stock the same evening. If we interpret Galpin's circles as representing one hour's travel time from the trade center, the rectangular road grid and a speed of 5 miles per hour generate trade areas measuring 5 miles from center to corner and oriented at a 45-degree angle to the road grid.

THE AUTOMOTIVE REVOLUTION AND THE EXPANDED COMMUNITY, 1966

When Galpin began his survey (1911), there were about 600,000 passenger automobiles in the entire United States. As of 1966, there are more than 60 million—an increase of more than a hundred fold!

The effect of the automobile on the spatial pattern of the United States economy has been greater than that of any other technological innovation of the twentieth century. Not only were large numbers of people employed in the production of automobiles themselves, but many others were employed in improving and modernizing roads and in building suburban housing in areas that would not have been sufficiently accessible to the business districts with earlier forms of transportation.

Passenger automobile registrations exceeded one million for the first time in 1913; by 1929, the number had risen to 23 million! Truck registrations passed the 100,000 mark in 1915, and exceeded 3.5 million in 1929. The automobile was not perfected overnight, and the road systems were slow to respond. There was an interaction between manufacturers, businessmen, and consumers on the one hand, and public officials on the other. The development of faster automobiles put pressures on public officials to design and build roads to accommodate the higher speeds; and limitations in the prevailing quality of the road systems put limits on the speeds for which automobiles were designed.

By the time of the 1960 census, the automobile and the road

builder had been at work on a significant scale for half a century. Although major improvements in road systems are still being made, it seems reasonable to assume that the patterns of shopping centers, trade areas, towns, and cities existing in agricultural regions as of 1960 reflected a fairly mature adjustment to the requirements and possibilities of the automobile age, in the same sense that Galpin's communities represented a mature adjustment as of 1911 to the limitations and possibilities of the horse and wagon.

HUMAN ECOLOGY AT 50 MILES AN HOUR

As of 1966, the automobile is the almost universal means of shopping and home-to-work travel in the Midwest. Man has become a four-wheeled species; through the magic of technology his speed has been multiplied tenfold in the short space of two generations. He cannot walk faster or sleep faster than before, but he can now trade an hour's time for 50 miles instead of 5.

Figure 5 shows some implications of this automobile revolution for the state of Iowa. Perhaps 95 percent of the total land area of Iowa is in farms. The distribution of the farm population over the state is fairly uniform. With minor exceptions, the road grid is rectangular. The grid is virtually complete in the sense that nearly every section of farmland in Iowa has access to public secondary roads on all four sides. Each mile of road serves one side of each of two adjacent sections of land, so a complete system of rural roads would contain 2 miles of road for each square mile of land. The completeness of the road system is suggested by two statistics: the area of the state is 56,290 square miles, and as of 1966 the highway commission presided over 112,000 miles of roads.

There are very few diagonal roads in the state. The implications of a diagonal highway constructed between Des Moines and Marshalltown in the 1930's were so disturbing to those concerned with efficient use of farmland that the state legislature passed a statute prohibiting the further construction of diagonal roads radiating from Des Moines; this statute remained in effect until the 1950's. By 1960 the road system was of relatively high quality, and workers and shoppers could drive their automobiles through most parts of Iowa at an average speed of about 50 miles per hour.

The principle underlying Figure 5 is precisely the same as that underlying Figure 4. The size of the trade areas hypothesized rep-

FIFTY-MILE COMMUTING DISTANCES FROM THE CENTRAL BUSINESS DISTRICTS OF ALL FEA (INCLUDING SMSA) CENTRAL CITIES IN OR NEAR IOWA

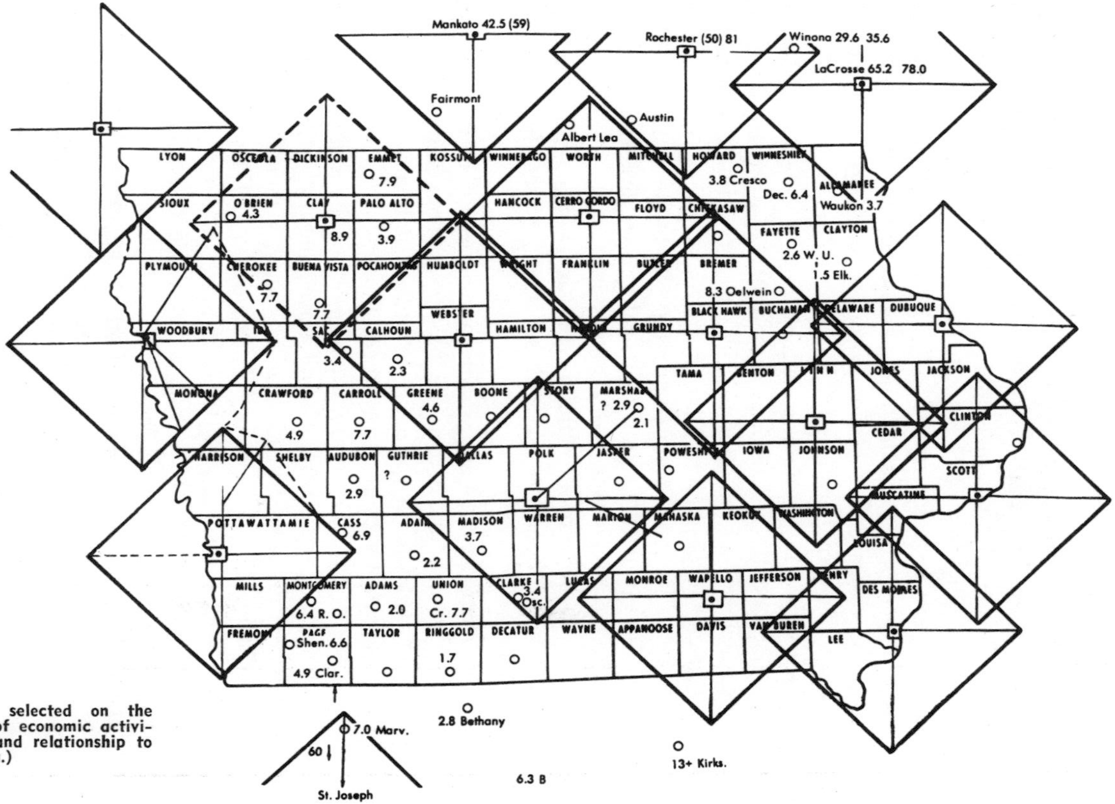

(Central cities selected on the basis of range of economic activities performed and relationship to surrounding area.)

resents one hour's travel time by the prevailing mode of transportation. In Figure 4 we assume that horses and wagons could travel 5 miles an hour; in Figure 5 we assume that automobiles can travel 50. The area of Walworth County is 576 square miles; the area of Iowa is 56,290 square miles. Each of the trade areas in Figure 5 covers 5,000 square miles, equivalent to 8 or 10 counties. Galpin's areas averaged about 50 square miles, less than one-tenth as large as a typical county.

Each square in Figure 5 is centered on a city, which is the dominant trade center in the area; these cities also provide a large and diversified array of job opportunities. It is 50 miles by road from the central city of an area to each of the four corners of the surrounding square. To travel from the central city to the northwest boundary of the square, the rectangular road grid requires that one go, for example, 40 miles west and 10 miles north. The generalization X miles west and (50-X) miles north (depending on the particular point on the boundary we wish to reach) states this relationship precisely.

If convenience and accessibility are measured in minutes rather than miles, it is just as easy for modern workers and consumers to get around in one of the areas delineated in Figure 5 as it was for the residents of Galpin's areas to get around their own "rurban communities" in 1911. Of course, the majority of the residents of a trade area live much less than an hour's travel time from the central city.

The central cities in the areas of Figure 5 include 3 urban centers (Omaha–Council Bluffs, Des Moines, and Davenport–Rock Island–Moline) with a population of more than 200,000 each. They include 4 other urbanized areas in Iowa (Cedar Rapids, Sioux City, Waterloo, and Dubuque) of 50,000 to 125,000 in population, and 4 smaller Iowa cities (Burlington, Fort Dodge, Mason City, and Ottumwa) of 30,000 to 35,000 population. The square with a dashed outline in northwestern Iowa centers on a town of about 10,000 people, which has been growing rapidly and has an unusually large volume of retail sales in relation to its total population.

Figure 6 gives us a close-up picture of the distribution of towns in the Fort Dodge area. The area involved is the one surrounding Webster County in Figure 5, a little north and west of the center of the state.

The areas of the shaded squares in Figure 6 are proportional to

FIGURE 6

DISTRIBUTION OF TOWN POPULATION SIZES IN THE FORT DODGE AREA

(Areas of squares are proportional to 1960 town populations. Only towns with retail sales of $2.5 million or more for year ending June 30, 1964 are shown.)

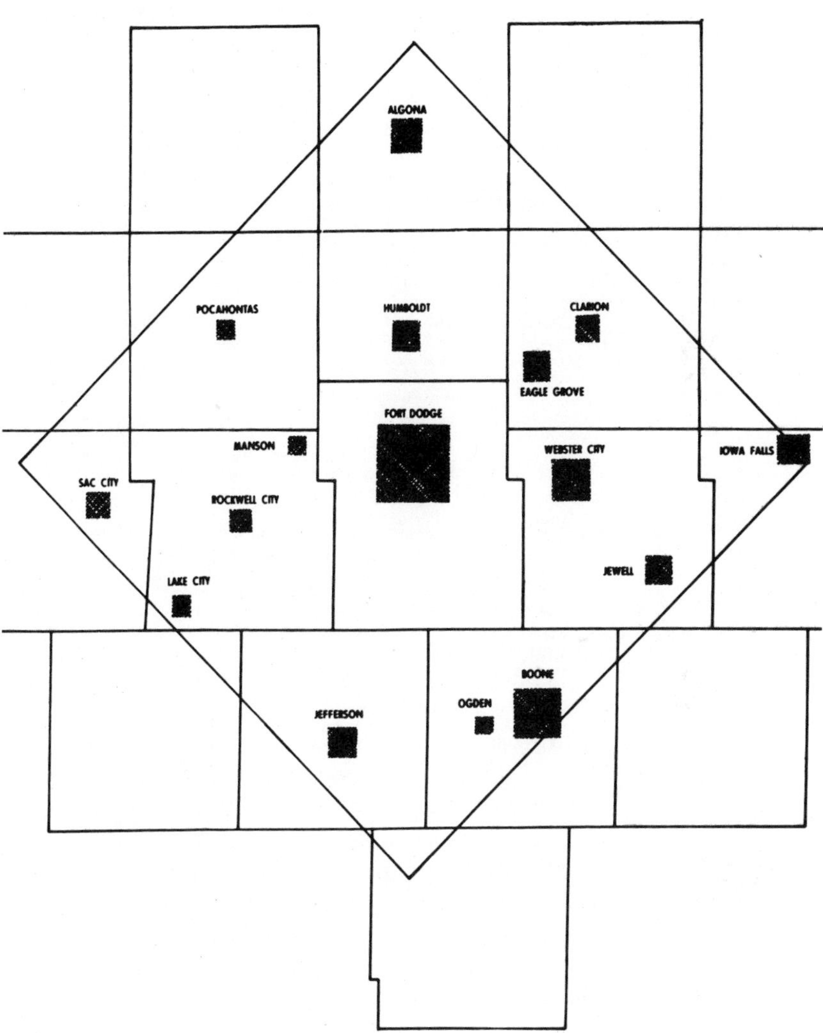

the populations of the different towns. The population of Fort Dodge is approximately 30,000; that of Boone, about 12,000; and that of Webster City, about 9,000. The other towns shown range from about 1,500 to 5,000 people. Not shown in Figure 6 are about 60 small towns with retail sales of less than 2.5 million dollars in the year ending June 30, 1964. Most of these towns had populations of less than 1,000.

It is interesting to compare the sizes of these towns with the trade centers Galpin studied in Walworth County, which he described as follows:

> Not all of the hamlet and smaller villages were surveyed. Twelve villages and cities were selected: Darien, population (1910) village and township 1,249 (village probably about 500); Delavan city, 2,450; East Troy village, 673; Elkhorn city, 1,707; Genoa Junction village, 709; Honey Creek village, not incorporated, about 200; Lake Geneva city, 3,079; Millard hamlet about 75; Lyons, not incorporated, about 500; Sharon village, 879; Walworth village, 755; Whitewater city, 3,224. This selection gave in the same class of small cities, Delavan, Elkhorn, Lake Geneva and Whitewater. Though under city government, and under the impetus of city ideals, these centers are still fundamentally agricultural, and of village type. A few industries of city type are beginning to prosper in these centers. Of the typical village type, still without city ambitions, are Darien, East Troy, Genoa, Lyons, Sharon, and Walworth. Honey Creek is nearly of village type. Though small in population, it has a bank, a one-year high school, lumber yards, and railway transportation. Millard is a neighborhood center of the one-store type, with a milk factory, school, and one church. It was selected from among many others in the county because of its availability, and its typical character.[18]

Galpin's 12 trade centers, then, were not all of the same type. From Figure 2 (which was also Galpin's Figure 2) it is evident that no one in the immediate trade areas of Millard (population 75) or Darien (population about 500) seemed completely satisfied with the shopping facilities in those places; all residents of these areas did some of their shopping at other, larger trade centers. (Incidentally, Darien was connected to Delevan, population 2,450, by a diagonal road that brought it within 4 miles of the larger place.)

Galpin commented that his trade map "was made first by merging the dry goods and grocery maps which nearly coincided." Most farm people seemed to be fairly well satisfied with the range of goods

[18] Galpin, *op. cit.*, p. 4.

they found in the towns of 700 to 1,000 population, given their traditions, the difficulties of travel to larger places, and the constraints of family income.[19]

AREAL EXPANSION TRANSLATED INTO INCREASES IN SCALE

Very few Iowa families as of 1966 would find all the consumer goods and services they require in a town of less than 1,000 people. A large proportion have come to rely to some extent on shopping facilities and services found only in a central city of the Fort Dodge type or larger.

In the modern economy, the central city of a trade area of the type shown in Figure 6 is also the center of a labor market, which is approximately coextensive with the trade area. The great majority of workers will contrive to live within far less than one hour's drive from their jobs, but a limited number are willing to drive as much as one hour a day each way.

It is our view that the city, town, and open-country populations of the area in Figure 6 are members of a highly interdependent community, the boundaries of which coincide at least roughly with those shown. The population of Fort Dodge itself is only 30,000, but the total population included within commuting distance of Fort Dodge exceeds 60,000 workers, whereas the labor force residing within the city limits of Fort Dodge is less than 15,000.

The central cities of the areas shown in Figure 5 accounted for most of the total growth of Iowa's population from 1900 to 1960. These 11 cities showed the following changes in population:

	1900	1960
Cedar Rapids	25,656	92,035
Council Bluffs	25,802	55,641
Davenport	35,254	88,981
Des Moines	62,139	208,982
Dubuque	36,297	56,606
Sioux City	33,111	89,159
Waterloo	12,580	71,755
Burlington	23,201	32,430
Fort Dodge	12,162	28,399
Mason City	6,746	30,642
Ottumwa	18,197	33,871

[19] Galpin makes no mention of mail-order purchases; presumably he would have if he had regarded them as quantitatively important.

The population increases in these cities total almost 500,000. If we add the increases in a few suburbs of cities such as Des Moines and Cedar Rapids, the total rises to 540,000, more than equal to the net increase (533,000) in the population of the state as a whole.

A good many other Iowa towns have shown population increases, but these have not quite offset the decrease in numbers of farm people and others who are living in the open country or in small towns.

There is no reason to believe that the pattern of agricultural communities in Iowa as of 1911 was much different from the pattern Galpin found in Walworth County, Wisconsin. As of 1911, most rural residents of Iowa got along quite well with the shopping facilities available in towns of 1,000 people or so, and were pleased indeed with the range of goods and services available in county seat towns of 2,000 to 3,000 people, about the size of the 4 small cities in Galpin's study. The selection of goods and services was well suited to disposable income and to limited transportation facilities. But as the automobile multiplied the potential shopping and commuting radius of rural people by a factor of ten, the potentiality of larger-scale service centers came into being. The history of commercial as well as of governmental services in the past six decades has been one of steady increase in virtually all fields.

The country store of horse and wagon days was succeeded by the cash and carry grocery of the 1930's and the supermarket of the 1960's. Each store provided a richer selection of goods; each was dependent on a larger shopper population. And the one-room school, which had provided an entire education to most of its pupils in 1900, gave way to the consolidated elementary school covering several of the original districts. The high school, which was not intended to serve everyone in 1900, provided terminal educational experience a generation later. By 1966, more and more students were thinking of 2 years of post-high school training as a necessity and a 4-year college education as a norm.

Popped corn cannot be crammed back into the kernel. The extended community cannot be collapsed back into a town of 300 people; an elementary, junior high, high school, community college complex cannot be somehow distilled into a miniaturized "package" without the loss of the very scale of services that allows it to serve many diverse needs well.

If a community is defined as an entity that can supply all or nearly all the needs of its members, a town of 300 people can no longer serve as a "community." On the basis of the present locations of department stores, factories, community colleges, vocational and technical schools, daily newspapers, radio and television stations, and other facilities, the modern community requires a town of about the Fort Dodge size or larger to satisfy the needs of its residents. In predominantly agricultural regions, communities will generally be of the type and size (but not necessarily shape) of those in Figures 5 and 6.

For example, in choosing locations for new community colleges, junior colleges, and vocational and technical schools, administrators in a number of states are using rules of thumb such as "not more than one hour's drive for the most distant students" or "not more than 40 or 50 miles." Students making such long trips would form a distinct minority, but a considerable number might be commuting from distances of 30 to 40 miles.

HIERARCHIES OF TRADE CENTERS IN THE EXPANDED COMMUNITY

Different kinds of retail businesses have different optimal sizes. In the large metropolitan areas of the United States there are 3 categories of modern shopping centers. The *neighborhood* center serves about 15,000 to 30,000 people, with a supermarket as the chief tenant. The *district* center serves about 60,000 to 120,000 people, with a department store as the chief tenant. The *regional* center serves as many as 500,000 people, usually with the chief tenant a branch of a large department store.[20]

A regional center may also contain a supermarket. Its regular patrons, however, will be drawn from a relatively small area—a neighborhood containing 15,000 to 30,000 people. Such a regional center will also contain smaller department or variety stores of the kinds found in district centers. These district-level stores will tend to draw from a surrounding area containing 60,000 to 120,000 people.

---

20 See article on "Shopping Centre" in the *Encyclopaedia Britannica* (1965 edition), Vol. 20, pp. 575–576. Such large numbers of patrons are, of course, possible only in our densely populated cities.

Thus, the largest kind of shopping plaza is a regional center for about 480,000 people, a district center for 120,000 people, and a neighborhood center for 30,000 people. The intermediate kind of shopping plaza is a district center for 120,000 people and a neighborhood center for 30,000 people. With the figures we have chosen, there will be four times as many district centers as regional centers, and there will be four times as many neighborhood centers as district centers.

Some geographers and economists have referred to this pattern as "a nested hierarchy of central places." The actual pattern of shopping centers, of course, always contains distortions and haphazard elements.

Interestingly enough, a rectangular grid of city streets would logically tend to build a multiplier of 4 into the sizes of trade areas at successive stages in this hierarchy. A rectangular road grid in the open country would tend to produce the same effect. If towns of the Fort Dodge class were located 100 road miles apart, towns of the next smaller class should tend to be located 50 road miles apart, and towns of the next smaller class about 25 road miles apart. The "radius" of the trade area surrounding a town of the Fort Dodge class would be 50 miles, compared with 25 miles and 12.5 miles for the next 2 size classes. The areas would be 5,000 square miles, 1,250 square miles, and about 312 square miles respectively. The smallest area would be roughly half as large as an Iowa county and there might be areas that would contain a population as small as 5,000.

It is not surprising that the real-world pattern of central places does not fit an arbitrary form. The tendency toward nested hierarchies is both exciting and interesting. Tendencies similar to those discovered by Galpin can be found in the structure of today's urban areas.

Under urban conditions, 15,000 to 30,000 people may live within 15 minutes of a neighborhood shopping center. In rural areas the number of people living within 15 minutes of a town providing similar goods and services would be much smaller, but the same principles would be at work.

In 1963 John R. Borchert and Russell B. Adams published the results of an extensive study of cities and small towns in the Upper Midwest—an area including Montana, Wyoming, North Dakota,

South Dakota, Minnesota, and northern Wisconsin. Figure 7 is reproduced from the Borchert and Adams study.[21]

DEFINITION BY RETAILING AND WHOLESALING FUNCTIONS

Borchert and Adams classified the hundreds of small towns and cities in the upper Midwest into several categories or hierarchical steps on the basis of the retailing and wholesaling functions they performed. A *minimum-convenience center*, for example, would contain a gasoline service station, a grocery, a drugstore, a hardware store, a bank, an eating place, and any two of four other specified kinds of retail stores. These requirements might be met by a small town of about 1,000 people.

The Borchert and Adams categories fit the Iowa situation rather well. Broadly speaking, the *full-convenience center* has a population of 1,000 to 2,500 and an annual volume of retail sales of $2.5 million to $5 million. The *partial shopping center* has 2,500 to about 5,000 people and retail sales of $5 million to $10 million. A good many of the small and medium-size county seat towns in Iowa fall in this category. During the year ending March 31, 1963, Fort Dodge and and less than 25,000 population, has retail sales of $10 million to $40 million annually. The complete shopping centers have relatively full ranges of consumer goods and services. They include any 9 or more of the 13 kinds of specialty stores listed in Figure 7.

Borchert and Adams define two larger trade center types in terms of a combination of retail and wholesale criteria. The smaller of the two types they call *secondary wholesale-retail centers*, characterized by more than $40 million of retail sales annually, more than $40 million of wholesale sales, and 10 to 13 types of specified wholesale functions. Several of the smaller central cities in Iowa fall in this category. During the year ending March 31, 1963, Fort Dodge and Mason City each reported $65 million worth of retail sales, Ottumwa $55 million, and Burlington $62 million.

Finally, Borchert and Adams define *primary wholesale-retail centers*, which must have at least $75 million of retail sales annually, at least $75 million of wholesale sales, and all 14 of the wholesale business functions specified in Figure 7. In most cases, Iowa cities

[21] Reproduced from page 4 of John R. Borchert and Russell B. Adams, *Trade Centers and Trade Areas of the Upper Midwest*, Upper Midwest Economic Study, Urban Report No. 3, September 1963.

FIGURE 7

TRADE CENTER TYPES DEFINED BY BUSINESS FUNCTIONS

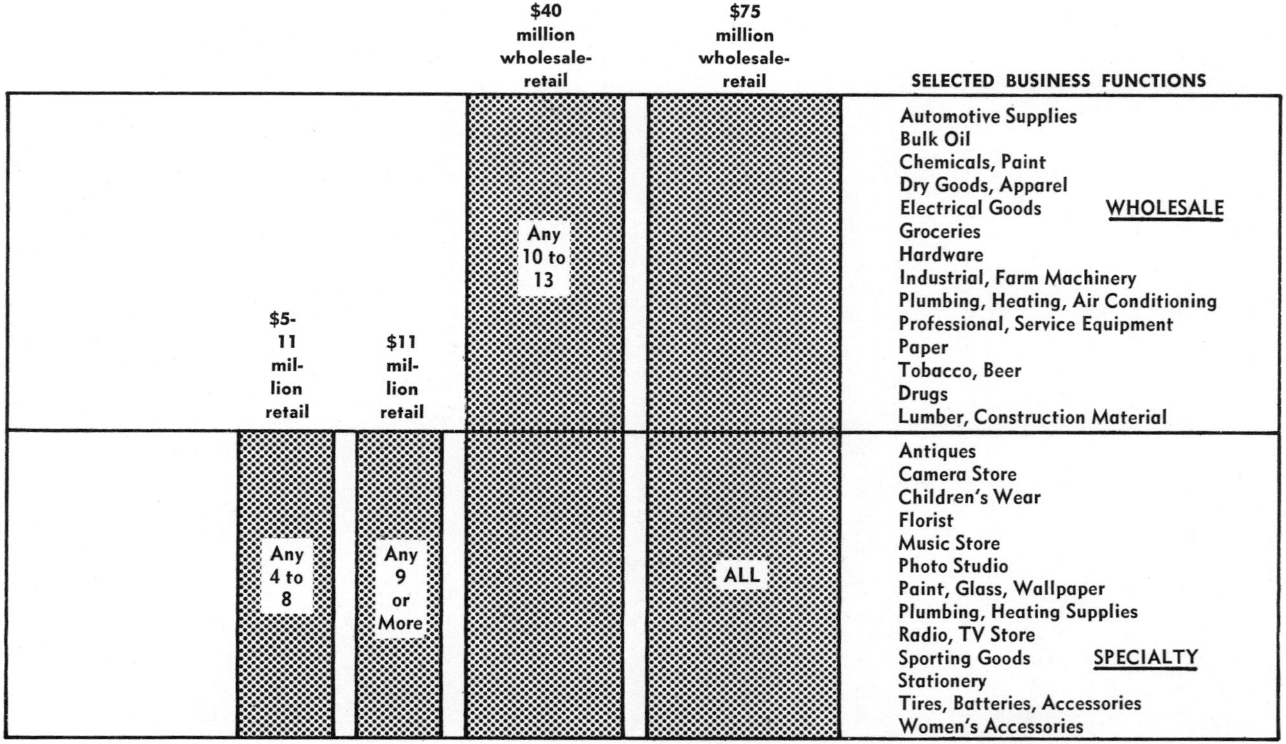

$5-11 million retail	$11 million retail	$40 million wholesale-retail	$75 million wholesale-retail	SELECTED BUSINESS FUNCTIONS	
		Any 10 to 13		Automotive Supplies Bulk Oil Chemicals, Paint Dry Goods, Apparel Electrical Goods Groceries Hardware Industrial, Farm Machinery Plumbing, Heating, Air Conditioning Professional, Service Equipment Paper Tobacco, Beer Drugs Lumber, Construction Material	WHOLESALE
Any 4 to 8	Any 9 or More		ALL	Antiques Camera Store Children's Wear Florist Music Store Photo Studio Paint, Glass, Wallpaper Plumbing, Heating Supplies Radio, TV Store Sporting Goods Stationery Tires, Batteries, Accessories Women's Accessories	SPECIALTY

Minimum Convenience	Full Convenience	Partial Shopping	Complete Shopping	Secondary Wholesale-Retail	Primary Wholesale-Retail	
	Any 3			ALL		Family Shoe Store Farm-Garden Supplies Lumber, Building Materials Hotel-Motel Mortuary
			ALL			Appliances or Furniture Jewelry Men's or Boy's or Women's Clothing Laundry, Dry Cleaning
Any 2		ALL				Garage, Auto, Implement Dealer Variety Store Meat, Fish, Fruit General Merchandise
ALL	ALL					Gasoline Service Station Grocery Drug Store Hardware Store Bank Eating Places CONVENIENCE

TRADE CENTER TYPE

Graphic summary of characteristics of six levels in the Trade Center hierarchy. Type of center is indicated at base of each bar. Types of business are listed in right-hand column. Businesses which were required and optional in defining each type of Trade Center are indicated by markings on each bar. Width of bar is proportional to dollar volume as indicated for Partial Shopping Centers and above.

of 50,000 population or more would meet these requirements. Thus, for 1962-1963, Dubuque reported $85 million in retail sales, Council Bluffs (overshadowed by adjacent Omaha) about $73 million, and Waterloo $134 million. Retail sales of the remaining central cities of Iowa trade areas ranged from $160 million each for Sioux City and Davenport to more than $200 million for Cedar Rapids and more than $450 million for Des Moines.

There is, then, a division of labor among towns of different sizes in trade areas of the type shown in Figure 6. If the region is an agricultural one, settled in the tradition described by Morris Birkbeck and past the mature horse-and-wagon state of Galpin's study, the complex of towns and small cities is intimately and integrally related to its agricultural and agri-business base.

Roughly speaking, the business districts of the two largest types of centers in Figure 7 perform the same functions as do regional shopping plazas in large cities. The complete shopping centers of Figure 7 correspond with the district shopping centers found in large cities. The full-convenience centers of Figure 7 evidently correspond with the neighborhood shopping centers of the large city. The partial shopping center may be a transitional type on its way toward complete shopping center status.

FUNCTIONALLY DEFINED URBAN CENTERS

We normally think of a city as an area covered by buildings and divided and subdivided into use areas by streets. Cities are distinguishable from countryside by the presence of buildings.

But suppose we define a city as a cluster of "urban functions." The shopping centers in a metropolitan area are separated from one another by several or many blocks of residences. Metropolitan areas also contain factories, which produce goods for "export" to other cities as well as for local consumption. These activities are sometimes called the *export base* of the area. The functions oriented primarily toward serving residents of the area itself are called *residentiary* activities.

Figure 8 is a map of an actual midwestern city with about 50,000 residents. The heavy crosshatching identifies the industrial plants that constitute most of the export base of Center City. The black oblongs are supermarkets. When the map was drawn, there were about 10 supermarkets, each serving on the average about 5,000 peo-

FIGURE 8

MAP OF CENTER CITY

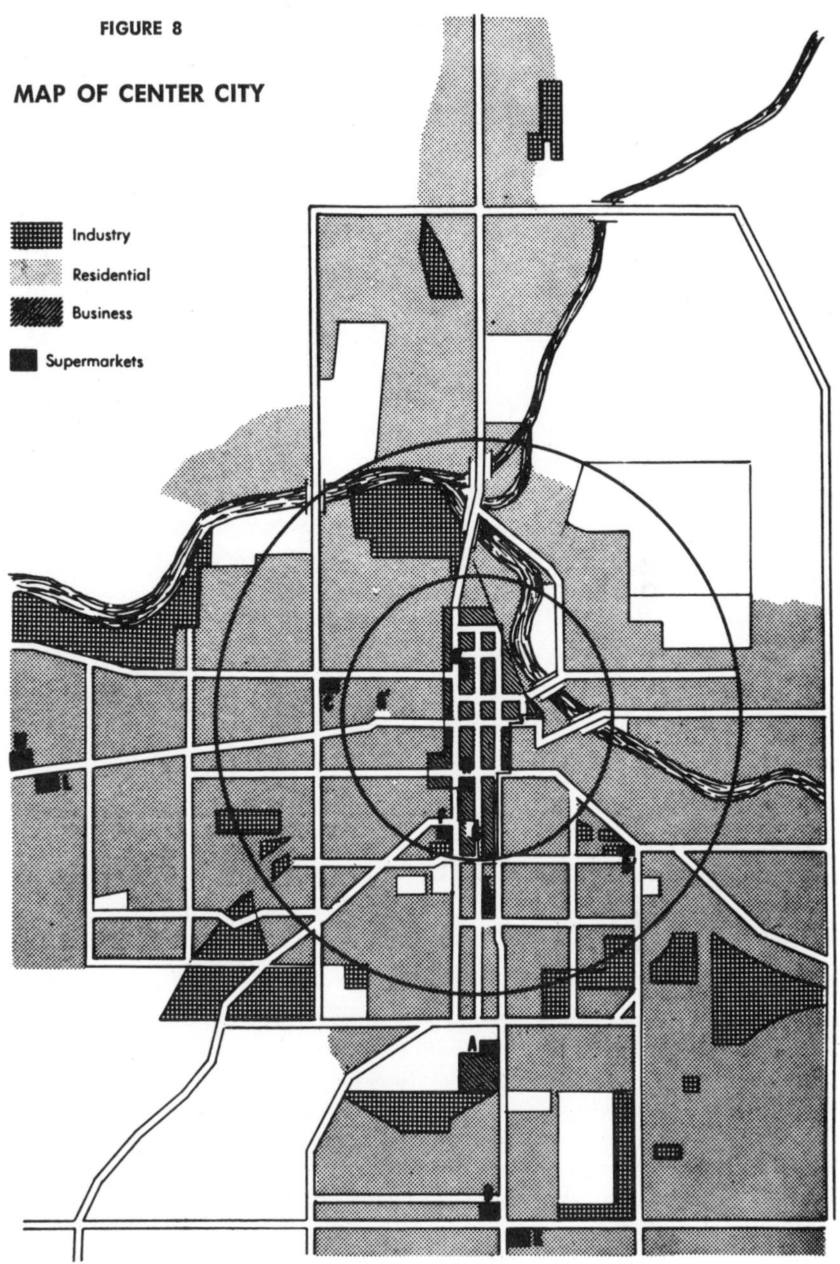

Source: Bob R. Holdren, *The Structure of a Retail Market and the Market Behavior of Retail Units.* © 1960 Prentice-Hall, Inc. Adapted by permission.

ple. The central business district is contained in the inner circle of one-half-mile radius. Not shown on the map are the small neighborhood stores and other convenience enterprises, which can subsist on the patronage of a few hundred customers.

The 10,000 Center City industrial workers require only 2 or 3 square miles of land for their production activities *and* their residences. The same number of export-oriented workers deployed on farms would spread out over 5 or 6 midwestern counties. To serve such a dispersed population, the neighborhood stores, barber shops, and gasoline stations must fan out into small towns and villages, many of less than 1,000 people. The supermarkets and other units requiring large volume for low-cost operation are found in county seat towns and others of about 1,000 to 5,000 population, while the central business district is typically found in a city of 25,000 or larger.

Regional economists seem to have no difficulty with this projective transformation of the structure of a city into the structure of a multi-county area. It seems useful to compare an area like that in Figure 6 to a city spatially extended to accommodate a low-density pattern of land use and residential location over the bulk of its area.[22] Furthermore, agriculture, despite its space-filling and eye-catching qualities, is simply another export industry and source of employment from the standpoint of a functional classification scheme.

THE EXPANDED COMMUNITY AND THE NATIONAL ECONOMY: A SYSTEM OF LOW-DENSITY CITIES OR CITY-STATES?

Although this book is concerned primarily with the small community, it will be useful to digress briefly to suggest how expanded communities fit into the United States economy.

As of 1960, there were a total of 213 urbanized areas (i.e. cities as clusters of buildings) with populations of 50,000 or larger. There were 7 such urbanized areas in, or partly in, Iowa, each the center of a labor market and trade area. Another 200 or more labor market and trade areas could be delineated around cities of about 20,000 to

[22] In an informal discussion, Wilbur Thompson reformulated my hypothesis as stating that "the United States is made up not of states but of city-states."

50,000 people, though in very sparsely populated areas towns with as few as 10,000 people can serve as area centers.

By taking careful account of local conditions and making a limited number of arbitrary but reproducible decisions, we should be able to delineate a set of 400 to 500 areas that would completely cover the United States. The populations of these areas would range from about 40,000 in parts of the Mountain states and the western Great Plains to 150,000 or more in the Midwest. The same system of delineation might, for some purposes, be extended to include even the largest metropolitan area. It is also possible that the trade areas of regional shopping plazas in the large cities—each containing perhaps 200,000 to 500,000 people—would be useful as administrative districts or subdivisions for various kinds of public and private services oriented toward residences rather than toward places of employment.

This complete set of areas forms a national system; geographers and economists often speak of it as a national system of *cities*. Brian J. L. Berry describes its function and logic as follows:

1. We live in a specialized society in which there is progressively greater division of labor and scale of enterprise, accompanied by increasing degrees of specialization.

2. There is an increasing diversity of people as producers. But as consumers they are becoming more and more alike from one part of the country to another, consuming much the same "basket of goods" whereever they may live, as well as increasingly large baskets because of rising real incomes.

3. The physical problem in the economic system is therefore one of articulation—insuring that the specialized products of each segment of the country are shipped to final consumers, seeing that consumers in every part of the country receive the basket of goods and services they demand and are able to purchase, and bringing demands and supplies into equality over a period of time.

4. Articulation requires flows of messages, of goods and services, and of funds. The flows appear to be highly structured and channeled and major metropolitan centers serve as critical articulation points. These flows are as follows: products move from their specialized production areas to shopping points in the locally dominant metropolitan centers; over the nation, products are transferred between metropolitan centers, with each metropolitan center shipping out the specialized products of its hinterland and collecting the entire range of specialized products from other metropolitan centers to satisfy the demands of the consumers residing in the area it dominates; distribution then takes place from the metropolis to its

hinterland through wholesale and retail contacts. In the reverse direction move both requests for goods and services, and funds to pay for goods and services received, so that the flows are not unidirectional.[23]

Berry's remarks emphasize the critical role of the central cities, of trade, and of labor market areas in the articulation (joining together) of the national economy. As Borchert and Adams indicate, a distinctive feature of the kind of central city we have described is the cluster of wholesaling activities that link it, and hence the retail businesses in its trade area, to the national economy. These wholesaling functions are not significantly developed in the smaller cities and towns of the area.

The linkages of shopping, commuting, and deliveries from wholesalers to retailers make the central city an integral part of its trade and labor market area; its wholesaling, manufacturing, and other functions also link it to the system of cities that stretches across the nation.

The areas containing large stretches of farming territory are particularly relevant to our small community. The hypothesis suggested here is that the smallest "communities" that satisfy nearly all the needs of their residents are areas delineated on the principles we have discussed, containing 40,000 to 150,000 people. If we look at small towns, schools, or churches in any narrower frame than this, we fail to perceive the real community of which they are parts. The problems of the small town can be understood only if we know its spatial and functional relationships to the whole system of farms, small towns, large towns, and central city that comprise the larger community.

"CREEPING URBANIZATION": RURAL-URBAN GRADIENTS IN THE EXPANDED COMMUNITY AS EVIDENCES OF PROCESS AND CHANGE

Figure 9 shows percent changes in total population from 1950 to 1960 for each of Iowa's 99 counties. A few of the 50-mile squares are drawn in. Careful examination will show that, in almost all cases, the population of the county containing the central city has increased more (or decreased less) rapidly than any other county wholly or

[23] Berry, Brian J. L., "Approaches to Regional Analysis—A Synthesis," *Annals, Association of American Geographers,* Vol. 54, 1964, p. 10.

FIGURE 9

PERCENT CHANGES IN TOTAL POPULATIONS OF IOWA COUNTIES, 1950-1960

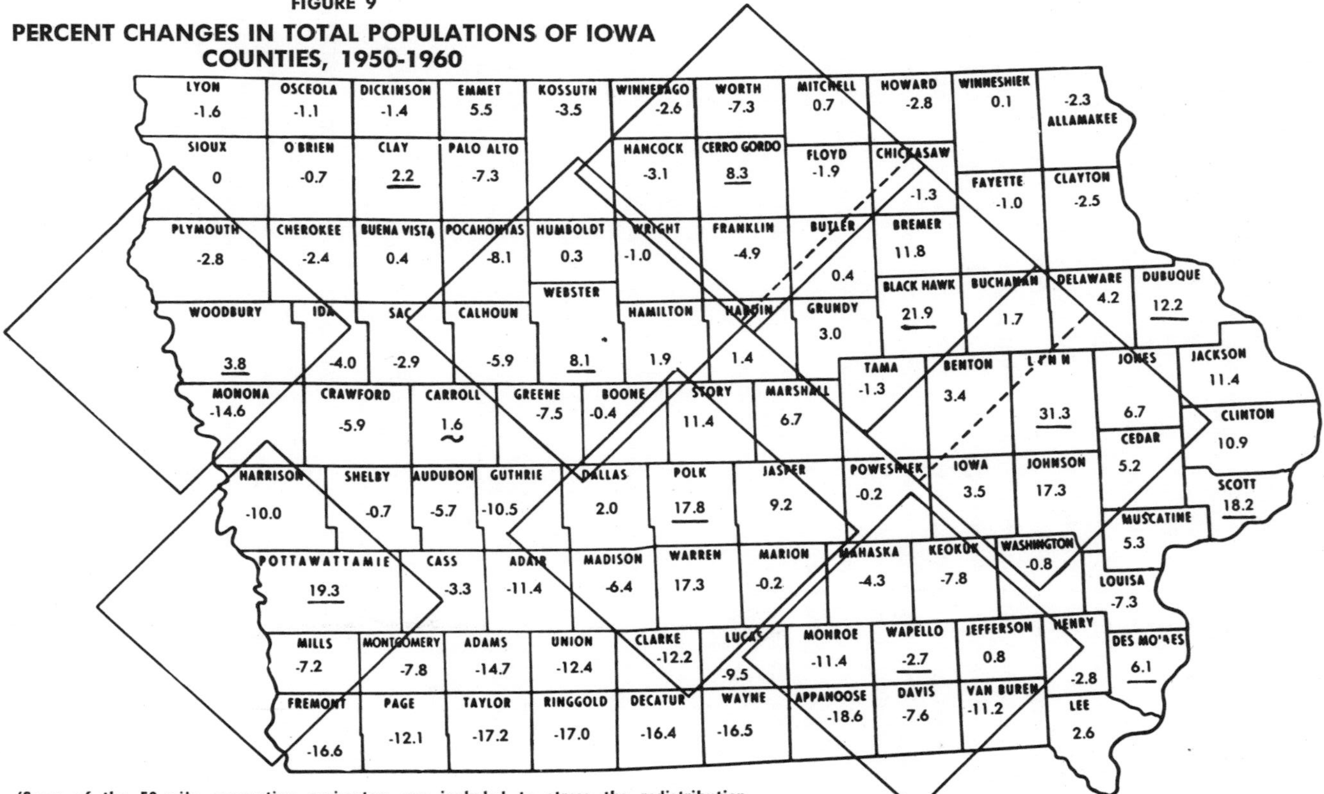

(Some of the 50-mile commuting perimeters are included to stress the redistribution of population occurring within functional economic areas.)

partly within the square. This fact suggests that there is an increasing concentration of economic functions in the central cities, that population density gradients from the perimeters toward the centers of the areas are tending to become steeper, and that in general the boundaries between adjacent areas are becoming more sharply defined.

According to the 1960 census, 80 percent of the residents of Fort Dodge and Mason City had been born in Iowa. This is consistent with the other evidences of "creeping urbanization," which may be synthesizing farms, small towns, and urban centers into low-density cities or urban community-of-interest areas. The total number of jobs has expanded in the central cities of such areas and has declined on farms and (typically) in towns of less than 1,500 people. The more specialized, more responsible, and higher-paying jobs have also tended to develop and concentrate in the central cities, where the decision-making responsibility is most typically located.

The age distribution of the male labor force in the age range from 25 to 64 offers some concrete illustrations of employment concentration.

PERCENT OF MALE LABOR FORCE AGE 25-64
IN EACH AGE GROUP

Age Group	*Cities of 10,000 or more*	*Urban places, 2,500 to 10,000 plus rural nonfarm*	*Rural farm*
Total, 25-64	100	100	100
25-34	29	27	22
35-44	29	27	28
45-64	42	46	50

One way to dramatize these figures is to look at this age distribution from the standpoint of a young man in the 25-34 age group. In cities of 10,000 or more there are 2.4 older workers (34-64) for every worker aged 25-34. In the towns smaller than 10,000 and among the rural nonfarm population, this "seniority ratio" is 2.7. But for the worker aged 25-34 in the rural farm population, the "seniority ratio" is 3.6. The ratio for all rural and urban categories combined is 2.76, a much more optimistic figure than the 3.6 confronting the young rural farm resident.

These figures can be further elaborated by comparing the number of people involved in economic activities that result in "exported" goods and services to the number of those who serve the residents of the low-density city. Rural farm residents are very strongly concentrated in export-oriented industries. Rural nonfarm residents (in towns of less than 2,500 people) and residents of towns in the 2,500 to 10,000 population class show high concentrations in retail trade establishments, which serve as neighborhood and district shopping centers for the farm population as well. Manufacturing employment increases from smaller to larger urban places, because manufacturing establishments most typically require relatively larger and more easily accessible supplies of available labor.

In 1960, about 45 percent of the workers in the state of Iowa were in export and 55 percent in residentiary industries. Similar percentages should be found in any subdistrict that can satisfy nearly all the needs of its residents, as we can see in the following sequence of figures:

Workers, by place of residence	*Percent of employment in residentiary activities*
1. Rural farm residents	16
2. Rural farm plus rural nonfarm	40
3. Rural farm, rural nonfarm, and urban places of 2,500 to 10,000	48
4. Item 3 plus urban places of 10,000 to 50,000	52
5. Total Iowa population	55

Our estimate of residentiary employment for an 8-county approximation to the Fort Dodge area of Figure 6 was 53 percent of total employment. Under 1960 conditions in Iowa, there is a strong inference that areas containing no cities of more than 10,000 people were unable to supply the full range of consumer goods and services (including public and professional services) desired by their residents. Roughly speaking, they would have contained one or more *district* shopping centers but would not have contained a *regional* shopping center.

When income distribution and education are taken into account, the concept of the low-density city is further substantiated. There is a pronounced upward trend in median family income from the farm and rural nonfarm categories to the larger urban places, as well as a strong upward trend in the percentage of adults who are college graduates. Both of these gradients may be summarized in the following manner:

Residence category	Median family income, 1959	Percent of persons 25 years of age or older having 4 or more years of college, 1960
Rural farm	$3,352	2.1
Rural nonfarm	4,626	5.1
Urban		
2,500–10,000	5,159	7.6
10,000–50,000	5,820	10.1[24]
Over 50,000	6,421	8.8

HIERARCHIES OF SCALE IN SMALL TOWNS AND LARGER CITIES

The concept of a labor market and trade area (like that of Figure 6) as a low-density city helps to explain these various gradients. In a town of 1,000 people, for example, most of the establishments are small—few have more than half a dozen or a dozen employees. The level of education and administrative ability required for most of these jobs is limited. The only school in a town of this size is likely to be an elementary school, covering 6 grades and employing perhaps 6 or 7 teachers.

Studies of organizational behavior have demonstrated the effectiveness and utility of teams made up of several workers and a supervisor. These elementary producing mechanisms are the basic units from which our great corporate and bureaucratic agencies are built. While the smallest production unit would be the one-man farm or one-man store, it is the establishment that involves a proprietor or manager and about 4 employees that manifests primary economies of scale. The next-larger unit would be constituted of perhaps 4 production teams, headed by foremen and linked together by a team of managers and assistant managers. Next would come a 4-level hierarchy with a total of 85 persons involved, and the next stage would be an organization with a 5-stage hierarchy and a total staff of 341 persons.

The maximum size of food stores that can be supported by a given trade area depends on the population of the area and its per capita expenditure for food. A population of 1,000 making food expenditures of $300 per person could support retail food sales of $300,000 a year. The labor force of this store might consist of the proprietor and 4

[24] Omitting Ames and Iowa City, which contain major universities and have thousands of students in graduate and professional schools, plus faculty members.

employees. The next-larger food store in the pattern just discussed would have a labor force of 21 persons.

If it takes a population of 1,000 to support the first store, a population of about 4,000 will be required to support the larger one. This store would have a retail sales volume of about $1,250,000, still relatively small according to urban standards. The next-larger supermarket in our hypothetical series would have a labor force of 85 people and a gross sales volume of $5 million a year. It would be a sizable modern enterprise, requiring the patronage of more than 16,000 persons at an average food expenditure of $300 each.

Lines of business characterized by increasing returns to size (economies of large scale) will gravitate to the larger population centers in an area. The more challenging opportunities for proprietors will tend to be found in the larger places, as will the higher-salaried positions for managers, assistant managers, school principals, and school superintendents.

Highly educated people are likely to be highly specialized and to require larger organizations, towns, or cities to accommodate their degree of specialization. As Adam Smith observed in 1776, "the division of labor is limited by the extent of the market." Except for farmers themselves, the ladder of advancement and opportunity for specialized people runs from smaller organizations to larger ones and also inward from the smaller towns to the central city of the trade area. The central business district of the trade area's largest city would provide the central place functions for a low-density city.

This conception would lead us to expect a progression in median incomes from the small towns toward the central city; the percentage of families with incomes of $10,000 and more would also increase, as would the percentage of adults with college educations. Small towns would show below-average median incomes even if workers in each kind of job there received exactly the same wages as workers doing the same jobs in the central city. The large number of more specialized jobs in the central city, which require more education or training and/or more administrative ability, will raise the average income level in the central city above that in the smaller towns. The performance of the economy of such an area cannot profitably be measured county by county or town by town. Rather, the performance of the area as a whole should be compared with that of other areas delineated on the same basis.

All these gradients and distributions substantiate the hypothesis that a synthesis of rural and urban populations is far advanced, at least on the economic level.

SOME IMPLICATIONS OF THE EXPANDED COMMUNITY

Recently, the Iowa Extension Service announced its plans to reorganize its field operations as rapidly as possible on the basis of 12 multi-county areas instead of 99 individual counties. Also, groups of contiguous counties have organized districts for the administration of area vocational-technical schools. These school districts have now elected the members of their school boards, and several of the multi-county areas have hired superintendents to administer the area vocational-technical schools.

The ecology of the functional area may be beginning to make itself felt in our bureaucratic arrangements.

In July 1966 the Committee for Economic Development published a report on *Modernizing Local Government*. One of its recommendations was that in "metropolitan areas" covering a single county, the city and county governments should be fused. A second was that the 2,700 "nonmetropolitan counties" should be consolidated into not more than 500 governmental units.

The argument of this chapter would suggest that these two recommendations be synthesized to provide a political counterpart of the functional community or trade and labor market area.

If we visualize a functional area as a low-density city whose export-oriented workers are engaged in agriculture, food processing, and farm supply activities, perhaps the simplest and most direct approach is to suggest that functional areas of this sort be given municipal government responsibilities.

We may ask, then, which functions of local government could be better organized on a multi-county functional economic area basis than on a single-county or single-small-town basis? The following functions merit consideration:

a. School districts including junior and four-year colleges,

b. Centers for vocational education, training, and retraining,

c. University-wide extension programs, including extension programs for farmers and those engaged in farm supply or farm product processing and storing activities,

d. Police and fire protection,
e. Public health services,
f. Social welfare services,
g. The maintenance and construction of local streets and roads, as distinct from those connecting major population centers,
h. Urban and rural or regional zoning,
i. Public library services.

Further, legislative districts might be related to functional areas. The population of functional areas in the American Midwest will generally run from 150,000 to 500,000 people. The population of Iowa is 2,800,000 people. A state legislature of 100 persons might be composed of 5 or 6 representatives elected from each of the less populous functional areas. (The extremely large cities, such as Chicago, in some states would present a different problem and require larger numbers of legislators.) If state legislators were elected from subdistricts within functional areas, they could represent local constituents on narrow issues and cooperate with their colleagues on an area basis on broader issues.

United States congressional districts have populations of at least 400,000. A congressional district could be reconstituted to comprehend 2 or 3 of the less-populous functional areas.

Which functions of state or federal governments could be better organized and implemented on a functional area basis? Here we could consider programs of the Bureau of Employment Security; of the post office; of area economic development; of state planning for outdoor recreation facilities; and of state planning and operation of mental health and medical facilities to the extent that these are publicly supported; as well as the state activities that support such local services.

As we have seen, declining farm populations and increasing city populations made a great deal of ecological sense in an area framework. We could conceptualize, and perhaps measure within each functional area, continuous "surfaces" of house rentals, values of homes, rates of construction of new homes, and expected wage rates and income distributions reflecting costs of home-to-work commuting travel to the central city from each point in the area. To some extent, perhaps, the economic forces operating in a functional area result in certain age groups and labor force categories locating in concentric rings of commuting *minutes* around the central city.

Study after study has shown that substantial improvements in service can be obtained by the creation of hierarchies of program agencies to expand the scale of a program or activity. Schools manifest this principle in a familiar form. The 100 school districts in Walworth County (Figure 1) as of 1911 have no doubt undergone sweeping changes and consolidations. Schools do not sell their pupils, but they do pay their teachers. Costs per pupil in the one-room schools rose, they could not attract qualified teachers, or their pupils found themselves at a disadvantage when they entered high school—sometimes all three. The measures of the total performance of one-room schools no doubt contained some judgment elements, but these judgments were made. The sizes, designs, and locational patterns of school buildings today are very different from those of 1911.

The readjustment of school systems has not proceeded with scientific precision, but school administrators have had various kinds of "feedback" over the years about what happens to students with different amounts and kinds of education. Students may be denied admission to universities because of inadequate background, or they may have difficulty in getting jobs. Students from an inadequate elementary school may come to grief when they enter a junior high school. The different components of our educational system exert pressures for change on one another, and the national job market exerts pressures on the system as a whole.

The problems of other local institutions are less widely understood. To what extent should the sizes and locations of church buildings change over time? To what extent should their programs change? Many children who now live on farms or in small towns will inevitably move to larger towns or cities. Should the rural churches be preparing them for urban living? Will they find the urban churches so different from the rural that they will not remain active after they move to the city?

If there is justification for church administrators to regard the individual churches in a city of 200,000 to 500,000 people as forming a system that should provide services in an effective (and efficient) manner and be sensitive to the mobility of families within the city, there is perhaps equal reason to view the churches in a functional area in the same light.

One can reasonably hold that the city, as an economic and cultural entity, has surrounded the countryside. Urbanism will probably engulf most rural areas in a short time. Economic institutions are rapidly adjusting their sizes and locations to this fact. One chain store executive explained his company's policy of building larger stores and locating them in larger towns as follows: "We found that the farmers were moving into town, and so we decided to move in with them."

Perhaps as people move the social, political, and religious institutions aspiring to serve them should migrate, or at least reform themselves. Political reapportionment represents a belated adjustment to the rural-urban population movement. It is reasonable to believe that churches—and particularly churches that were located during the nineteenth century to serve rural people—are also confronted with a reapportionment problem. If the hypothesis projecting the integration of rural and urban areas into functional "rurban" areas is substantiated, there is reason to believe that the rethinking from which the "new church" must emerge might be undertaken with these functional units as the primary service areas.

SUGGESTIONS FOR FURTHER READING

Berry, Brian J. L., "Reflections on the Functional Economic Areas," pp. 56-64 in *Research and Education for Regional and Area Development*, Iowa State University Center for Agricultural and Economic Development. Ames: Iowa State University Press, 1966.

Borchert, John R. and Russell B. Adams, *Trade Centers and Trade Areas of the Upper Midwest*. Upper Midwest Economic Study, Urban Report No. 3, September, 1963.

Duesenberry, J. S., Gary Fromm, L. R. Klein, and Edwin Kuh (eds.), *The Brookings Quarterly Econometric Model of the United States*. Chicago: Rand McNally, 1965.

Fox, Karl A., "The Study of Interactions Between Agriculture and the Nonfarm Economy: Local, Regional and National," pp. 1-34, *Journal of Farm Economics*, Vol. XLIV, No. 1, February 1962.

Fox, Karl A., and T. Krishna Kumar, "Delineating Functional Economic Areas," pp. 13-55 in *Research and Education for Regional and Area Development*, Iowa State University Center for Agricultural and Economic Development. Ames: Iowa State University Press, 1966.

Fox, Karl A., and T. Krishna Kumar, "The functional economic area: delineation and implications for economic analysis and policy," pp. 57-85 in the Regional Science Association *Papers*, Vol. 15, 1965.

Fox, Karl A., J. K. Sengupta, and Erik Thorbecke, *The Theory of Quantitative Economic Policy: With Applications to Economic Growth and Stabilization*. Chicago: Rand McNally, 1966.

Change in the Small Community

Galpin, C. J., *The Social Anatomy of an Agricultural Community*. Agricultural Experiment Station of the University of Wisconsin, Madison, Research Bulletin No. 34, May 1915.

Johnstone, Paul H., "Old Ideals Versus New Ideas in Farm Life," *An Historical Survey of American Agriculture*. Yearbook Separate No. 1783, United States Department of Agriculture, Washington, D. C., 1941, pp. 129-130.

Article on "Shopping Centre" in the *Encyclopaedia Britannica* (1965 edition), Vol. 20, pp. 575-576.

CHAPTER 4

THE LITTLE COMMUNITY IN THE UNITED STATES:

A Combination of Opposites

ART GALLAHER, JR.

Several years ago Robert Redfield proposed a number of viewpoints from which to study a particular kind of human whole, which he called "the little community." One such viewpoint Redfield defined as "a combination of opposites," and he raised the question of whether the little community "may be described not as having just this content but as having also that content—that it may be two things of the same kind: two views of the world, two types of personality, two sets of emphasized values, two kinds of social relationships."[1]

My own experience and reading lead me to believe that this viewpoint depicts accurately the state of affairs in the little community in the United States today. In all communities, there are kinds of behavior that have the quality of "insideness" associated with them, and at the same time kinds of behavior that have an "outsideness" quality. *Classification* of the detail in such opposites is not important. Rather, there are substantive differences in the culture inventory of every little community, and these are not necessarily the same for all communities. Thus, I will deal here with the *dynamics*—the centrifugal and centripetal tendencies—which to a great extent structure and give meaning to the opposites, however classified, that are present in the little community.

Art Gallaher, Jr., is Associate Professor of Anthropology and Deputy Director, Center for Developmental Change, at the University of Kentucky, Lexington.

[1] Robert Redfield, *The Little Community: Viewpoints for the Study of a Human Whole*. Chicago: University of Chicago Press, 1955, p. 133.

As an anthropologist, I have limited myself mainly, though not exclusively, to substantive materials on the American community that have been collected by anthropologists, particularly to analyses that attempt rather complete examination of single little communities. I have reviewed these "community studies" individually and collectively to see what they say about what is happening in the little community in the United States and have balanced my judgments against some of the general works on the American community.

My understanding of community, then, large or small, is that of an anthropologist. Anthropologists have traditionally approached the study of communities as a total pattern of living, a whole made up of parts. Their assumption is that the community can be viewed, conceptually at least, as a minimum total culture isolate. Professor Redfield says:

> It is this "context of the whole" that is the characteristic of method often claimed by anthropologists who have studied so many communities, and have so often in each instance taken responsibility for finding out about all aspects of life of the community.[2]

And addressing himself specifically to community studies in anthropology, Julian Steward says of their methodology: "It is ethnographic; the culture of a tribe, band or village is studied in its totality, all forms of behavior being seen as functionally interdependent parts in the context of the whole."[3]

A major concern for this "whole," consistent with the foregoing assumption, has been to induce from it knowledge of the contemporary condition of a larger region or even nation. Steward tells us that this is, in fact, most often the intention of what anthropologists have come to call "community study."[4] And the result, more often than not, has been to use the community as a convenient laboratory for studying specific problems. This writer tends to agree with Stein's judgment that this kind of study is the more significant contribution of community studies. Referring to studies by Park, the Lynds, and

---

[2] Redfield, *op. cit.*, p. 156.

[3] Julian Steward, *Area Research: Theory and Practice*. Social Science Bulletin 63, 1950, p. 21.

[4] *Ibid.*

Warner, for example, all of whom made assumptions about the "representativeness" of the communities they studied, Stein says:

> The point is not that Chicago, Muncie, and Newburyport were representative communities in any statistical sense but rather that they were undergoing processes of structural transformation that affected all American cities and towns to one or another degree, and therefore could be used as laboratories in which to study these representative social processes.[5]

These assumptions, combined with others, bear on a conception of the nature of community that has come to be identified strongly with anthropologists and attributed mainly to their empirical involvement with primitive peoples. Stein, in an excellent piece on the anthropological perspectives on the modern community,[6] traces this view particularly in the writings of Sapir, Benedict, and Radin.[7] He points out their concern (held by most anthropologists) that society provide its members with full opportunity for the experience necessary for social growth and individual satisfaction.

> It almost seems as if community in the anthropological sense is necessary before human maturity or individuation can be achieved, while this same maturity is, in turn, a prerequisite for community.[8]

There is, then, etched into the anthropological tradition the now widely shared view that in the community the individual confronts the larger society and culture. This view of community is derived mainly from historical and comparative knowledge of other times and many places, and it bears on the nature of the human condition itself. The sociologist Roland Warren, long a student of contemporary community matters, puts this position very well:

> It is in his own locality, characteristically, that, throughout most of mankind's history and to a very great extent today, the individual confronts his society's institutions, its manner of religious expression, its ways of

---

[5] Maurice Stein, *The Eclipse of Community*. Princeton: Princeton University Press, 1960, p. 94.

[6] *Ibid.*, Ch. 10.

[7] *Selected Writings of Edward Sapir*, David G. Mandelbaum. Berkeley: University of California Press, 1949. Ruth Benedict, "Continuities and Discontinuities in Cultural Conditioning," in *A Study of Interpersonal Relations*, Patrick Mullahy, (ed.). New York: Hermitage Press, 1949. Paul Radin, *The World of Primitive Man*. New York: Henry Schuman, 1953.

[8] Stein, *op. cit.*, p. 248.

socializing the young, its way of providing sustenance, its ways of aesthetic expression.[9]

Even though for analytical purposes we conceptualize the community as a whole, it is itself a part of some larger whole. Depending on the analytical concerns and level of abstraction, this larger whole might be a regional subculture;[10] a historically derived subcultural continuum;[11] an ethnic category, such as Negro or Latin American; the nation-state; or any of a number of other ways of conceptualizing the social differentiations of a large heterogeneous society. However we conceptualize the larger whole, though, it is important to keep in mind that a particular community does not present a carbon copy of that whole. *The little community does, in fact, present to us a combination of opposites.*

"WE–THEY": INTERACTIVE OPPOSITES

The combination of opposites is not a characteristic that is new to the little community. Quite the contrary, in our kind of society it has been there all along and is, in fact, a normative condition for communities large and small. Furthermore, my own experience reinforces the theme that the internal dynamics of the community are to a great extent an effort to come to grips with kinds of activity that appear as opposites in the community setting. There are on the one hand fields of activity that carry the connotation of "we," and on the other hand those that initially carry with them the connotation of "they."

The *we* and *they* dichotomy can be seen in many substantive areas. It might be in matters of value, for example when the *local* work ethic is not considered a relevant criterion for participation in a *federal* welfare program; or in the conception of charity as a function of the local community, as contrasted to "our" participation in a

---

[9] Roland Warren, *The Community in America*. Chicago: Rand McNally, 1963, p. 21.

[10] Conrad M. Arensberg, "American Communities," *American Anthropologist*, 1955, Vol. 57, No. 6, Pt. 1, pp. 1143–62; and Marion Pearsall, "Cultures of the American South," *Anthropological Quarterly*, 1965, Vol. 39, No. 2, pp. 128–141.

[11] Evon Z. Vogt, "American Subcultural Continua as Exemplified by the Mormons and Texans," *American Anthropologist*, 1955, Vol. 57, No. 6, Pt. 1, pp. 1163-72.

charitable cause that originates, is administered, and distributes its rewards in *another place.* On the other hand, the dichotomy may appear in social relations: "In our town we are friendly and show it by speaking on the streets, whereas the government bureaucrats among *us* who are *outsiders* cannot give themselves over to such friendly ways"; or, "When I trade with a *local* independent storekeeper I can pay when I have the money, but if I buy from the local representative of a *national* chain I must pay cash." These are only a few of the myriad examples one can draw from even the smallest community in the United States today.

More important here is the fact that the structure and meaning of these and other substantive differences derive from underlying processes that are themselves opposites. There are in all communities centripetal tendencies to support the "we" feeling and centrifugal ones to pull the community out from itself in the direction of "they." Again, this situation is part of the nature of community, rather than exceptional or unusual. This concept is more than intellectual footwork. Most of our thinking has assumed an equilibrium model of community, in which there is a high level of "we" autonomy combined with the tendency to think that external stimuli have negative implications. Nowhere has this been more evident than in the preachments of early social scientists, social workers, and others, that the country life was the good life and the city life was the bad. They reasoned that the city with its sinful ways was a major stimulus to change in the pristine countryside. Related to their ideas was the implicit fear that the centrifugal impact of urban influences would dominate the centripetal tendencies toward inner consistency in rural life.

In the little community in the United States, there have always been fields of activity that force the view "in" to exist beside, and sometimes come into conflict with, the view "out." The internal dynamics of the community mainly involve *converting* behaviors that are initially of the "outside" functions into behaviors that serve "inside" functions; this characteristically involves converting into internal norm directives the norm directives embedded in the linkages to extra-community systems. This *is* the nature of the little community that exists as part of a larger whole.

This chapter, then, is an attempt to come to grips with the dynamics of linkage between the little community and the greater society of which it is a part. The processes that are delineated comprise the background phenomena against which decisions about the little community—either by those who live there or by those who live elsewhere but influence what goes on there—must be taken. As a whole they do not substantiate our traditional attachments to an equilibrium model; they seem to suggest that change is a normative condition of the little community.

THE LITTLE COMMUNITY: A CHANGING NET OF "WE–THEY" LINKAGES

Studies by anthropologists in American communities during the past 30 or so years make it clear that the little community is being increasingly pulled into the social and cultural mainstreams of the larger wholes with which it is identified. It may be more a reflection of the analytical biases of those of us who do our studies in the community context, but to read the author's *Plainville Fifteen Years Later*,[12] West's[13] earlier study of the same community, and the studies done by Vidich and Bensman, Pearsall, Goldschmidt, Rubin, Vogt, and Warner,[14] to name only some, is to gain the impression that the little community finds it increasingly difficult to maintain coherence and autonomy. These and other studies show an increased leveling of culture patterns in little communities. And at the broader level this is given focus in such works as those by Olson, Nisbet, and Warren,[15] again to name only a few.

The mechanism that conveys the greater culture to the little community is diffusion. It is useful to distinguish between *market* and

---

[12] Art Gallaher, *Plainville Fifteen Years Later*. New York: Columbia University Press, 1961.

[13] James West, *Plainville, U.S.A.* New York: Columbia University Press, 1945.

[14] Arthur J. Vidich, and Joseph Bensman, *Small Town in Mass Society*. Princeton: Princeton University Press, 1958. Marion Pearsall, *Little Smokey Ridge*. Tuscaloosa: University of Alabama Press, 1959. Walter Goldschmidt, *As You Sow*. New York: Harcourt, Brace, 1947. Moron Rubin, *Plantation County*. Chapel Hill: University of North Carolina Press, 1951. Evon Z. Vogt, *Modern Homesteaders*. Cambridge, Mass.: Harvard University Press, 1955. W. Lloyd Warner and Associates, *Democracy in Jonesville*. New York: Harper and Brothers, 1949.

[15] Philip Olson, *America as a Mass Society*. New York: The Free Press, 1963. Robert A. Nisbet, *The Quest for Community: A Study in the Ethics of Order and Freedom*. New York: Oxford University Press, 1953. Warren, *op. cit.*

administered types.[16] Market diffusion is relatively unplanned, and it accounts for the wide distribution of many aspects of material and nonmaterial culture in our own or other society. A crucial variable is, of course, social and physical isolation. If either or both of these are diminished, we can expect an acceleration in market diffusion. All the studies done in little communities indicate that this is, in fact, happening in the United States.

Administered diffusion is the *deliberate* introduction of innovations into the little community. The administering unit may be part of the community, for example, the public school, a denominational church, or the local branch of a national firm. On the other hand, administered diffusion may take place through agencies external to the community, which are especially efficient when they have access to the mass media. The increased interest of the central government in social planning, the increased bureaucratization in all segments of our society, and the refinement of mass media techniques have combined to intensify administered diffusion. The little community is subject to this kind of impact more now than at any prior period in our history. Significantly, administered diffusion has a more explicit content and direction than does market diffusion, and it therefore accelerates the tempo of change in the little community. Furthermore, diffusion administered through the bureaucracy is often accompanied by built-in rewards and/or sanctions, which are designed to facilitate the acceptance of innovations.

SOURCES OF CHANGE IN THE LITTLE COMMUNITY

Let us turn our attention now to some of the major processes at work in the little community in the United States. We have seen that the little community is related to the larger society and culture. It remains to point out that this relationship is not between entities, as of one whole to another, but rather between diverse elements of culture in the greater society. This qualification is necessary, to show that the following processes do not influence the community merely in diffuse ways, but that in all cases there may be, and frequently are, logical paths along which such influences travel.

[16] Cf. Warren, *op. cit.*, pp. 260–266.

CONJUNCTION OF CULTURAL DIFFERENCES

The first process, the *conjunction of cultural differences,*[17] brings together market and administered diffusion. We have seen before that the person who lives in the little community is now, more than ever, exposed to alternatives. I went to Plainville in 1954 prepared to believe that this was the situation. James West, fifteen years before me, had already written of government reform programs, the appearance of "scientific" farming, and diminishing isolation, among other innovative features, and he had put the case quite strongly when he said of that place and others like it:

> For better or for worse, they are doomed as "traditional" communities. As their ancient value systems crumble under the blows of a new "tradition" imposed from outside, their problem is to learn to participate more fully in the cultural rewards of the greater society.[18]

A similar point is made by another researcher about a very different kind of community, in the plantation South:

> The effect of the mass culture in promoting cultural and social change in the plantation area has been to create forces which are causing the new patterns to be dysfunctional and inconsistent with the old ones. . . . Old ways are being redefined, but compromise is slow. The young people of the plantation area will have to examine the old ways and the new ways with clear and analytic minds in order to discover that goal of a good life they want and deserve.[19]

And writing of still another kind of community, in the Appalachian south, Pearsall[20] states the matter simply but strongly: "The Outside Is Here to Stay." Perhaps the process can best be illustrated by turning to a community the writer knows well and exploring its reaction to the massive input of alternatives from the greater society surrounding it.

West wrote of Plainville, correctly, that change was not easy for the people there in 1939, and that there was considerable resistance and hostility to the alternatives being introduced. So it came as

---

[17] Cf. Homer G. Barnett, *Innovation, the Basis of Cultural Change.* New York: McGraw-Hill Book Company, Inc., 1953, pp. 46–56.

[18] West, *op. cit.*, p. 225.

[19] Rubin, *op. cit.*, pp. 204–205.

[20] *Op. cit.*, Ch. IX.

something of a surprise to find that Plainvillers did not resist change in 1955 to a great extent. By then, most of the people in this community seemed accustomed to confronting an environmental situation saturated with alternatives. By 1955, these alternatives, and those to which the people had been exposed over the preceding fifteen-year period, fell into three main categories: the reform programs that had proliferated since the New Deal era, improved communications both locally and with the larger society, and developments associated with World War II.

To talk about the massive confrontation with alternatives which the people in Plainville had experienced is not to imply that they either accepted or rejected change. We are concerned here only with the fact that *the tempo of diffusion has increased*, and that most of the people have accommodated to it by accepting the situation as normal. There are some, though, who are disturbed by the sheer magnitude of alternatives, and who because of their fears are spokesmen for conservatism. This is particularly true of the older-aged category which made up a third of the village during the time of our study. Their influence, however, was minimal, and their protestations that the world was moving by too quickly were not heeded—in fact, they were sometimes ridiculed, or rationalized away with the facile explanation that it is the nature of all old people to be that way.

In all communities, there are local units that belong to both the community and the extra-community systems. Every community is therefore subject to controls from within and without; and neither type of control can ever operate completely independently of the other. The local branch of the bureaucracy, the schools, various voluntary associations, the branch firms are at one and the same time local and extra-local, we-oriented and they-oriented. Depending on the situation, however, one set of controls will usually carry more weight than another in any given instance.

The church provides a particularly good example. Within the denominational hierarchy, there are matters of concern to the local body that must be transmitted to the local church. At the same time, there may be religious sentiment in the local congregation, perhaps in the region, that must be considered, especially by official functionaries of the community church. In Plainville, there are four churches, three of which are interdenominational; and they all served as primary public forums for discussing people's confrontation with alternatives in their daily lives.

In any such discussion, the view of the specialist leaders tends to be oriented toward the view of the small community. While they have one foot in the community and one foot in the greater society, they are likely to be vulnerable to the demands of the local community because it is there they are most intimately involved. Hence it is in these terms that they are likely to define survival. Because they are performing a *balancing* role, as systems linkers between the "we" and the "they," they tend not to perform as many innovative functions as we might otherwise expect. Yet they do serve as vital connecting links to the greater society and, community conditions permitting, can serve as an innovative or at least an initial accepter's elite. We cannot assume, however, before a policy problem is articulated, that church leadership will automatically take an innovative position. In Plainville, the clergy felt more strongly the need for local support; thus, they responded to aspects of the issues that could be identified most easily as lying in the community.

GROWING EXPECTATION OF CHANGE

A second major process at work in the little community is the *growing expectation of change.*[21] In all societies there are, of course, expectations of change in certain elements of community. In the United States, for example, we expect change in our technology. In fact our interest in some new technology often implies a desire to change, for technological innovation is a means of ameliorating difficulties. Such expectations are manifest in the way we define progress, and in the "style" and "fad" concerns in many segments of the national culture.

On the other hand, though our political organization is geared to orderly change, which generates a steadily increasing flow of innovations, the evidence seems to indicate that, publicly at least, we do not view these institutions as primary innovative mechanisms. In such findings as we have there seems to be an even more rigid assumption of stability in family organization and in religion. Plainville and other little community clergymen are likely to speak on the side of conservatism because they represent an area of stability, and they

---

[21] Cf. Barnett, *op. cit.*, pp. 56–64.

are *expected* to play roles consistent with latent needs for conserving that which constitutes the "we" component of the United States little community.

Generalizations about the expectations of change characteristic of our society do not suggest that all peoples are equally responsive to innovative stimuli. In fact, one axis of the rural-urban dichotomy involves the notion that the rural segment of the total society lags behind the urban. In this view, urban society is the heart of the innovative process, the fountainhead of culture in the greater society. And since the bureaucracy, industrial effort and mass media all originate or seem to rest in the urban segment of society, it makes sense that one of the major attempts to conceptualize the internal dynamics of community is a process called "urbanization."

The growing expectation of change in the little community is partly an outgrowth of the massive increase in alternatives that spring from diverse sources in the greater society. Just the presence of so many alternatives is enough to make people sensitive to the possibility of change. Sensitivity takes on definite meaning, however, when we consider that the increase in available alternatives has not been a random process, but rather reflects definite concentrations of ideas in the greater society. This means that sensitivity is most likely to be crystalized in aspects of culture that reflect the dominant concerns of the greater society—what Herskovits[22] calls the foci of a culture.

In such foci there "is lodged the greatest stimulus to thought and creative expression, the greatest proliferation of institutional forms."[23] Furthermore, these foci have special relevance for change, because it is in them that change is most likely to occur. "It [a focus] is an element making for the dynamic drives which bring about greater ease in change, and consequently greater diversity of manifestation in some aspects of a culture than in others."[24]

What we are saying, then, is that the increased alternatives made available to the little community are drawn mainly from the dom-

---

22 Herskovits, Melville, "The Processes of Cultural Change," in *The Science of Man in the World Crisis*, Ralph Linton (ed.). New York: Columbia University Press, 1945, pp. 164–170.

23 *Ibid*, p. 165.

24 *Ibid*., p. 168.

inant foci of the greater society, and therefore an expectation of change is generated in the little community. We should keep in mind, however, that the existence of an expectation does not mean that a particular change is necessarily welcomed. In fact, a change can be expected that would result in a sense of despair, frustration, loss of autonomy, or other negative consequences for the local community.

GROWING DEPENDENCE ON AUTHORITY

The growing expectation of change in the little community is further conditioned by the active role of the bureaucracy in administering diffusion. Since the 1930's particularly, the bureaucracy, through the political and legal processes available to it, has aggressively pushed for the clarification of what the planners felt to be important culture foci. The social and economic reforms of the New Deal in the 1930's comprised such an attempt; these were shortly followed by the explosive concerns for human rights begun during the 1940's, the push for educational reforms launched in the 1950's, and efforts in the 1960's to override poverty by a complex of programs given the label of the Great Society. These attempts to come to grips with social and psychological deprivation in the total society have resulted in the definition of a succession of cultural foci which have, at the local level, constituted urban impingements that typically resulted in community concern about the possibility of change.

Taken as a whole, these attempts have resulted in what Max Lerner calls the "revolution of access." He means by this the current dominant concern that all in this greater society of ours should have equal access to opportunity to maintain ourselves as viable social beings.

> It is a welfare society, a necessary effort to build a floor below which the human condition is not allowed to fall. Beyond welfarism there is potentially a spacious society. But it has to do not so much with achieving a consensus for legislation, as with forging a bond among Americans.[25]

The local reaction to these newly or more clearly defined culture foci depends mainly on local and/or regional subculture norms.

---

[25] Max Lerner, "Six Revolutions in American Life," in *The Revolutionary Theme in Contemporary America*, T. R. Ford (ed.). Lexington: University of Kentucky Press, 1965, p. 9.

The term "dependence on authority"[26] incorporates within it what many writers refer to as "bureaucratization." It is used here to denote something beyond bureaucratization, though, for it recognizes clearly that dependence is not a necessary consequence of bureaucratic maturation. In a society as complicated as ours, for example, where a highly developed division of labor results in extreme specialization, we are accustomed to relying on the authority of specialists to see us through the normal routines of social life. This is nothing new to our society, though again we have assumed the number and kinds of dependency to be less in the little community than in the larger one. Thus, an increased conjunction of alternatives and greater expectation of change broaden the little community's potential involvement in the greater society, and make the little community sensitive to the dependence upon authority that comes with participation in the more elaborate and specialized system of the greater culture. Involved in this whole process, and of special significance, is the critical view that turns in on the little community as its adequacy to satisfy expanding needs is assessed. The consequences of accepting a new standard of living, for example, can be disastrous for the merchant in a little community who has geared his investment to assumptions of traditional consumer behavior. Such situations threaten solidarity in the little community.[27]

In addition to the dependence on authority that accompanies specialization, there is also the authority that derives from bureaucratization. This ranges from political bureaucratization, which impinges on the little community, to bureaucratization that might come through the location of an industrial plant there, or the fact that there are voluntary associations, schools, and businesses tied formally to extra-community systems. Of course, there are always degrees of depersonalization, and the view of those associated with such units is less one that cuts across the community than one that looks out and away to the parent enterprise.

The impact of political bureaucratization on the little community is significant primarily because it threatens community autonomy by radically modifying local decision-making processes, perhaps even removing them entirely from the community.

---

[26] Cf. Barnett, *op. cit.*, pp. 65–72.

[27] Gallaher, *op. cit.*, p. 234.

We have already seen that the growth in expectations of change in the little community reflects the government's attempts to define or clarify significant foci of change in the greater society. To a great extent, the political bureaucratization of the local community is the implementation of these changes at the local level. The fact that there is frequent resistance at this level attests to a major dilemma: how can change be effected in a pluralistic society? The core of this dilemma is the determination of the locus of decision-making responsibility. Attempts to come to grips with this and related matters have had wide political, social, and judicial ramifications.[28]

Economic reforms, especially in such fields as agriculture, welfare, civil rights, educational reforms, and now the Great Society programs, have all had their impact. They have represented a steady barrage of innovations directed at the little community. In many cases, these programs have defined issues so complicated that the little community had no choice but to relinquish decision-making responsibilities to a bureaucratic level. In others, the threat to local or regional values was too great and resistance moves set in. This is currently true of emotion-charged issues such as civil rights, and of less emotion-tinged issues such as religion in the schools, educational reform, and community action programs of the War on Poverty.

Always, some voices from the little community say that, given the opportunity, we can show "our" way to be the best. Only recently the President of the United States went on record to support small-town life as good and desirable. Unfortunately, those who speak for the little communities, including the people who live in them, are seldom explicit about their virtues. The writer remembers asking the question of some Plainvillers who insisted that theirs was the best life, and receiving muted if not garbled responses. The program areas we have mentioned have undoubtedly linked the people more closely to the greater society. Looking at all the major programs to which Plainvillers had been exposed over the preceding 15 years, one could say of them:

> We need only emphasize one important feature which all of them hold in common: they substitute external for internal authority in areas of Plainville life where decision-making responsibility has heretofore been

---

[28] Cf. Herman C. Pritchett, "The Judicial Revolution and American Democracy," in T. R. Ford, *op. cit.*

considered autonomous. And this, as we have indicated, represents probably the most significant change in the Plainville subculture—the people not only accept but are dependent on external authority, particularly the federal government, as a directive source of change.[29]

A similar but much more incisive examination of a small community was put forth by Vidich and Bensman in their excellent *Small Town in Mass Society*. They tell us that the people in this community still cling to the traditional image of their life as eminently more desirable than the life of the city. Still the urban culture is much more a part of Small Town than the people who live there will permit themselves to believe. This condition exists because the people have accommodated successfully to their situation by developing two systems of social control. One of these supports the small-town ideology, and the other, through a well-integrated leadership group, insures that local affairs will be adapted to the pressures of the greater urban society.

The Small Town case certainly represents a more extreme reaction to the greater society than do studies of Plainville or other little communities. Whereas the Small Towners seem bent on keeping the small-town ideology alive, even if it is mythical, and organize their community to permit doing so, the others seem more content to verbalize the ideology and in their behavior rather passively accept the greater society. Plainvillers may not be as committed to the small-town ideology; or they may be committed just as strongly but have some structural defect, such as political sophistication, that does not permit them to come to grips with maintaining the myth. On the other hand, there may not be economic, social, and other kinds of viability sufficient to sustain the ideology that equates the good life with small-town life styles.

A related factor, the transmission of dependency status, has yet to receive the analytical attention it deserves, but it will become increasingly important for those who plan for others. It can be seen most easily in those communities farthest removed from the mainstream of American economic and social advantages, where dependency is likely to become so complete as to be normative, and therefore transmitted. Transmission, if it occurs, will pose a special problem for those who assume that innovations are "naturally" judged against the ground of social and psychological deprivation. There is

[29] Gallaher, *op. cit.*, p. 255.

reason to assume that an awareness of relative deprivation can serve as an incentive to change; but if dependency status becomes normative and is transmitted to succeeding generations, deprivation may be more apparent than real.

ACCELERATED URBANIZATION

A fourth major process at work in the little community is accelerated urbanization. There are many ways of conceptualizing urbanization. Because we are concerned with urbanization at the level of process, rather than substantively, we shall use the definition of Bennett and Tumin: "The transformation of rural communities within Western society into specialized and dependent communities serving the whole national socio-economic system."[30]

Thus, people in little communities throughout the United States are almost daily entering into relationships drawing them into ever-widening circles of awareness of, participation in, and dependency on the surrounding urban culture. All studies of little communities support this statement, from the extreme urban impact upon highly industrialized farm communities in California,[31] to the lesser impact experienced by isolated communities in the Appalachian mountains,[32] and even less in an ethnic enclave in New Mexico.[33]

Exposure to urban culture comes through both market and administered diffusion. The mass media, particularly advertising and the mass consumer behavior it attempts to direct, are part and parcel of the urban segment of our society. A formidable expertise exists to guide the presentation of massive alternatives to the greater society, and in the process—almost incidentally—to the little community, to focus expectations of change within alternatives, and to predispose us to depend on authorities to direct what we buy, read, and prefer. And since the bureaucracy and the programs developed through it are administered from the cities, they represent an urban point of view.

---

30 John Bennett and Melvin Tumin, *Social Life: Its Structure and Function*. New York: Alfred A. Knopf, 1948, p. 432.

31 Cf. Goldschmidt, *op. cit.*

32 Cf. Pearsall, *op. cit.*

33 Olen E. Leonard and C. P. Loomis, *Culture of a Contemporary Rural Community: El Cerrito, New Mexico*. Washington, D. C.: Bureau of Agricultural Economics, 1941.

In- and out-migration also serve as effective bridges for the movement of urban traits into the rural area. Pearsall, for example, offers an excellent discussion of how this process works in a remote Southern Appalachian region, the kind of community in which this kind of communication, more than all other forms, probably exposes urban traits to the little community.[34] Inescapably, most little communities are tied to agricultural and extractive resource economies, both of which have been undergoing severe constrictive modification over the past several decades. In fact, out-migration has been the population safety valve in such areas almost since their initial settlement. With the closing of the land frontier, the youth of little communities have turned almost as a body to the urban, industrial segment of our society.

The process just explained has been documented to the point of monotony, and no matter how the facts are manipulated there remains the inescapable conclusion that from a real and psychological viewpoint the city represents *opportunity dominance.* This is the hard and cold fact; probably it is the toughest of all the fibers woven into the process we call urbanization, and it is one with which centripetal tendencies in the little community have never come to grips.

Are the socializing agencies, such as family, school, and church, now present in the community equal to the task? Must there continue to be mobility in our society? The answer to the latter question, however, lies less in the community than does the answer to the former question.

We should not overlook the possibility that the rural-urban influence may not be as one-way as it first seems. Wood suggests that the small-town ideology may in fact be carried over into "suburbia."

> In any given suburban territory, small governments, truly local governments, remain to enhance the feeling of the small community in the modern world, to cling to the ideal of the republic in miniature, and to prevent the encroachment of the metropolis.[35]

And Bell suggests that the move to the suburbs is a reaction against specialization and impersonalization, that it:

---

[34] *Op. cit.*, Ch. 10.

[35] Robert C. Wood, *Suburbia: Its People and Their Politics.* Boston: Houghton, Mifflin, 1959, pp. 254–55.

expresses an attempt to find a location in which to conduct family life which is more suitable than that offered by central cities, i.e., that persons moving to the suburbs are principally those who have chosen familism as an important element of their life styles as over against career or consumership.[36]

A MOVING BALANCE OF OPPOSITES

In conclusion, it is worth reiterating the point that there are in little communities kinds of behavior that are part of the life of such communities, and at the same time there are elements of that life with a relative "outsideness" quality to them. We have concerned ourselves here with some of the forces that are transpiring to produce this condition. We have explored briefly some of the major processes which our studies tell us are contributing most heavily to the substantive changes occurring in little communities. The processes we have delineated are, of course, all related and occur simultaneously in the experiences of people. They are the background phenomena against which decisions about the little community, for whatever reasons, must be taken.

The implication of this analysis is that the "outsideness" dimension of the community weighs more heavily on the total dimension of community life with each passing day. And in all fairness to the data there seems no indication that this direction will be reversed. Therefore, the little community to survive must do more than simply "react," it must "act." It must integrate in a way that allows the "outsideness" in its behavior to become more of the "insideness." This is not to say that it should embrace totally all the new behavior that comes to it from the greater society; in fact, no one knows what should be ingested and what rejected among the multiplicity of alternatives that impinge upon it. Perhaps the greatest need is for qualitative assessment of alternatives. If this cannot somehow be managed, the "we" sentiment may be lost and with it the sense of *this community*. Our national statistics show that this does occur.

Whether or not the little community manages survival in ways that are satisfying to those who will live there depends to a great

---

[36] Wendell Bell, "Social Choice, Life Styles, and Suburban Residence," in *The Suburban Community*, William Dobriner (ed.). New York: G. P. Putnam's Sons, 1958, p. 231.

extent on how units with ties to both the community and the extra-community systems manage to maintain linkage. If the extreme position is taken, that is, if the lot is cast all the way with either inside or outside, the little community can only suffer. We need only look toward a recent alternative with high emotional content to see the implication. Racial desegregation of areas of community life, and the differential, inconsistent, and often-conflicting roles taken by in- and out-oriented groups such as church, school, law enforcement, business, and political, point up the kind of instability that an imbalance among these opposites can produce. There must be some middle ground, in which such institutions can more satisfactorily relate to each other in the little community setting, at the same time providing people in the little community with access to the greater society.

SUGGESTIONS FOR FURTHER READING

Arensberg, Conrad M. and Solon T. Kimball, *Culture and Community*. New York: Harcourt, Brace and World, 1965.

Foster, George, *Traditional Culture and the Impact of Technological Change*. New York: Harper and Row, 1962.

Goldschmidt, Walter, *Man's Way*. New York: Holt, Rinehart and Winston, 1959.

Hall, Edward T., *The Silent Language*. New York: Doubleday and Company, 1959.

Henry, Jules, *Culture Against Man*. New York: Random House, 1963.

Kluckhohn, Clyde, *Mirror for Man*. New York: McGraw-Hill, 1949.

Moore, Wilbert E., *Social Change*. Englewood Cliffs, N. J.: Prentice-Hall, 1963.

Pelto, Pertti J., *The Nature of Anthropology: Social Science Perspectives*. Columbus, Ohio: Charles E. Merrill, 1966.

Spicer, Edward H., *Human Problems in Technological Change*. New York: Russell Sage Foundation, 1952.

Wallace, A. F. C., *Culture and Personality*. New York: Random House, 1961.

CHAPTER 5

POLITICAL CHANGE IN THE SMALL AMERICAN COMMUNITY

BERT E. SWANSON

I approach a study of the small community with wistfulness. Many of my formative years were spent in one, and my research there has always been enjoyable. The people in these communities, whether a small Indian village or a one-company mill town, were often inspiring. These sentiments become all the stronger now that I live in and study a crowded, large city. In a sense, inventorying some of what we know about the polity of the small community involves looking at the past and feeling nostalgia for pleasant, bygone days. The small community seems a thing of the past, yet the U. S. Census Bureau reports that 4,680—85.9 percent of our cities—are under 25,000 in population. These same census reports indicate, nevertheless, that two-thirds of our population live in urban metropolitan centers (Standard Metropolitan Statistical Areas).

Our knowledge of American communities is confusing in two basic aspects. On the one hand, there is little conscious effort to distinguish between small, medium, and large places. Differences or similarities of size are assumed, seldom stated. This undifferentiated approach to the study of politics gives rise to many ambiguities about the dynamics of political behavior in small and large places. Is power widely shared? Are public officials responsive to citizen preferences? Do

---

Professor Swanson teaches political science at Sarah Lawrence College, Bronxville, New York, where he also serves as coordinator for its Institute of Community Studies. The author wishes to acknowledge the help of his graduate assistant, Edith Corton.

citizens participate freely and effectively? Is political controversy functional or dysfunctional? Does government assume its proper responsibilities to assure or achieve a viable system? Is the bureaucracy sufficiently skilled and efficient at the day-to-day operations of public affairs?

So pervasive is this ambiguity that we can almost conclude that knowledge of behavior patterns gained from small-town experience is authoritative enough to account for what is happening in our big cities. Our conceptions of the small-town operations guide our political behavior in large urban places. Such attitudes should be seriously questioned, and distinguishing characteristics of the small political system should be sorted out. At the same time, such knowledge may assist some participants in the political process to prepare their communities to make necessary adjustments as their towns grow in size and complexity. They may find it advisable, in order to survive, to modify or abandon their conceptions and myths about democracy.

Paradoxically, small-town America today is being transformed even while its mode and concepts are more and more coming to serve as referents against which we measure and evaluate what we do in the great urban centers. In fact, many insist that city politics currently reflect the verities of rural America and the small town—free of corruption, simple in nature, narrow in function. Not only have the reformers partially succeeded in achieving these conditions; they have also evolved an ideology of community conservation that sees the community as a complex of mutually interdependent parts wherein the individual and the common good are compatible, if not identical.[2] They see the values of community life maximized when the leaders represent the public at large rather than the "special interests." They value professionally trained public administrators and hold the professional politicians in disrepute. They oppose "dirty politics" and generally speaking they are aligned on the side of re-

---

[2] For a detailed discussion of the prevailing political ideologies, see Robert E. Agger, Daniel Goldrich, and Bert E. Swanson, *The Rulers and the Ruled: Political Power and Impotence in American Communities*. New York: John Wiley and Sons, 1964, pp. 14–32.

form, primarily in order to stress long-range planning in the public interest.

Another source of confusion in our attempts to understand small communities has grown out of the laissez-faire strategy we have used in research. That is, little of what we know is based on any systematic, comprehensive, theory-based inquiry. Rather, we have a scattered ad hoc collection of case studies by numerous individuals —practitioners and academicians—who proceed with little more than a convenient and manageable set of concepts and only a casual regard for the gap between these bundles of concepts and the knowledge our difficulties require. We need a useful and theoretical approach. We have been overwhelmed with statistics compiled by the "brute empiricists," who present the facts but provide no general perspective on the meaning of the data they have generated.[3] Even the insights gained through participant observation have seldom been formulated into warrantable assertions about the conditions of political life in small communities.

This last point requires elaboration. Lacking a comprehensive, theoretical approach, we ought at least to encourage those practitioners who wish to learn from their experience to develop ways of testing out our limited knowledge and our many assumptions about small political systems. In other words, the data, knowledge, and insights discussed here should be probed for their significance and relevance to a better understanding of how small polities work and of how to improve present conditions in American small communities. Above all, we should be attempting to prepare these communities for the conditions and problems that generally accompany urban growth and change. This was Lincoln Steffens' position in *The Shame of the Cities*,[4] a book touted as an exposé of political corruption. Actually, the author himself was interested both in reform and in understanding a condition, created by apathy and tolerance,

---

[3] Several recent studies attempt to inventory our general political knowledge. See Robert Lane, *Political Life*. New York: The Free Press, 1959; Wendell Bell, Richard J. Hill, and Charles E. Wright, *Public Leadership*. San Francisco: Chandler Publishing Co., 1961; Charles Press, *Main Street Politics*. East Lansing: Michigan State University Press, 1962; Lester W. Milbrath, *Political Participation*. Chicago: Rand McNally, 1965.

[4] Lincoln Steffens, *The Autobiography of Lincoln Steffens*. New York: Harcourt, Brace & Co., 1931.

of a citizenry too busy to undertake the business of governing the local polity.

We shall attempt here to inventory the impacts and the implications of change in the political structure of the small community. Our immediate object is to classify our knowledge of changes that take place in the polity of the small community as it increases and/or decreases in size and complexity.

Because we need analytic conceptions rather than continued description of immediate or policy problems, we will not focus on the many concrete and practical issues facing American communities (increased public expenditures, taxes, and indebtedness) or on the many problems associated with specific policy issues involving public and mental health, urban renewal and housing, public education, and the like.

Instead, six concepts (or factors), each linked to the preceding ones to form a chain, will be offered as a frame of reference for analyzing the dynamics of change in the small community. These factors constitute the major issues associated with the political change. Each is typically both cause and consequence of larger changes in the social and economic structure of community. Indeed, these political factors may significantly affect the form and direction of social and economic change.

1. Power structure: the distribution of influence;
2. Political regimes: rules governing the competition for power, the rules of the "political game," so to speak;
3. Citizen participation: voting, discussion, and attending meetings;
4. Political competition: the degree of contention, controversy, and conflict;
5. Politicization: shifting or maintaining the scope of government;
6. Professionalization: the degree of specialization of the bureaucracy.

Each factor is related to the others in the chain of causation. For example, changes in the rate of citizen participation affect the type of power structure. A proposal to expand the scope of government may set off extended community controversy. Throughout this discussion the small communities of Farmdale and Oretown, where the author has had considerable first-hand experience, will be used to distinguish these factors and show how they function in an empirical setting.

THE SMALL COMMUNITY DEFINED

First, we will define briefly the small community and its political system. What characteristics best describe the small town—its population size and spatial arrangements, or its location and its degree of self-contained identity or autonomy? Or is there some other unique economic, social, political, or psychological property?

Plato preferred a *polis* of 5,040 persons, a figure derived from cosmological speculations. Modern estimates have expanded to Jane Jacobs' administrative districts within the large city, ranging from 30,000 to 200,000 population. Aristotle considered Plato's figure too large for satisfactory communal existence. Jacobs views anything larger than 200,000 as unable to be "comprehended both whole and in sufficient detail."[5]

Population size is a favorable measuring unit. Entities of local government have long been classified by population size, and with each designation of village, town, and city certain legislative rights and responsibilities have been assigned. Such a hierarchy of urban places assumes that communities of a certain size have certain public problems that require about the same kinds of legal authority to manage them. Villages in the state of New York, for example, have been classified by size: first class, 5,000 population; second class, 3,000 to 5,000; third class, 1,000 to 3,000; and fourth class, under 1,000. First-class villages, as well as cities, have "home rule" powers, with more local authority but generally not enough to handle all local problems. Likewise, state aid to school districts in New York is based on both population size and density. A district with greater density receives additional financial aid because larger-scale enterprises frequently have problems that are more expensive to ameliorate.

This legal classification of communities by state legislatures, based on population size, assumes that different problems, resources, and organizational forms are primarily a consequence of size. Small towns

---

[5] Jane Jacobs, *The Death and Life of Great American Cities*. New York: Random House, 1961, p. 425.

typically have certain *social* characteristics that are crucial in their operations and set them apart as essentially different from larger places manifesting constellations of factors. The running dialogue between the advocates of the garden city and the urbanists illustrates a kind of presupposition in policy making. The garden city proponent favors a small town of some 30,000 persons, situated on approximately 1,000 acres. The urbanist, on the other hand, is suspicious of any attempt to give the city a rural flavor. He prefers the heterogeneity of urban life and the wide variety of opportunities pointed out by Lawrence Haworth:

> The contrasts are indicated by such terms as integration and specialization, solidarity and independence, homogeneity and variety. Impersonality and anonymity, which the partisan of the small town regards as defects of urban life, are considered by the urbanist to be precious values.[6]

The almost universal use of arbitrary statistical population figures (such as number of inhabitants per square mile) to distinguish between different forms of urban places presents difficulties. One has only to make the transition once to become aware of this difference. Louis Wirth summarized the distinctive features of the urban mode of life

> . . . as consisting of the substitution of secondary for primary contacts, the weakening of bonds of kinship, and the declining social significance of the family, the disappearance of the neighborhood, and the undermining of the traditional basis of social solidarity.[7]

Ferdinand Tonnies developed a useful dichotomy between Gemeinschaft (community) and Gesellschaft (society) as representing stages in the historical development of a group of people. These two concepts allow us to contrast any two cultures at any given point in their development. While this typology specifies a wide range of social attributes, those of order, law, and morality have been selected for inclusion in the following comparison[8] because of their relevance to this discussion of political systems.

---

[6] Lawrence Haworth, *The Good City*. Bloomington, Ind.: Indiana University Press, 1963, p. 105.

[7] Louis Wirth, "Urbanism as a Way of Life," *American Journal of Sociology*, Vol. 44, No. 6 (July, 1938), pp. 1–24.

[8] Adapted from Ferdinand Tonnies, *Community and Society*. New York: Harper and Row, 1957, pp. 268–269.

Concept	*Gemeinschaft*	*Gesellschaft*
Order	Concord, family spirit	Convention
Law	Folkways and mores, law of custom	Legislation, law of contracts
Morality	Religion	Public opinion

While America has essentially reached the Gesellschaft stage of society, many pockets of the Gemeinschaft stage of community still remain. The small community has a political system based more on concord than on convention, more on custom than on legislation, regulation, and contracts, and more on religious ethos than on public opinion. In fact, this sense of community continues to guide political behavior and reform in any urban place where there is some effort to recapture the basic qualities of community decision making so that the citizen can more effectively participate and have his preferences prevail.[9]

THE SIX FACTORS OF POLITICAL CHANGE

This section will discuss each of the six factors of political change as they relate to change in small communities.

POWER STRUCTURE

The term community power structure refers to an analytic conception of the relationships between, the give-and-take among, those who seek to influence community policy. Because the pattern of influence is subject to frequent change, it must be considered at a stated point in time.

Two attributes of community affect the distribution of political influence. One is the system of legal institutional arrangements for law and order in the community; the other is the system of "who gets what, when, and how." Information about the first is obtained in a formal description of local government. Information about the second is found in an examination of the informal display of power and influence in the decision-making processes through which power holders or influentials determine when local government shall function in the interest of the local polity and when in the interests of the commonwealth as a whole. Although the government has a

[9] See Bert E. Swanson, "The Concern for Community in the Metropolis," *Urban Affairs Quarterly*, Vol. 1, No. 4 (June, 1966), pp. 33–44.

monopoly on the legal prerogative to make laws and enforce them, there are a number of centers of political, economic, and social power in the community that seek to define the character of local government, to identify who will govern, and to decide what policy positions the governmental agencies at the community level will take.

American communities have been ingenious in developing various institutional and extra-legal forms of local government. One of the first devices—the New England town meeting—impressed de Tocqueville as a mainstay of democracy.

> The activity of the township is continually perceptible; it is daily manifested in the fulfillment of a duty or the exercise of a right; and a constant though gentle motion is thus kept up in society, which animates without disturbing it.[10]

But as the nation and the cities grew in size and complexity, responsible local government began to deteriorate, leading Lord Bryce to call municipal government "the one conspicuous failure in the United States." Three major forms of local government developed. (1) The mayor-council form may have a weak or a strong mayor (an important distinction for reformers who generally propose to strengthen executive leadership). The weak mayor form, prevalent during the early nineteenth century and present today in small communities, diffused administrative power. The strong mayor form, developed before the turn of the twentieth century and used in larger cities, relegated more administrative authority to the mayor. (2) The commission plan, founded after the near-destruction by fire of Galveston, Texas, conducts its business under the guidance of elected commissioners, who divide functional areas of responsibility. (3) The council-manager plan, a twentieth century phenomenon found in many small and middle-sized cities, is the culmination of a municipal reform movement to eliminate corrupt local government and bring efficient, professional, and businesslike managerial talent to the conduct of local affairs. A corollary development in the large city has been the creation of a chief administrative officer to serve as the alter ego of the mayor and to bring professional administrative talent to the top structure of local government.

---

[10] Alexis de Tocqueville, *Democracy in America*. Vol. I. New York: Random House, 1945, p. 70.

Change in the Small Community

Many political scientists have devoted their attention to introducing uniform operations in structures of the same type, but it can probably be said that no two cities have exactly the same government structure. Nor, more importantly, do those in official positions operate in exactly the same manner in structures of the same type.

Still, certain patterns appear. Most modern communities have begun to emphasize professionalized administrative decision making in place of the uneven efforts of part-time politicians. Municipal elections are mainly nonpartisan, particularly in the West and the Midwest. Even where they still remain partisan, the reformers have attempted to free the mayor from his party. With the development of the "administrative state," apathy on the local level has developed among citizens who no longer feel that they can "fight city hall."

These efforts to depoliticize the decision-making process often create a power vacuum, where officials may govern with little reference to popular election. Thus, the concentrated focus on legal form has led researchers to examine the informal political processes and the community power structure. Because their findings indicate that these extra-institutional arrangements result in real changes in the dynamics of the polity, political analysts are raising once again the classic questions about the distribution of power, reclassifying the polity as oligarchic or democratic. Much discussion has centered on the "ideal-type" models of community power structures, ranging from the most *monolithic* or *power elite* systems to the more *pluralistic* or *open* systems.

In a monolithic political system, power is concentrated in the hands of a few, with fairly rigid barriers between the leaders and the nonleaders, with private citizens rather than government officials constituting the largest proportion of the top leadership, and with a high level of political manipulation by the leaders. In a polity dominated by a power elite, power is monopolized by a few, and there is little prospect that it will ever be widely shared so long as the elite sustains and regenerates itself. Control is exercised by a few men who dominate the institutional and organizational vehicles in the community. For example, the one-company town, which has not experienced a population influx with diverse ethnic or racial backgrounds, can exercise considerable economic leverage in public affairs. In 1953 Floyd Hunter found Atlanta, Georgia, to be a classic example of a city under the control of "economic dominants."[11] He discovered that the will of these men, leaders of finance and industry, prevailed on all the big issues and most small ones. They comprised a more or less homogeneous group, united in their operations. There were cliques among them which were more like cooperating subgroups of an integrated whole than competing factions, each seeking dominance over the others.

In a pluralistic political system, on the other hand, power is actually or potentially widely shared, there are relatively permeable power strata, government officials comprise a large proportion of the top leadership, and the level of manipulation by leaders is comparatively low. The open community is generally associated with a pluralistic social structure, which has a diversified industrial base, a bureaucracy both specialized and differentiated, and a heterogeneous population. Even more important, power is divided among competing political parties and other social and civic organizations, which reflect differing political ideologies.

Robert Dahl found in New Haven, Connecticut, a New England oligarchy transformed into a democratic polity wherein leaders of a number of countervailing sectors of society, from the old Yankees to the newly arrived ethnic groups, all contended to govern the city. New Haven leaders were found bargaining with each other within a consensual system. Dahl does not agree, however, with de Tocqueville's notion that there is a universal belief in the basic rules of the democratic game. Rather, in his search for an explanation of stable American communities, he believes political leadership to be significant and hypothesizes how it works.

> Suppose the rules, procedures, and essential characteristics of this system are strongly supported by a minority which, in comparison with the rest of the population, possesses a high degree of political skill. Suppose further that a majority of voters would prefer rules different from those prevailing, though they might not all prefer the same alternatives. Suppose finally that the majority of voters have access to fewer resources of influence; that their preferences for other rules are not salient or strong; that because of their relative indifference they do not employ what potential influence they have; and that they are not very skillful in using their

---

[11] Floyd Hunter, *Community Power Structure.* Chapel Hill: University of North Carolina, 1953.

TABLE 1

COMPARATIVE STUDY

Community[c]	Region	Size[b]	Economic Base	Whether Industrial
a. Redwing	N Cent.	B	Diversified	Yes
b. Bakerville	South	A	Narrow	No
c. Bennington	N East	B	Diversified	No
d. Cibola	N Cent.	B	Narrow	Yes
e. Springdale	N East	A		No
f. Northville	West	B	Diversified	No
g. Algona	South	B	Diversified	No
h. Milton	N Cent.	B		No
i. Norwood	N East	B	Narrow	Yes
j. Cerebrille	N Cent.	B	Diversified	Yes
k. Burlington	South	B	Diversified	Yes
l. Orange Point	South	A	Narrow	No
m. Floriana	South	B	Narrow	No
n. Eastborne	South	A	Narrow	No
o. Westborne	South	B	Narrow	No
p. Dorado	South	A	Narrow	No
q. Edgewood	N East	A	Narrow	No
r. Riverview	N East	A	Narrow	No
s. Midway County	South	A		No
t. Beach County	South	B		
u. Farmdale	West	A	Narrow	No
v. Oretown	West	B	Diversified	Yes
w. Oberlin	N Cent.	A		No

a Adapted from an article by John Walton, "Substance and Artifact: The Current Status of Research on Community Power Structure," *The American Journal of Sociology*, Vol. 71, No. 4 (January, 1966), pages 430-438. Used by permission of the University of Chicago Press and the Editor.

b A=population up to 10,000; B=population 10,000 to 50,000.

c The original studies are as follows: (a) Donald W. Olmstead, "Organizational Leadership and Social Structure in a Small City," *American Sociological Review*, XIX (June, 1954), 273-81; (b) Alexander Fanelli, "A Typology of Community Leadership Based on Influence and Interaction within the Leader Sub-system," *Social Forces*, XXXIV (May, 1956), 332-38; (c) Harry Scoble, "Leadership Hierarchies and Political Issues in a New England Town," in Morris Janowitz (ed.), *Community Political Systems* (Glencoe, Ill.: Free Press, 1961), pp. 117-45; (d) Robert O. Schulze, "The Bifurcation of Power in a Satellite City," in Janowitz, *op. cit.*, pp. 19-80; (e) Arthur J. Vidich and Joseph Bensman, *Small Town in Mass Society* (Princeton, N. J.: Princeton University Press, 1958); (f) Ted C. Smith, "The Structure of Power in a Suburban Community," *Pacific So-*

ALL AMERICAN COMMUNITIES[a]

Population Growth	Social Composition	Influentials	Structure	Number of Leaders
Stable	Homogeneous		Factional	
Stable	Heterogeneous	Nongovt.	Pyramid	25
Stable	Homogeneous	Govt.	Factional	69
Increase	Homogeneous	Govt.	Factional	35
Increase	Homogeneous		Pyramid	5
Increase	Heterogeneous	Nongovt.	Pyramid	16
Increase	Heterogeneous		Factional	
Stable	Homogeneous		Amorphous	
Stable	Homogeneous		Amorphous	
	Homogeneous	Govt.	Coalition	49
Increase	Heterogeneous	Nongovt.	Pyramid	16
Increase	Heterogeneous	Nongovt.	Pyramid	
Stable	Heterogeneous	Nongovt.	Factional	
Stable	Homogeneous	Govt.	Pyramid	
Increase	Homogeneous	Nongovt.	Pyramid	
Increase	Homogeneous	Govt.	Factional	
	Homogeneous	Both	Coalition	36
	Heterogeneous	Both	Factional	35
		Govt.	Factional	20
		Govt.	Pyramid	18
Stable	Homogeneous	Both	Pyramid	14
Increase	Homogeneous	Both	Coalition	38
		Both	Factional	

ciological Review, III (Fall, 1960), 83-88; (g) Ernest A. T. Barth, "Community Influence Systems: Structure and Change," *Social Forces*, XL (October, 1961), 58-63; (h) *Ibid.;* (i) *Ibid.;* (j) Delbert C. Miller, "Town and Gown: The Power Structure of a University Town," *American Journal of Sociology*, LXVIII (January, 1963), 432-43; (k) Charles M. Bonjean, "Community Leadership: A Case Study and Conceptual Refinement," *American Journal of Sociology*, LXVIII (May, 1963), 672-81; (l) Gladys M. Kammerer *et al.*, *The Urban Political Community: Profiles in Town Politics* (Boston: Houghton Mifflin Co., 1963); (m) *Ibid.;* (n) *Ibid.;* (o) *Ibid.;* (p) *Ibid.;* (q) Robert Presthus, *Men at the Top: A Study in Community Power* (New York: Oxford University Press, 1964); (r) *Ibid.;* (s) Ralph B. Kimbrough, *Political Power and Educational Decision Making* (Chicago: Rand McNally & Co., 1964); (t) *Ibid.;* (u) Robert E. Agger, Daniel Goldrich, and Bert E. Swanson, *The Rulers and the Ruled: Political Power and Impotence in American Communities* (New York: John Wiley & Sons, 1964); (v) *Ibid.;* (w) Aaron Wildavsky, *Leadership in a Small Town* (Totowa, N. J.: Bedminster Press, 1964).

political resources anyway. Such a political system, it seems to me, might be highly stable.

On the other hand, if any of the characteristics of this hypothetical minority were to shift to the majority, then the system would surely become less stable. Instability would increase, then, if the minority favoring the system no longer had superior resources, or if it became less skillful, or if the question of rules became salient and urgent to a majority of voters.[12]

How prevalent is any type of power structure in America? This question has been dealt with by John Walton.[13] In a recent survey of 33 studies covering 55 communities, Walton found a fair representation of several types of power structure: 19 "pyramidal, monolithic, or elite systems"; 17 "factional," with at least 2 durable factions; 14 "coalitional," with fluid coalitions of interest usually varying with the issues; and 5 "amorphous," with no pattern of leadership.[14] Table 1 illustrates some of the social, economic, and governmental characteristics of those communities.[15] Among Walton's list of communities there are essentially the same distributions of power structures in the small (between 10,000 and 50,000) and the smallest (under 10,000), except that the coalitional form occurs most often in the larger of the two groups.

Walton found that the method of study was a major factor in typing the communities and that socio-economic characteristics seemed to have little effect on the type of power structure. With the exception that the pyramidal systems had decidedly fewer leaders (less than 20, as compared to more than 20 for factional and coalitional systems and mainly nongovernmental leaders), there were no striking differences between the types of power structures, based on the ecological data Walton examined. The analysis underlying *The Rulers and the Ruled* corroborates this finding: there was "no evidence of any general relationship between economic trends and po-

---

[12] Robert A. Dahl, *Who Governs?* New Haven: Yale University Press, 1961, p. 315.

[13] John Walton, "Substance and Artifact: The Current Status of Research on Community Power Structure," *The American Journal of Sociology*, Vol. 71, No. 4 (January, 1966), pp. 430–438.

[14] The terms factional, coalitional, and amorphous are comparable to the use of a pluralistic political system. Certainly they are nonelite.

[15] See footnote to Table 1.

litical change."[16] Nor was there substantial evidence of any relationship between the configuration of power relationships and population size or the rate of growth. Though these findings are based on a very limited sample of 4 communities, the evidence indicates that both the legal and political power institutions shape and are affected by the ideologies of the people, especially by the leaders who articulate the values of the community. Ideological differences sometimes cause contention and escalate into more serious disputes.

Disputes break out in all communities from time to time; they provide the content of most American politics. They may be about the degree of corruption in government, a change in public policy that increases the scope of governmental activity, or the relative sense of political efficacy of the participants.

The two small places, Farmdale (2,500) and Oretown (15,000), which appear as u and v in Table 1, illustrate some of these dynamics. Farmdale has an elite system with a narrow distribution of political influence (see Table 2), while that of Oretown is broader. Farmdale has a single clique, with a Jeffersonian conservative ideology, which dominates community affairs. Oretown has three quite viable leadership cliques—orthodox conservative, community conservative, and liberal—all vying for control of the community. These ideological leadership groups construct the political regimes and thereby determine how decisions are made.

POLITICAL REGIMES

A political regime, as distinct from the distribution of power, is a representation of the rules of political decision making as they are understood by the citizens and interpreted and articulated by the political leaders. The classic question about the nature of leadership centers on the social background,[17] the personality, and the representative nature and responsive role of the leadership.[18] Virtually every study of American communities has shown that the leadership has a higher socio-economic status than the norm for the community.

---

[16] Agger, Goldrich, and Swanson, *op. cit.*, p. 682.

[17] See Donald Mathews, *The Social Background of Political Decision-Makers.* New York: Doubleday and Company, 1954.

[18] See Harold Lasswell, *Psychopathology and Politics.* New York: Viking Press, 1960.

TABLE 2

POLITICAL INFLUENCE STRUCTURES[a]

	Political Influence Score	Farmdale Percent	Oretown Percent
(High)	3	10	14
	2	20	29
	1	28	39
(Low)	0	42	18
Total		100	100
N		(254)	(138)

a Agger, Goldrich, and Swanson, *op. cit.*, p. 273. (This table is to be read, "of the 254 influentials in Farmdale 10% were judged to be highly influential while 42% were judged to have little political influence.")

Our society is sufficiently stratified to produce leaders from the upper middle classes, which are determined by income, education, and occupational status. The disagreement among community analysts has arisen over which institutional groups are most influential or dominant in our cities. Most sociological studies have found "economic dominants" at the top of the power structure, while political scientists have identified politicians and mayors as key influentials.[19] Other major actors may include the educator, the clergyman, the editor, and the union leader, but they play mainly their specialized roles of the pamphleteer, the moralist, or the individual who has unusual ability to reach the masses.

In most small towns the leaders have held economic, social, and political power simultaneously, serving the business or economic interests of the community. Robert Dahl discovered that an interesting transformation of leadership took place as New Haven, Connecticut, grew. In its early period as a small town, the Patricians ruled

[19] See particularly Chapter V, "Sociology of Knowledge—A Test," in Claire W. Gilbert, "Community Power Studies: Why the Difference in Findings?" unpublished Master's thesis, Northwestern University, 1965, pp. 25-34. She also found that sociologists mainly identified elite power structures, which may be a result of their method.

the city. They were men of white Anglo-Saxon Protestant (WASP) background. As the community diversified its economy and became industrialized, the Entrepreneurs took over. Then the ethnic minorities—from Italy and Poland—came to the city, and it was not too long before their representatives, the Ex-Plebes, became the leaders.[20] This transition in leadership probably reflects the quality, though not necessarily the kinds, of changes that we shall find in most American communities.

The final aspect of our examination of political regimes is the procedural "rules of the game." The degree to which leaders are representative and responsive is heavily influenced by the procedures through which they are chosen and by the ways in which the citizens' preferences are determined. The term "electoral potency" denotes the degree to which voters feel they can influence leadership through their own efforts. Because the individual's sense of political potency depends on his belief that he will not be subjected to penalties or punishment if he makes his preferences known, potency must be considered in relation to the probable degree that illegitimate sanctions will be applied to those who express themselves. As Harold Lasswell has said, people in a democratic government "must be free of intimidation. Moreover, they must have confidence in their capacity to exert effective control over decisions, whether or not they vote on any given occasion."[21]

Illegitimate political sanctions include loss of employment opportunities and extreme social ostracism. They also include the arbitrary, capricious, unpredictable, and discriminatory exercise of legal authority. These sanctions are likely to have more devastating effects in a small community than in a large city. There are few protections against their use in a small place and many more ways for the urbanite to avoid or be less affected by them. The operation of the rule of law in small towns as a consequence of a spirit of fraternity has its dangers. According to Robert Wood: "The individual depends on the sanction of the group and remains uncertain of his

[20] Dahl conceptualized five leadership patterns: (1) covert integration by economic notables; (2) an executive-centered "grand coalition of coalitions"; (3) coalition of chieftains; (4) independent sovereignties with spheres of influence; (5) rival sovereignties fighting it out. See his *Who Governs?*

[21] Harold D. Lasswell, *The Analysis of Political Behavior*. New Haven: Yale University Press, 1949, p. 8.

rights and prerogatives. In the end he has no fixed standard to indicate how he stands in the face and eyes of his neighbors."[22]

The citizens of a fully developed democracy would have a high sense of electoral potency, and there is a low probability that illegitimate sanctions would be used against them following their expression of political preferences. People in an oligarchy, on the other hand, would have a low sense of electoral potency and there is a high probability that illegitimate sanctions would be used to block their efforts toward political change.[23] The citizens of Farmdale have a high sense of electoral potency, but there is also a high probability that illegitimate sanctions might be used by the leadership regime to delay or block political change. The three-member Jeffersonian conservative clique, all from the same family, use the local Lions Club to regulate community affairs and a small in-group "poker club" to make key decisions before they are publicly confirmed. This town has the atmosphere of a guided democracy. The citizens have an unrealistically high sense of electoral potency. There is generally a high turnout for mayoralty elections (sometimes more than 70 percent), even when only *one* candidate is running and the outcome is certain. The citizens of Oretown also have a high sense of electoral potency, but there is a low probability that illegitimate sanctions will block their efforts to change. The competition between the three leadership groups makes the system extremely open, especially because the rate of citizen participation is high.

CITIZEN PARTICIPATION

Citizen participation is the action taken by the participants to maintain or alter the shape, character, policies, and programs of the political system. It is a major factor and correlate in shaping, maintaining, and reforming any given political regime. A political democracy presupposes high rates of citizen participation, free of intimidation, with each citizen having essentially equal access to political resources and equal opportunity to use them, and to express and obtain his policy preferences.

Participation takes many forms. Numerous legal and political

---

[22] Robert C. Wood, *Suburbia: Its People and Their Politics*. Boston: Houghton Mifflin Company, 1958, p. 280.

[23] For a more complete discussion, see Agger, Goldrich, and Swanson, *op. cit.*, pp. 82–90.

channels have been established through the constitutional and traditional means open in most American communities. Some political regimes attempt to minimize the effective development and use of the political channels of expression and (as in a guided democracy) are able to manipulate the citizenry enough to reduce the intensity and extent of citizen participation. Elections are the most widespread means of participation in the political processes provided by the constitutions or local charters. These include the selection of such key public officials as mayors, councilmen, school board officials, and others serving in special districts, such as water boards and fire districts. Locally, numerous policies are referred to the people—budget and special bond elections or special issues involving community controversy, such as fluoridating the water supply, establishing a municipal utility or a park and recreation program.

Voter turnout in the United States is generally low but widely variable. In some communities, and for some elections, it is extremely low. While more than 75 percent of the eligible citizens are registered in Oretown, and more than 60 percent voted in the last mayoralty election, one recent school board election had an 8-to-8 tie vote. As an example of how administrative control can dampen citizen interest, when the superintendent of schools asked a teacher to come to the school to vote and break the tie, and the teacher asked for whom she should vote, he replied that it made no difference, because both were his chosen candidates.

More important in shaping community attitudes and policy preferences are the many informal means of participation. These include taking an active part in election campaigns, attending meetings where community issues are discussed, and maintaining a series of communication linkages in the community, where the citizens discuss community problems, policies, and issues with public officials, neighbors, friends, and members of their own families. Table 3 shows the descending order of the forms of participation utilized in Farmdale and Oretown. They range from discussion with friends to the less-prevalent form of taking an active part in a campaign. The table also shows that participation is far more extensive and intensive in democratic Oretown than in elite Farmdale.

Almost every community study shows significant differentials as to which citizens participate in the political process. The most active

TABLE 3

PROPORTION OF COMMUNITY ENGAGING IN POLITICAL PARTICIPATION[a]

Participation Items	Farmdale (N=255) Percent	Oretown (N=742) Percent
Discuss with friends occasionally	56	81
Discuss with civic leaders occasionally	18	32
Discuss with local officals occasionally	15	21
Attend one or more meetings	7	12
Take active part in campaigns	5	15

a Agger, Goldrich, and Swanson, *op. cit.*, p. 268.

participants are those with the greatest resources and socio-economic status in the community. This fact has ramifications not only for who is selected to govern but what interests they represent and how perceptive and responsive they are in meeting the needs of the people in developing and maintaining a viable system.

POLITICAL CONTENTION, CONTROVERSY, AND CONFLICT

Community problems and issues can be (1) invisible, (2) potential, (3) routine, or (4) controversial. A problem not visible to the public may be disposed of without the participation of the citizens, generally by the top leadership or administrators. A potential issue is one where there is public concern but where the dialogue through which policy is made has not yet been activated, either because the citizens have not translated their policy preferences into political demands or because the leadership has not deemed it necessary to respond to the particular problem. A routine issue involves a more or less habitual response, following the pattern of behavior according to which citizen preferences are managed administratively. A controversial issue develops where there is a lack of agreement among the major participants—making established decision routines irrelevant—or where they have decided to contend against one another in the hope of achieving their own policy preferences at the expense of others.

Controversy may erupt from clashes between economic interests, population shifts, or cleavages caused by past controversies. Controversies, like the weather, are continually changing. Religious controversy, for example, is hardly as prevalent today as in the 1920's. Recently James Coleman cited "revolts against an administration" as accounting for a large number of local disputes.

> In most school controversies, the critics oppose the school administration or school board.
>
> In desegregation disputes, those who refuse to accept desegregation oppose the local school authorities.
>
> In fluoridation disputes, a group against fluoridation opposes the community administration which initiated the plan.
>
> In disputes over the city-manager plan, those attempting to overthrow the plan oppose the city manager and the council.
>
> In labor-management disputes, labor, the insurgents, oppose management, the authorities.
>
> In southern political disputes, the insurgent veterans oppose the entrenched machine.[24]

On the other hand, local administrators have also shown their capacity to control and regulate controversy. Oretown's city manager, for example, deliberately set about to reduce community conflict by asking the mayor to stop attacking the representatives of industry over such issues as annexation, air pollution, and a public versus private electric power fight. In its place, the manager substituted a more harmonious policy agenda of "tree planting" and requests for a new city hall and a library. This approach reduced controversy; it also reduced citizen participation.

> There was a relatively heavy decrease in the extent to which the citizens of Oretown reported discussing local government or community affairs with friends, civic leaders, and local government officials. This decrease in policy or decisional discussion was greater for the less educated than for the well educated in their respective friendship groupings, but there was even a decrease in such discussion with friends among the well educated. There were substantial decreases in such discussion with civic leaders and local government officials among the well educated as well as among the less educated.[25]

Thus, community competition, controversy, and conflict are all

---

24 James S. Coleman, *Community Conflict*. New York: The Free Press, 1957, pp. 14–15.

25 Agger, Goldrich, and Swanson, *op. cit.*, p. 624.

likely to increase citizen participation, at least up to some undetermined level of strife where the people will grow apprehensive and withdraw from the political process. It is also probable that as the community increases in size and becomes heterogeneous, different policy preferences will become manifest and diverse ideologies will begin to be articulated. Some fear these developments and even attempt to retain the small-town character of their communities in order to avoid what they consider turmoil. The political regime of Farmdale, for example, used severe economic sanctions against the editor of the weekly newspaper, who began to organize a new Chamber of Commerce to bring new industry to the town, which it was predicted would change the character of the community and perhaps be less controllable by the small elite.

The search for the good life, the ideal community, and the well-adjusted individual has led both political participants and political scientists to focus their attention on mechanisms that will produce harmony, consensus, and stable political systems. Participants, reluctantly drawn into controversial situations, are often aware of the utility of conflict in resolving contentious issues.

Need conflict be conceived as dysfunctional to political systems? George Simmel would have us appreciate the "positive character of conflict." Ralf Dahrendorf, in his reexamination of a theory of conflict, suggests that creativity, innovation, and development in the life of the individual and his group are caused to a great extent by the "operation of conflict." "This fundamental fact alone seems to me to justify the value judgment that conflict is essentially 'good' and desirable."[26] Whether it is conceived as good or bad, positive or negative, functional or dysfunctional, conflict exists and, as Robert Dubin has stated, "cannot be wished out of existence. It is a reality with which social theorists must deal in constructing their general models of social behavior."[27] Certainly the civil rights movement has adopted this strategy in American communities, north and south, today. Once they are accepted, however, these groups may very well modify their strategy to one of political coalitions and begin to work within prescribed institutional arrangements.

---

[26] Ralf Dahrendorf, *Class and Class Conflict in Industrial Society*. Stanford, Calif.: Stanford University Press, 1959, p. 208.

[27] Robert Dubin, "Approaches to the Study of Social Conflict: A Colloquium, *The Journal of Conflict Resolution*, Vol. 1, No. 2 (June, 1957), p. 184.

POLITICIZATION AND THE SCOPE OF GOVERNMENT

Just as community controversies generally serve as vehicles for realigning public attitudes, politics, in the broadest sense, serve to introduce changes into the administrative patterns of governmental officials. If the bureaucratic changes needed to implement a new configuration of public attitudes require adjustments in the working relationships between several local agencies, it is often considered a *political* decision. If it requires only changes within an agency (or within several agencies not linked to each other), it is considered an *administrative* decision. The former will be emphasized here and the latter in the following sections.

A political demand for change involves either a major review of an existing policy or a new decision that bears on significant value judgments or political preferences of a substantial proportion of the citizenry. Politicization is a person's *awareness* of the relevance of government to his own life. Participation is his *involvement* in politics, motivated by a set of expectations articulated in demand statements. What one person expects may reflect merely his own hopes, or it may reflect a hope shared by a large number of others. These preferences in themselves, whether expressed or implied, seldom activate a policy dialogue. There must be some perceived discrepancy between the need or preference and its realization, or between the *actual* and the *ideal,* articulated as a "strain" or disturbance of the expectational system, which in turn activates a dialogue oriented toward rebalancing expectations. This discrepancy must be recognized in some specific form and expressed through overt communication processes. The result will be the development of "political tensions," which relate perceptions of human needs and desires to sets of actual events and conditions.

The actual feelings and expressions of political tensions, however, must arise from some sense of a need for change and a belief that change can be effected.[28] In addition, or in correlation, there must be a problem orientation. Americans, for instance, are especially receptive, from a cultural perspective, to the notions of progress and

---

[28] For a thorough discussion of human and social needs and political tensions, see James Davies, *Human Nature in Politics*. New York: John Wiley and Sons, 1963, p. 2. He offers the formula B=f (SO) where "behavior (B) is a function of the interaction of the situation (S) and the organism (O)."

the "problem" concept. H. G. Barnett points out in his study of the cultural background of innovation:

> We are concerned with all sorts of situations which we interpret as being unnecessary. . . . They are eradicable discomforts or social evils. They need not or should not be; hence we should do something to alter them to conform to our specifications. Instead of accepting things as they are because they have always been that way, as many people do, we seek to change them. Problems are such an important stimuli to change because we make them out of the substance of our wishes. We have become accustomed to ask for solutions almost as freely and as often as the reality in our experience conflicts with our hopes.[29]

The reformer, for example, perceives the discrepancy between machine politics and lofty democratic ideals. The problem for him is an institutional one; the party machinery no longer represents or responds to the needs of the people.

There is a classic concern to differentiate public from private problems and action. John Dewey proposed a very simple test to distinguish between private and public transactions. He would evaluate human acts, and

> . . . when indirect consequences are recognized and there is effort to regulate them, something having the traits of a state comes into existence. When the consequences of an action are confined, or are thought to be confined, mainly to the persons directly engaged in it, the transaction is a private one.[30]

Thus, when the interests of the third party are affected and there is some need to regulate the impact of this action, a public interest has been developed and declared. Acceptance of what constitutes a public problem is often no easy matter, for much depends on a combination of such factors as frustration and expectation, opportunities to express these feelings, anticipated solutions, and the leadership and other resources to organize support.[31]

What, then, is the proper scope of government? The primary concern of government, David Easton states, is the "authoritative

---

[29] H. G. Barnett, *Innovation: The Basis of Cultural Change*. New York: McGraw-Hill, 1953, p. 36.

[30] John Dewey, *The Public and Its Problems*. Chicago: Henry Regnery Company, 1946, pp. 12–13.

[31] For a more detailed discussion see William C. Mitchell, *The American Polity*. New York: The Free Press, 1962, p. 281.

allocation of values."[32] So defined, the scope of government has two interrelated aspects. The first is its constitutional and legitimate right to perform functions that satisfy people's needs—whether these be needs for group harmony, with the government acting as mediator for less-comprehensive social or economic groups, or needs for greater income, with the government acting as producer or employer. The second is the extent and the manner of the government's exercising of constitutional authority. Political conflict may center on either the extension or the restriction of government's authority, or on the way government does or does not exercise its existing authority.

Government functions may include providing education; moderating, adjusting, or improving race relations; stimulating business; helping to attract new business and industry to the city; providing recreational facilities; eliminating slums and redeveloping rundown areas of the city; providing housing for certain groups; producing and/or distributing electric power; providing hospital facilities; and performing other equally important tasks.

Such functions of local government have become imperative as the small town has grown. While law and order were of the greatest importance on the frontier and are an increasingly important function in the enlightened modern metropolis, and a municipal water works was of prime importance to the settlers in arid portions of the country as well as for Los Angeles today, the character of modern city life has given added importance to these and the new functions of local government. It may be worth identifying the policy areas where government activity may be expected as the small town grows into a full-blown urban center. All these functions are currently being performed by local governments, to a greater or lesser degree. A total inventory of such functions in the large city includes:

1. Public safety (police, fire, juvenile authorities)
2. Public works (streets, sidewalks, drainage)
3. Health (hospitals, health inspection, air pollution)
4. Education (kindergarten, primary, secondary, and higher education)
5. Recreation (parks, playgrounds)

---

[32] David Easton, *The Political System*. New York: Alfred A. Knopf, 1953, p. 129.

6. Cultural facilities (community centers, libraries, museums, art galleries)
7. Welfare (public housing, aid to the indigent)
8. Renewal and redevelopment (slum clearance, improving the central business district)
9. Planning (subdivision control, zoning, master plan)
10. Utilities (water, electricity, sewage disposal, garbage)
11. Expansion (annexation, extension of services outside the city)
12. Regulation and stimulation of business (off-street parking, traffic, licensing, taxes, franchises)
13. Industrial development (industrial sites, promotion)
14. Intergroup relations (race relations, relations between political antagonists, labor-management relations)

Perhaps it bears repeating—as the small community matures the spectrum of services it offers increases. Thus Farmdale provides the first four services; in the somewhat larger Oretown several others are available.

PROFESSIONALIZATION OF THE BUREAUCRACY

The preceding list of public services and programs makes obvious the need for a bureaucracy to provide for the day-to-day affairs of the local political system. The trend is to refine the administrative machinery through the professionalization of its personnel and the development of performance standards. At the same time there has been a move toward an administrative arrangement which discourages, though it does not preclude, citizen participation.

Administrative decision making involves the routine implementation of previous and generally applicable established policies. Minor values of a technical nature involve few persons—the technically trained experts.

> When administrators engage in the policy-making, they may . . . engage in a process of depoliticization—the removal from consideration of the anticipated effects on people's needs of a projected shift in the scope of government, the making in technical terms of the different patterns of benefits and costs for citizens in different circumstances that may be expected from alternative solutions to policy problems. Rather than a policy being selected by the open working of politics, by the open exercise of political influence, the decisional process is determined by other consid-

erations. Thus, the location of a new city facility may be removed from the open political arena and entrusted completely to a consulting "specialist." Or pupils may be assigned to schools on the basis of technical criteria developed and applicable (and understood) only by educational administrators.

. . . .

This does not mean that decisions are done away with when "specialists" effectuate policy. Rather, the decisions may develop an aura of being beyond the competence and grasp of laymen, as decisions that must be made by "experts." To be sure there are, there always have been, and there probably always will be complicated technical problems in effectuating policy that lie outside the range of comprehension by masses of men. But this is not to argue that depoliticization ought to go unchallenged or that a political democracy in the middle of the twentieth century must be based on that process.[33]

The professionalization of the bureaucracy is an effort to meet three conditions. The first, best reflected in the city manager movement mentioned earlier, is the long-lasting effort to make local governments run as efficiently as corporate enterprise. The second is to insure that even though more and more policies are formulated beyond the public view, the making of policy remains responsive to public sentiment and at the same time free from dominance by any particular public interest. American communities assume that high levels of training and skill will make the bureaucracy not only efficient but responsive to community needs. The third is the development of specialization as the scope of government expands and more and more public services are offered in response to the increase in size of community and complexity of administrative function. In theory, at least, increasing specialization should lead to increased quality in those services offered to the public.

A PARADIGM OF POLITICAL CHANGE

This chapter began with a comparative note on small towns and urban places and the possible use of our political knowledge to engage in reform and change of the political system. Also, throughout the discussion of the six factors, we have alluded to political changes and their effects on one another. The paradigm of political change presented in Table 4 summarizes the interrelationships between the

---

[33] Swanson, "The Concern for Community in the Metropolis," *op. cit.*, pp. 41–42.

six factors and suggests what factors the reformers may decide to use to secure community action to gain their policy preferences.

The first column in Table 4 assumes that we must consider change in communities that are growing more complex, remaining as they are (stable), or becoming less complex. Because complexity in its common sense is not what we are concerned with, and because the researchers who devised a very sensitive and meaningful measure of this phenomenon labeled it *magnicomplexity*, this is the term that heads the first column in the table. Magnicomplexity is associated with population change, size, density, and heterogeneity; economic base, growth, and diversification, including wholesale trade and retail sales gain; educational plant size; government complexity; and relief expenditures.[34] These factors are more amenable to quantification than some others. It seems likely that someday someone will show us how the transformation from Tonnies' Gemeinschaft to Gesellschaft is accomplished in terms of these factors.

In addition, the paradigm accepts and develops the fact that small communities have both monolithic (or elite) and pluralistic (or open) power structures, and that these may lead to different rates of change in the other factors—political regimes, citizen participation, political controversy, the scope of government, and the professionalization of the bureaucracy.

The citizens of a stable elite system, such as Farmdale, have an accurate sense of their low political potency. The low rate of citizen participation corresponds to a low level of controversy, a government of limited scope, and the development of a modest professional bureaucracy. The citizens of such stable pluralistic systems as Oretown accurately assess their medium political potency. A political system of this magnicomplexity has a medium degree of citizen participation, as well as of political controversy. Its citizens approve of a minimum scope of government with a minimum professional bureaucracy. As such communities grow in complexity and diversity (magnicomplexity), there is a tendency toward increased political potency, accurately assessed by the citizens in a pluralistic system, but an inaccurately sensed low efficacy in cities graced by an elite

[34] Christen T. Jonassen and Sherwood H. Peres, *Interrelationships of Dimensions of Community Systems: A Factor Analysis of Eighty-two Variables*. Columbus: Ohio State University Press, 1960.

TABLE 4

A PARADIGM OF POLITICAL CHANGE IN SMALL COMMUNITIES

Community Magnicomplexity	Power Structure	Political Regime	Citizen Participation	Political Controversy	Scope of Government	Professionalization of Bureaucracy
Increase	a. Elite	Low efficacy (inaccurate)	Medium	Medium	Medium expansion	Higher specialization
	b. Pluralistic	High efficacy (accurate)	High	High	Medium expansion	Medium specialization
Stable	a. Elite	Low efficacy (accurate)	Low	Low	Minimal	Medium specialization
	b. Pluralistic	Medium efficacy (accurate)	Medium	Medium	Minimal	Minimum specialization
Decrease	a. Elite	Lower efficacy (accurate)	Lower	Low	Stable	Stable
	b. Pluralistic	Medium efficacy (inaccurate)	Medium	Medium	Stable	Stable

power structure. Citizen participation and political controversy increase moderately in the elite system and greatly in the pluralistic system.

The paradigm in Table 4 indicates that the scope of government is more likely to expand in a city where power is pluralistically distributed and the bureaucracy to become more specialized in communities with elite structures of power.

The decreasing need for elite control in a community in decline reduces the sense of political efficacy, citizen participation, and political controversy, while the scope of government and the degree of professionalization of the bureaucracy hold constant. The citizens in a pluralistic system, however, tend to have an inaccurate sense of medium electoral potency. They participate only to a medium degree, and political controversy is also medium. As one might expect, the scope of government remains rather stable, as does the degree of professionalization of the bureaucracy.

Structural change is the most fundamental and long lasting, but it is also the most difficult to achieve. Therefore, to change the structure of power relations in the small community and increase the probability of securing community action, a person can either wait for a basic change to occur in the complexity of the town, including its social and economic system, or proceed to change the other factors identified in Table 4. Of course, he cannot rely completely on a natural change to occur in complexity of community. But if he desires political reform, he can make the most of ongoing community change by giving it direction, or by taking the initiative and stimulating change (for instance in the economic base by means of industrialization), or by rearranging social relationships between social classes or ethnic groups. Certainly it is easier to change the political regime and stimulate a change in citizen participation. One can insist on and work for equality before the law, as stipulated by the constitutional provisions of a democratic system. Also, one can prepare the citizenry to develop a realistic sense of electoral potency and to use legal and other remedies to reduce the use of illegitimate sanctions. The rates of meaningful citizen participation can be increased, which would affect both the political regime and the power structure, by putting before them as a community agenda for discussion and decision issues that will meet much more closely the needs of the citizens. Such a move could generate enough controversy to bring the citizens out to the polls, to the meeting places, and to the rallies. This can be accomplished by proposing meaningful change—increase and/or decrease—in the scope of government.

Professionalizing the bureaucracy could depoliticize community decision-making, so that the citizen no longer desires or feels the need to participate. Reduction of controversy and citizen participation could lead to a low sense of political efficacy and the maintenance of elite power structures that may not be responsive to the needs of the people or prepare the community for change.

It seems as though most large urban systems in America have grown too rapidly and have been unable to retain the essence of democracy. Their social and economic structures have so factionalized the polity that there is a low sense of political efficacy among the people and a low rate of participation in community affairs, as well as a fear of community contention, controversy, and conflict. The scope of government has expanded slowly and often too late to meet the citizens' real needs. The administrative officials are increasingly removed and insulated from the people whom their programs are to serve.

A few words of advice, then, are in order. If leadership desires to prepare a community to meet the political change that lies ahead of most American towns, it should provide its people with an *accurate* and increasingly high sense of political efficacy; encourage mass citizen participation by and for *all*; risk political controversy; shift the scope of government to meet the needs of the people; and professionalize the bureaucracy to serve the public but not to govern the system. To do otherwise is to countenance the growing deterioration of democratic myths in a world of oligarchic reality. Even if it is impossible to move on all six factors, we can anticipate change not only as a matter of political and moral reform but as a most effective way to learn how the system works. Then perhaps practical reform and community action will be both possible and probable.

SUGGESTIONS FOR FURTHER READING

Agger, Robert E., David Goldrich and Bert E. Swanson, *The Rulers and the Ruled*. New York: John Wiley and Sons, 1964.

Banfield, Edward C. and James Q. Wilson, *City Politics*. Cambridge, Mass.: Harvard University Press, 1963.

Change in the Small Community

Coleman, James S., *Community Conflict*. New York: The Free Press, 1957.
Dahl, Robert, *Who Governs?* New Haven: Yale University Press, 1961.
Hunter, Floyd, *Community Power Structure*. Chapel Hill: University of North Carolina Press, 1953.
Jennings, M. Kent, *Community Influentials: The Elite of Atlanta*. New York: The Free Press, 1964.
Presthus, Robert, *Men at the Top*. New York: Oxford University Press, 1964.
Swanson, Bert E., *The Struggle for Equality: School Integration Controversies in New York City*. New York: Hobbs-Dorman, 1966.
Vidich, Arthur J. and Joseph Bensman, *Small Town in Mass Society*. New York: Doubleday and Company, 1960.
Wildavsky, Aaron, *Leadership in a Small Town*. Totowa, N. J.: The Bedminster Press, 1964.
Wood, Robert C., *Suburbia: Its People and Their Politics*. Boston: Houghton Mifflin Company, 1959.

CHAPTER 6

THE CHURCHES OF MIDWEST, KANSAS AND YOREDALE, YORKSHIRE: Their Contributions to the Environments of the Towns

ROGER G. BARKER, LOUISE S. BARKER, AND DAN D. M. RAGLE

The aim of the larger study[1] of which this chapter is a part is to describe in a quantitative way the environments that two small towns, Midwest, Kansas and Yoredale, Yorkshire, provide for their inhabitants, and to determine some of the consequences for the behavior and ultimately for the personality and adjustment of their inhabitants. The research, an excursion into psychological ecology, is an attempt to systematize some of the existing relationships between human behavior and its nonpsychological, or ecological, context.

In this chapter we shall be concerned with the contributions of the churches to the environments of Midwest and Yoredale, and with changes in the churches' contributions between 1954 and 1963. We shall raise such questions as: What proportions of the towns' environments do the churches provide? How many and what classes of residents inhabit these parts of the towns? What are the attributes

---

Professor Barker is a member of the Psychology faculty, University of Kansas; Mrs. Barker and Dr. Ragle are associated with him in the Midwest Psychological Field Station where a classic study of a small community has been in process for almost two decades.

[1] The data were collected and the report was prepared in connection with a research project supported by the National Science Foundation (GS-116) and the National Institute of Mental Health (M-1513). The contribution of the University of Kansas Computation Center and the special cooperation of the Midwest Methodist Church are gratefully acknowledged.

of the environmental areas furnished by the churches? Midwest and Yoredale will be described as behavior habitats, and we will assess what the churches bring to the environments in which the people of the towns spend most of their days.

There is evidence, some of which is given in this chapter and some in other publications,[2] that Midwest and Yoredale are not atypical towns, but have many characteristics of other small communities in the United States, England, Canada, and Norway. The significance of the data is by no means limited to these two communities, and the concepts and methods of the study have general relevance for the assessment of churches and of their contributions to their communities.

Midwest and Yoredale are both rural trading and government centers. Midwest is a county seat, and Yoredale is the seat of a rural district council; both towns are centers of regions of about 400 square miles inhabited by about 11,000 people. The population of Midwest during the years when studies were made was 700 to 800 and the population of Yoredale varied closely around 1,300. Data were collected during two year-long periods separated by 9 years: September 1954–August 1955 and September 1963–August 1964.

UNITS OF THE ENVIRONMENT: BEHAVIOR SETTINGS

The first question to be answered is: how is the environment of behavior to be identified, described and measured? Almost any descriptive fact about Midwest on Sunday, April 19, 1964—the amount of rain that fell, the duration of the Methodist High School Sunday school class, the number of buildings in the town, the location of the benches around the courthouse square—had an influence on the behavior of some resident of the town on this day. The list of relevant facts about the environment Midwest provides for its inhabitants is endless. We have discovered, however, a limited number of community parts, which together encompass the other facts about

---

[2] Barker, R. G. and H. F. Wright, *Midwest and Its Children*. New York: Harper and Row, 1955; and Barker, R. G. and Louise S. Barker, "Behavior units for the comparative study of cultures," in B. Kaplan (ed.), *Studying Personality Cross-Culturally*. New York: Harper and Row, 1961, pp. 457–476.

the town and hence constitute the environment. These parts we have called *behavior settings*.[3]

The Presbyterian Church Worship Service is an example of a behavior setting, and of its characteristic attributes.

1. It has a space-time locus, the sanctuary of the United Presbyterian Church at Midwest, Kansas, 11 A.M. to 12 noon each Sunday.

2. It is composed of a variety of things and events: people (adults and children, men and women), objects (pews, walls, a pulpit, candles, a microphone), behavior (preaching, listening, singing), and other processes (air circulation, sound amplification).

3. The widely different components of the Worship Service form a bounded pattern, which is easily discriminated from the pattern on the outside of the boundary.

4. Its component parts are obviously not a random arrangement of independent classes of entities; if they were, it would be surprising that all the pews are in the same position with respect to the pulpit, that all members of the congregation happen to come to rest upon the pews, and that the lights are not situated helter-skelter from floor to ceiling. Although many of the parts can be found in other settings, in this setting they are arranged to carry out the program of the Worship Service.

5. The Worship Service is a part of a nesting structure; it has components (hymnals, organ console), which have parts (pages, keys); and the setting itself is contained within a more comprehensive unit, the Midwest Presbyterian Church.

6. It is an objective unit, in the sense that it exists independently of anyone's perception of it, though not independently of the people who are a part of its pattern.

7. The Worship Service consists of both behavior (singing, preach-

---

[3] Barker, R. G., "Ecology and Motivation," in M. R. Jones (ed.), *Nebraska Symposium on Motivation*. Lincoln: University of Nebraska Press, 1960, pp. 1–49. Barker, R. G., "On the Nature of the Environment," *Journal of Sociological Issues*, Vol. 19, No. 4, 1963, pp. 17–38. Barker, R. G. and P. V. Gump, *Big School, Small School*. Stanford, Calif.: Stanford University Press, 1964. Barker, R. G., "Explorations in Ecological Psychology," *American Psychologist*, Vol. 20, No. 1, 1965, pp. 1–14. See also Footnote 2.

ing) and objects (hymnals, organ); both are essential; the setting is a phenomenon which consists of interdependent objects and behavior.

8. An important factor is the space-time boundary; there is a physical boundary (the walls and doors of the church) and there is a temporal boundary (11 A.M.-12 noon).

9. Within the boundary of the setting, the behavior of individuals conforms to the pattern characteristic of the setting. This fact is a function of other people in the setting and of the physical arrangements of the setting. At the Worship Service members of the congregation do not converse loudly (social pressure) or sit in the aisles (physical arrangements).

10. The Presbyterian Church Worship Service is but one of a set of behavior settings that blanket the town; no behavior occurs outside of a behavior setting.

11. The Worship Service and other behavior settings are recognized by laymen in their daily living, but the precise identification and enumeration of behavior settings is a technical task; many reasonable, common-sense parts of a community can be identified which are not behavior settings.

12. The Presbyterian Church Worship Service, and other settings, have a multitude of other characteristics; the ones listed here are common, defining attributes of all behavior settings.

Behavior settings are units of the environment that have relevance for behavior. They provide the primary data of the study to be reported here. We have dealt only with the settings that occur outside the homes of the community, that is, the public behavior settings. The number of public behavior settings in a town is a measure of the size of the town's public environment.

We must emphasize that a behavior setting coerces people and things to conform to its temporal-spatial pattern. This is not an incidental or accidental characteristic. The person or persons who maintain and control the setting (the performers) make a deliberate effort to insure that this is so, and that the setting therefore fulfills its function. This aspect of a setting we call its *program*. Two settings are said to have the same program when their parts and processes are interchangeable. When this is true, two or more settings belong to the same *genotype*. Two grocery stores, for example, could exchange stock, personnel, bookkeeping systems, shelving, and so forth, with little interruption in their operation. They belong to the same genotype. A Methodist and a Presbyterian minister could, and sometimes do, exchange pulpits. The number of behavior setting genotypes in a town is a measure of the variety of the town's environment.

We now turn to what behavior settings tell us about the contribution of the churches to the environments that the towns of Midwest and Yoredale provide for their inhabitants. There were 4 churches in Midwest in both years of the study: Methodist, United Presbyterian, Southern Baptist, and African Methodist. In Yoredale there were 4 churches in 1954–1955: Methodist, Church of England, Roman Catholic, and Congregational; in 1963–1964, the Congregational Church had ceased to function.

SIZE OF THE TOWNS AND THEIR CHURCHES

We shall consider, first, some environmental dimensions of Midwest and Yoredale and of their church-related[4] parts. We have made use of three measures of size.

1. Number of behavior settings (BS): the total number of behavior settings occurring in a town (or church) during a year, that is, the differentiation of the town in terms of behavior settings.

2. Number of daily occurrences of behavior settings (O): the number of days in a year on which each behavior setting occurs, summed for all settings of a town (or church), that is, the number of setting days. Behavior settings occur on different numbers of days: daily (Trafficways, O = 365 days); on weekdays (most stores, for example, Sherwin Furniture Store, O = 312); weekly (Presbyterian Church Worship Service, O = 52); monthly (some organization meetings, for example, Methodist Woman's Society of Christian Service, O = 12); on a single day (Presbyterian Church Installation of Pastor, O = 1).

3. Number of hours during which behavior settings occur in a year (H): the sum of the hours in a year during which the behavior settings of a town (or church) occur, that is, hours of duration, or number of setting hours. Setting hours vary widely (Trafficways, H = 8760; Sherwin Furniture Store, H = 2763; Presbyterian Worship

[4] Behavior settings that are initiated by, maintained by, or that occur only with the permission of the central, governing settings of the churches of the towns are referred to *in toto* as church settings or church-related behavior settings; separately they are called Methodist settings, Roman Catholic settings, etc.

Service, H = 52; Methodist Woman's Society of Christian Service, H = 24; Installation of Pastor, H = 2).

These dimensions of a town, and of its parts, have important consequences for a town's inhabitants. For example, it was a matter of considerable importance for Midwest when the behavior settings under the control of the county commissioners were changed from a 6-day, 44-hour week to a 5-day, 40-hour week. At that time, the occurrences (O) of each county setting changed from 312 to 260 (a reduction of 17 percent), and the hours of duration (H) changed from 2288 to 2080 (a reduction of 9 percent). The number of behavior settings (BS) remained constant. It was important for the town, too, when the number of dental office settings doubled, from BS = 1 to BS = 2, even though the other dimensions of the dental settings changed relatively little.

The significance of these dimensions of a town's environment varies with the particular concerns of the inhabitants. The reduction in the number of occurrences of the county office settings was probably more significant for the employees, because it added one office-free day per week, than was the reduction in number of hours duration, which added 4 office-free hours per week. But the latter was probably more important to the county commissioners, who were faced with the necessity of increasing the work staff or reducing the work load by 9 percent.

The number (BS), occurrence (O), and hours of duration (H) of behavior settings in a town (or church) are measures of the extent of the behavioral environment, the behavior resources, that the town (or church) provides for its inhabitants. The extent of this behavioral environment can be changed by changing any of its dimensions. In general, though, it is easier to change the occurrences and hours of behavior settings than to change the number of settings. Most behavior settings have built-in procedures for increasing and decreasing occurrences and hours of duration, which require little effort; for example, there may be provision for adjourned meetings and for motions to adjourn. But a comparatively much greater force is needed to establish and terminate most behavior settings. This often requires concurrence and/or assistance of external authorities. To establish a Sunday school class, for example, it is necessary to have a teacher, pupils, a room, equipment, and materials; persons outside the setting have to approve of or supply most of these. To end a Sunday school class, places have to be found for the pupils within other settings; here again, the setting is not autonomous.

Since conditions outside particular behavior settings, within communities, have a hand in establishing, maintaining, and removing them, behavior settings are in a real sense community behavior resources. Without behavior settings, behavior that is an integral component of settings does not occur; without the behavior setting church weddings, there is no marrying in church.

It is important to elucidate the differences between the BS, O, and H measures of environmental size. An analogy in the form of a conundrum may help to do this. A philanthropist endows a number of display galleries in 4 museums and fills them with art treasures. These permanent exhibits amount to 13, 15, 18, and 22 percent of the exhibits in the museums. The museum directors, for administrative reasons, place restrictions on the days the galleries are to be open to the public. Counting each day a gallery is open to the public as one gallery day, it turns out that the philanthropist's galleries are open for 4.5, 5, 3.6, and 7 percent, respectively, of the museum's gallery days. But the galleries, when open, are not always open for full days, so that the philanthropist's galleries account for 0.7, 0.9, 0.8, and 1.7 percent of the museum's gallery hours. The question is: What is the extent, then, of the philanthropist's contribution to these museums?

To the museum directors, who see themselves as conservators of art treasures and who are aware of the transitoriness of gallery practices and donors' wishes, he contributed 13 to 22 percent of their collections, of their museum resources. But to museum visitors with limited days of freedom, the philanthropist contributed 3.6 to 7 percent of the exhibits, because wandering freely through the open galleries on their occasional museum days they would find these proportions of the galleries acknowledging his gift. And to museum administrators who provide the supervisors, guards, and lights for the galleries when open and account for their costs, the philanthropist is the source of 0.7 to 1.7 percent of gallery operations; without his galleries the hours of supervising, guarding, and lighting the museums' possessions would be so much reduced.

So there are three answers to the conundrum: the philanthropist contributed 13 to 22 percent of the museums' resources, he contributed 3.6 to 7 percent of the museums' daily accessible exhibits, and he contributed 0.7 to 1.7 percent of the gallery hours of operation.

Two important questions are not answered by these hypothetical museum data: What kinds and quality of art objects did the philanthropist contribute? To what extent were his galleries actually visited and the exhibits viewed?

Data regarding the contributions of the churches (analogous to the philanthropist) to the behavior settings (analogous to the museum galleries) of Midwest and Yoredale in 1954–1955 and 1963–1964 (analogous to the four museums) are shown in detail by the figures in Table 1. The church-related behavior settings of Midwest and Yoredale:

—constituted 13 to 22 percent of the behavior settings of the towns;

—accounted for 3.6 to 7 percent of the daily occurrences of behavior settings in the towns; and

—comprised 0.7 to 1.7 percent of the hours of duration of the towns' settings.

We conclude that the churches provide a greater proportion of the behavior setting resources of the towns than of days and hours of access to these resources. To the guardians of the churches' teaching and ceremonies (as to the museum directors) the churches provide a maximum of one in 5 of the towns' behavior setting resources; but to participants in community religious behavior (as to museum visitors) the resources provided by the churches are accessible on a maximum of only one in 14 of the towns' behavior setting days, and in only one in 60 of their behavior setting hours. The churches are more generous in providing behavior resources for the towns than in making them accessible.

Some comparative data are available for 8 other small, vigorous towns ranging in population from 166 to 1200, 2 in England, one in Canada, one in Norway, and 4 in the United States. From 18 to 29 percent of the behavior settings of these towns were church-related. The church-related behavior settings of 4 Canadian and one American community which were *not* vigorous, and which showed signs of disorganization and decay, varied from 0 to 49 percent of these towns' settings. This evidence suggests that within a considerable range of Western culture, churches provide thriving small towns with 15 to 30 percent of their community behavior resources, but

TABLE 1

SIZE DIMENSIONS OF MIDWEST AND YOREDALE, OF THE CHURCHES AND OF THE METHODIST CHURCHES, 1954-1955 AND 1963-1964

	MIDWEST				YOREDALE			
Number of Behavior Settings (BS) and Percent of Town Settings (%)								
	1954-1955		1963-1964		1954-1955		1963-1964	
	BS	%	BS	%	BS	%	BS	%
Town	576	100	884	100	504	100	758	100
All Churches	103	18	193	22	78	15	95	13
Methodist Church	46	8	63	7	30	6	46	6
Daily Occurrences of Behavior Settings (O) and Percent of Town Occurrences (%)								
	O	%	O	%	O	%	O	%
Town	49,562	100	53,258	100	52,483	100	65,155	100
All Churches	1,778	3.6	3,677	7.0	2,701	5.0	2,938	4.5
Methodist Church	725	1.5	895	1.7	294	0.6	314	0.5
Hours of Duration of Behavior Settings (H) and Percent of Town Hours (%)								
	H	%	H	%	H	%	H	%
Town	283,656	100	286,909	100	301,049	100	337,318	100
All Churches	2,148	0.8	4,909	1.7	2,594	0.9	2,291	0.7
Methodist Church	792	0.3	857	0.3	380	0.1	483	0.1

that when towns decline in vigor, the contributions of the churches may become abnormally large or small.

Comparative data of another kind are available for Midwest. They refer to the Agricultural Extension Service which, like the churches, is a contributor of behavior settings to the town. In 1963–1964 the Agricultural Extension Service provided 5 percent of Midwest's behavior settings; these occurred in 0.7 percent of the town's total number of setting days and for 0.9 percent of its setting hours. Comparison with the Midwest Methodist Church is revealing. Table 1 shows that in 1963–1964 the Methodist Church contributed 7 percent of Midwest's behavior settings, that they occurred on 1.7 percent of the town's setting days and for 0.3 percent of its setting hours. In extent of contributions to Midwest's environment, the Agricultural Extension Service and the Methodist Church were within the same range.

CHANGES IN THE SIZE OF THE TOWNS AND THE CHURCHES BETWEEN 1954-1955 AND 1963-1964

Over this 9-year period, population increased in Midwest from 715 to 830, and in Yoredale from 1300 to 1310. Changes in the environmental dimensions of the towns are reported in Table 1. Both towns increased substantially in number and occurrence of behavior settings, and they increased to a smaller extent in hours of behavior setting duration. Midwest and Yoredale are in this respect like museums, which increase their galleries and their open gallery days but change their overall number of hours of exhibition very little.

What happened to the churches over this period? Did their contributions keep pace with the changes in the towns? We can summarize the relevant data of Table 1, *in relation to the changes in the towns*, as follows:

—Midwest's church-related settings increased from 18 to 22 percent of the town's settings;
—daily occurrences of Midwest church settings increased from 3.6 to 7 percent of all the town's setting days; and
—duration of Midwest church settings increased from 0.8 to 1.7 percent of the town's behavior setting hours.

—Yoredale's church-related settings decreased from 15 to 13 percent of the town's settings;
—daily occurrences of Yoredale's church settings remained almost constant at 5.0 to 4.5 percent of all the town's setting days; and
—the duration of Yoredale church settings was similar at 0.9 and 0.7 percent of the town's setting hours.
—The Methodist Church in both towns was almost unchanged in these measures relative to the town as a whole.

In general, the churches kept pace with the towns. The number of church-related behavior settings, occurrences, and hours of duration increased in Midwest a little more than in the town as a whole, and they increased in Yoredale slightly less than in the town as a whole. But these differences are small.

DIFFERENCES BETWEEN MIDWEST AND YOREDALE IN THEIR CHURCHES' CONTRIBUTIONS

The data of Table 1 show that the contributions of the churches to the behavior setting resources of the two towns, and to their days of occurrence and hours of duration, were surprisingly similar. The greatest difference is in 1963–1964, when Midwest churches were the source of 22 percent of the town's behavior settings and Yoredale churches were the source of 13 percent of Yoredale's settings. On 4 of the 6 measures, the percent contribution of Midwest churches was greater than that of Yoredale churches. Furthermore, among the 10 vigorous small towns, Midwest was in the middle range with respect to the percent of settings contributed by churches and Yoredale was in the low range. Thus, there is some reason to believe that Yoredale churches are the source of fewer of the town's behavior resources than is true of Midwest.

OCCUPANCY OF THE TOWNS AND OF THE CHURCHES

The community has a hand in establishing and maintaining most behavior settings, and the behavior settings themselves usually determine their days of occurrence and hours of duration. But it is the individual citizen of a town who enters or avoids, inhabits or stays away from, the town's settings, who does or does not participate in the behavior resources of the town. Having determined the extents of the towns' and the churches' behavior resources and their days and hours of accessibility, we now ask to what degree these behavior settings were inhabited.

The answer to this question is given by the *occupancy time* (OT) data of Table 2. The OT of a behavior setting is the amount of time in hours the inhabitants of the setting spend within its borders; it is the number of person hours of occupancy. The occupancy time is the summed OT values of all behavior settings.

The data of Table 2 show that the residents of Midwest and Yoredale spent 26 to 59 hours per year per person in the church-related behavior settings of the towns. This amounts to 2.3 to 4.5 percent of the time the residents were not at home, but were within the

TABLE 2

HOURS OF OCCUPANCY (OT) OF COMMUNITY BEHAVIOR SETTINGS, OF CHURCH-RELATED SETTINGS, AND OF METHODIST SETTINGS; OCCUPANCY PER TOWN INHABITANT (OT/P). MIDWEST AND YOREDALE, 1954-1955 AND 1963-1964

	MIDWEST				YOREDALE			
	Hours of Occupancy (OT)							
	1954-1955		1963-1964		1954-1955		1963-1964	
	Total Hrs.	%	Total Hrs.	%	Total Hrs.	%	Total Hrs.	%
Town	928,240	100	1,129,295	100	1,505,103	100	1,426,115	100
All Churches	42,150	4.5	33,176	3.0	34,028	2.3	34,228	2.4
Methodist Church	19,247	2.1	13,277	1.2	12,303	0.8	12,105	0.8
	Hours of Occupancy per Town Inhabitant (OT/P)							
Town	1,298		1,361		1,158		1,088	
All Churches	59		40		26		26	

towns' borders. In terms of the museum analogy, this is as if the philanthropist's exhibit galleries, 13 to 22 percent of all the galleries, received 2.3 to 4.5 percent of the total amount of museum visiting time. It is clear that the churches contributed behavior resources to the towns in greater abundance than they were used.

CHANGE IN OCCUPANCY OF THE TOWNS AND CHURCHES BETWEEN 1954-1955 AND 1963-1964

The occupancy of all Midwest's behavior settings by Midwest residents increased by 20 percent in the 9-year period, while the occupancy of the church-related settings of the town decreased by 21 percent. In the case of Yoredale, occupancy of all settings decreased by 5 percent, while the occupancy of the church-related behavior settings of Yoredale increased by less than one percent. Occupancy per person declined among Midwest residents from 59 to 40 hours per year, almost one-third; it remained constant at 26 hours per person for Yoredale residents.

DIFFERENCES BETWEEN MIDWEST AND YOREDALE IN BEHAVIOR SETTING OCCUPANCY

Midwest residents spent 1,298 hours per person in the community behavior settings of the town in 1954–1955, 12 percent more than did Yoredale residents. In 1963–1964 Midwest residents occupied community settings for 1,361 hours per person, 25 percent more than did Yoredale residents. In church-related settings the difference is greater; Midwest residents spent 127 percent more time in them in 1954–1955 and 54 percent more in 1963–1964 than Yoredale residents.

OCCUPANCY OF CHURCH-RELATED BEHAVIOR SETTINGS BY DIFFERENT POPULATION SUBGROUPS

We have discovered that less than 5 percent of the total hours of occupancy of the behavior settings of the towns occurred in church-related settings. Are these person hours of occupancy supplied by different population subgroups in proportion to their numbers in the towns, or are church-related settings differentially occupied?

Figure 1 reports the occupancy of church-related behavior settings in hours per person per year for these population subgroups.

Subgroup	*Identification*
Infants (Inf)	Under 2 years of age
Preschool children (PS)	2 to 5:11 years of age
Younger School ages (YS)	6 to 8:11 years of age
Older School ages (OS)	9 to 11:11 years of age
Adolescents (Adol)	12 to 17:11 years of age
Adults (Adu)	18 to 64:11 years of age
Aged (Aged)	65 years and over
Males (M)	
Females (F)	
Social Class I (SC I)	Social Classes I, II, and III, correspond fairly
Social Class II (SC II)	well to Warner's Upper Middle, Lower
Social Class III (SC III)	Middle, and Upper Lower Classes.[5]

[5] Warner, W. L., Marchia Meeker and K. Eells, *Social Class in America*. Chicago: Science Research Associates, 1949.

FIGURE 1

HOURS PER YEAR PER PERSON OF OCCUPANCY OF CHURCH-RELATED BEHAVIOR SETTING BY POPULATION SUBGROUPS

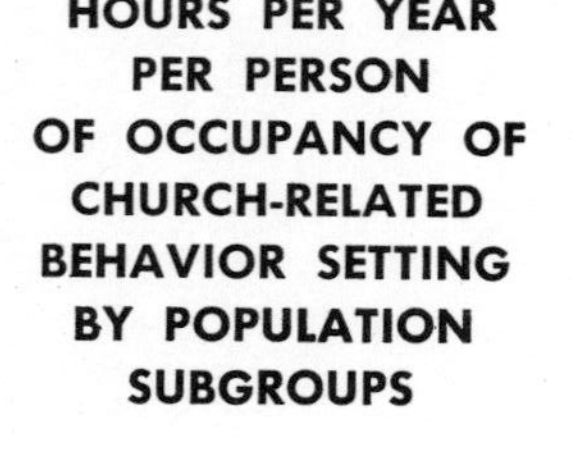

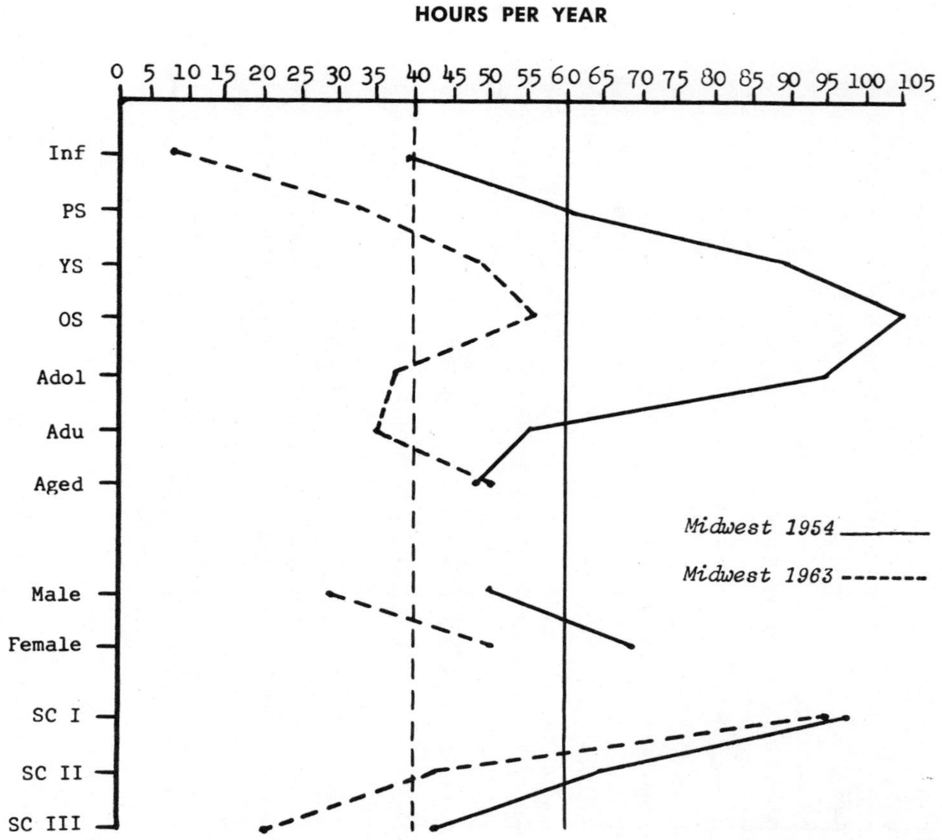

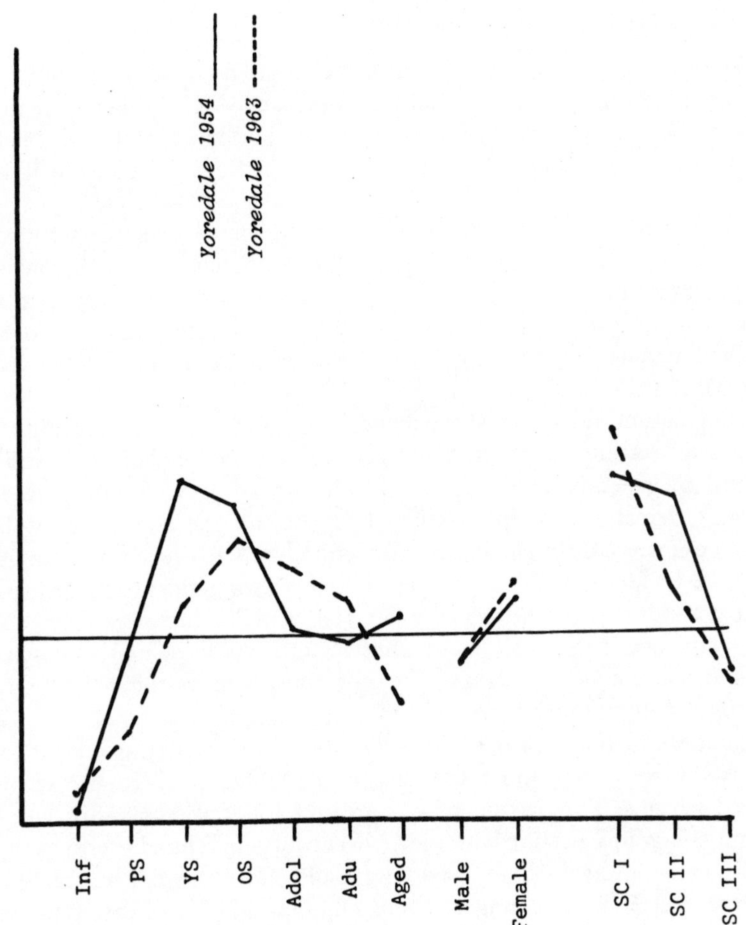
Yoredale 1954
Yoredale 1963
Inf
PS
YS
OS
Adol
Adu
Aged
Male
Female
SC I
SC II
SC III

Figure 1 shows, for example, that the mean occupancy of church-related behavior settings in the year 1954–1955 was 39 hours for infants and 61 hours for preschool children. The horizontal lines indicate the mean occupancy of church-related settings for all town residents.

It is clear, in the first place, that church-related behavior settings are differentially inhabited by population subgroups in both towns and years. The range in Midwest is from 9 hours per person for infants (Inf) to 105 hours for the older school ages (OS); in Yoredale the range is from 1.5 hours per person for infants to 52 for Social Class I.

Population subgroups whose members clearly inhabit church-related behavior settings for more hours per year per person than town residents in general are: younger and older school ages (6:00 to 11:11 years), females, and Social Class I. These are the church faithful. Subgroups whose members inhabit church-related behavior settings for fewer hours per year per person than town residents in general are: infants, males, and Social Class III. Many of these are strangers or only occasional visitors to church settings. Preschool children, adolescents, adults, and aged are not consistent in the towns and years as church inhabitants.

The mean hours of occupancy of church-related settings declined between 1954–1955 and 1963–1964 for all Midwest subgroups except aged persons. The decrement was greatest for adolescents. Six Yoredale subgroups declined in mean occupancy of church settings in the 9-year interval, 4 increased, and 2 did not change. The greatest decrement was for younger school children and the greatest increment for adolescents.

The general shapes of the mean occupancy curves of the population subgroups are similar for Midwest and Yoredale, but all the Yoredale values are lower than the corresponding Midwest values. Mean occupancy of church-related settings is less for all Yoredale subgroups.

Figure 1, which represents the relative amounts of time different categories of persons "go to church," does not tell the whole story. We would like to know, too, how much time people spend in church behavior settings relative to the time they spend in all community settings. When persons leave their homes they choose from the environmental resources the community provides. We have reported in

Table 2 that in 1954–1955 Midwest residents chose to spend 4.5 percent of their time in church-related settings. A person who spends in church-related settings more than 4.5 percent of the time he spends in all community settings *overinhabits* these settings relative to Midwesterners in general; he is *overexposed* to whatever occurs in church settings. Data of this kind for the population subgroups are presented in Figure 2. Here we find, for example, that 19 percent of the total hours Midwest infants spent in Midwest's community behavior settings in 1954–1955 were spent in church-connected settings. The horizontal lines show the occupancy of church settings by all town residents, that is, the *expected* values.

If Midwest infants had occupied church settings at the same rate as a random sample of Midwest residents, the point representing infants in Figure 2 would have been at 4.5 percent rather than 19 percent. This means that in 1954 the infants of Midwest overinhabited church-related behavior settings and were overexposed to their programs, relative to the population at large. Figure 2 shows that church-related settings are differentially inhabited in both towns in both years. The upper social classes, females, and the aged of both towns in both years inhabited church-related settings for more hours per year per person than the towns' residents in general—three times more than the population at large in the case of the Social Class I of Yoredale in 1963. Social Class III and males underinhabited church-related behavior settings in both of the towns in both years cited.

Changes in degree of exposure to church settings between 1954 and 1963 are not dramatic; in fact, Midwest's 1954 and 1963 curves appear to be remarkably parallel for the age span of 2 to 65 years. There are exceptions, however. Infants were transformed between 1954 and 1963 from overinhabiters of church-related settings to underinhabiters; and the old people were even more faithful church inhabitants in 1963 than in 1954. Careful inspection of the Midwest curves reveals that at all ages below adolescence the degree of overinhabitation of the church-connected behavior settings was less in 1963 than in 1954. When all childhood ages are treated as a single subgroup, the curves of Figure 3 result. From these it appears that in 1954 Midwest's church-related behavior settings were overinhabited by children and aged to about the same degree and that they were underinhabited by adolescents and adults to about the same degree.

FIGURE 2

PERSON-HOURS OF OCCUPANCY (OT) OF CHURCH-RELATED BEHAVIOR SETTINGS BY POPULATION SUBGROUPS

(Occupancy time reported in terms of the percent of the occupancy time of all town settings by each subgroup.)

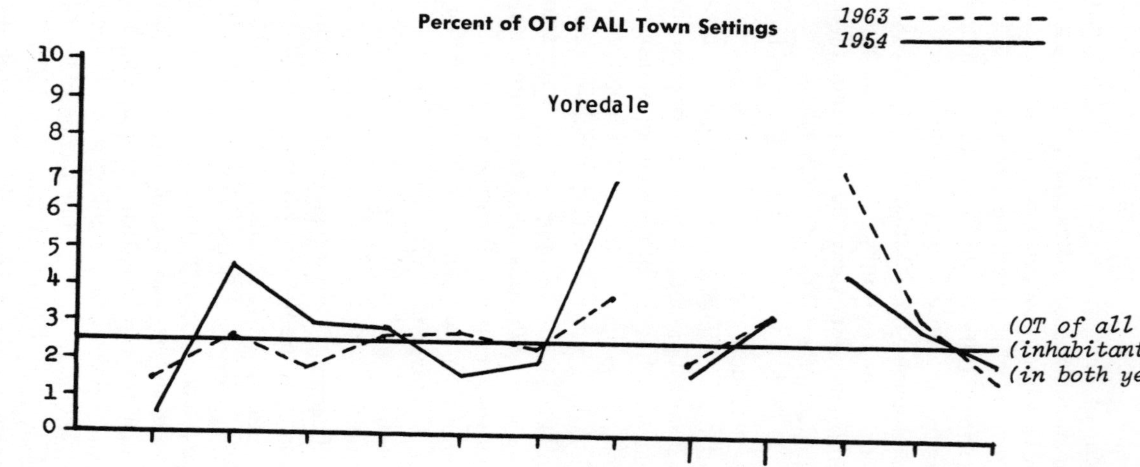

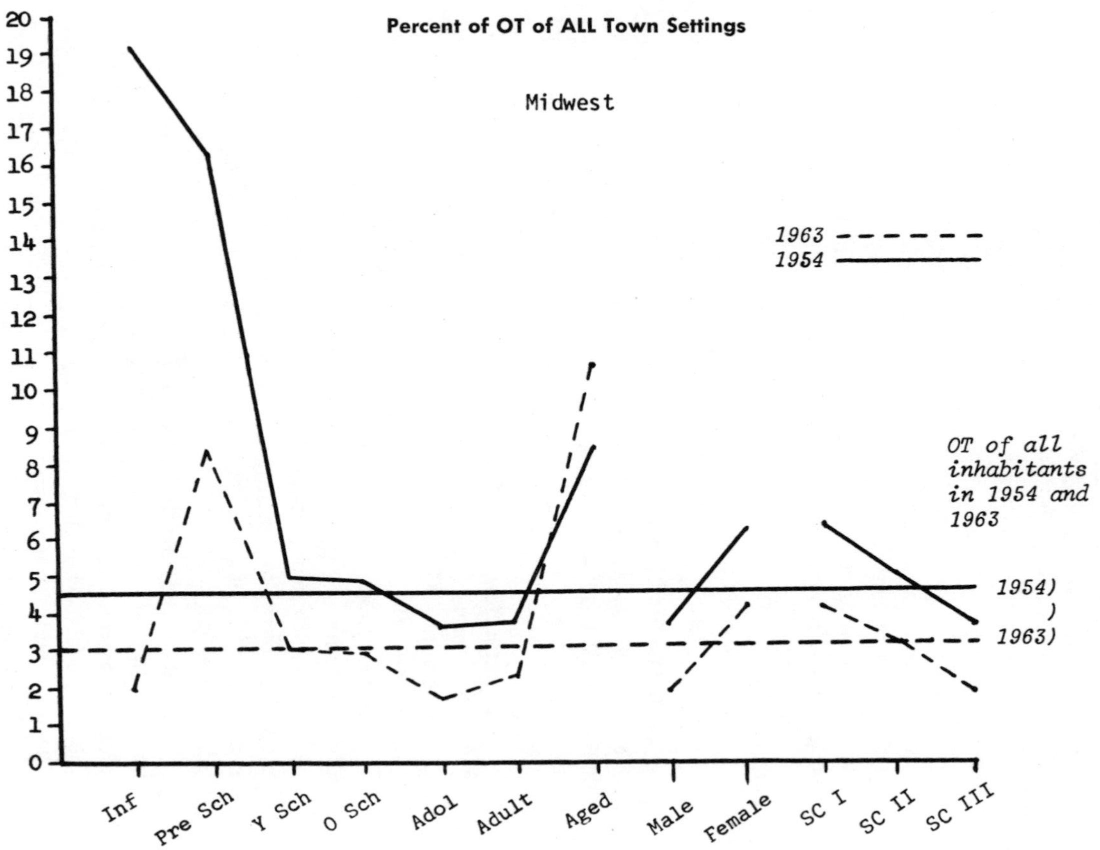
Percent of OT of ALL Town Settings
Midwest
1963
1954
OT of all inhabitants in 1954 and 1963
1954)
)
1963)
20
19
18
17
16
15
14
13
12
11
10
9
8
7
6
5
4
3
2
1
0
Inf
Pre Sch
Y Sch
O Sch
Adol
Adult
Aged
Male
Female
SC I
SC II
SC III

In 1963, the church-related behavior settings were no longer overinhabited by children, and they were overinhabited by aged persons at a higher rate than in 1954. In general, exposure to the church-related settings of Midwest shifted during the 9-year period from younger to older inhabitants. The changed picture is less systematic in Yoredale. In 1963 all Yoredale age subgroups came closer to the expected rate than they did in 1954; the greatest shifts are by adolescents, who overinhabited church settings in 1963 to a slight degree, and by the aged, who overinhabited the church settings to a smaller degree than in 1954. The direction of these shifts is opposite to those in Midwest.

RESPONSIBILITY AND LEADERSHIP IN CHURCH AND TOWN

Occupants of behavior settings have varying degrees of power and responsibility; there are attenders, performers, and leaders. Here are some data regarding power and responsibility in Midwest at large, in its churches as a whole, and more specifically in its Methodist Church.

The performers in a behavior setting are all the inhabitants who have responsibility of any kind for its functioning; for example, the performers in a Methodist Church Worship Service in Midwest are the preacher, the members of the choir, the ushers, the organist, and the candle-lighters. All performers are so essential to the program of the setting that substitutes must be found for missing performers or other adjustments made. Performers are important people. The proportion of the inhabitants of a behavior setting who are performers is an indication of the spread of responsible involvement among the inhabitants.

In Midwest, in 1963–1964, the mean percent of the inhabitants of behavior settings who were performers was 24.4. Of these performers, about 70 percent were adults, about 23 percent were adolescents, and about 7 percent were children. People are important in Midwest, but they are even more important in the church-related behavior settings. On the average, 31.4 percent of the inhabitants of church settings were performers in 1963–1964, and of these about the same proportion were adults as in settings at large (72 percent), somewhat fewer were adolescents (17 percent instead of 23 percent), somewhat more were children (11 percent instead of 7 percent). The churches of

FIGURE 3

PERSON-HOURS OF OCCUPANCY (OT) OF CHURCH-RELATED BEHAVIOR SETTINGS BY POPULATION SUBGROUPS

(Occupancy time reported in terms of the percent of the occupancy time of all town settings by each subgroup.)

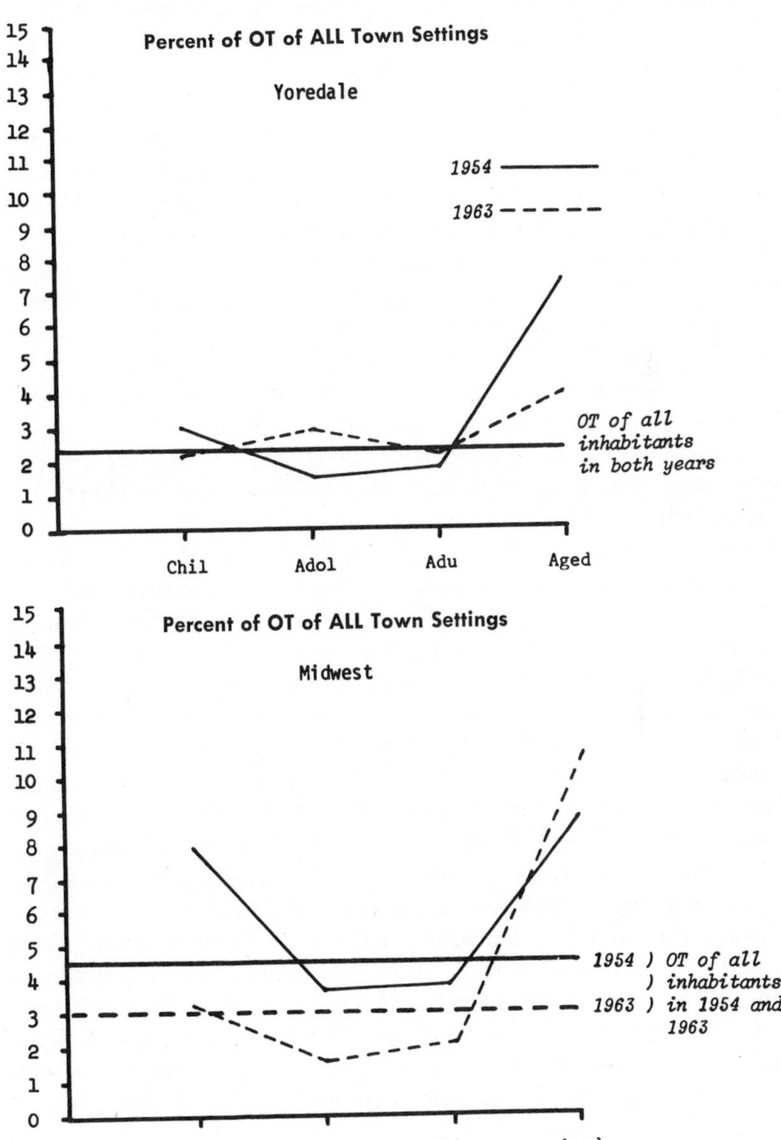

Midwest tend to shortchange adolescents and favor children in providing the experience of responsibility.

A person is a leader, according to our definition, when he is the single or joint head of a behavior setting, or is a member of an executive committee, that is, a behavior setting with authority over other settings. A person is a leader when he is in a position to exercise single or shared power over the total program in one or more behavior settings.

Forty-eight Midwest inhabitants were leaders in the Methodist Church in 1963–1964; this figure is 30 percent of those who were regular or irregular inhabitants of Methodist settings, and it is 39 percent of the inhabitants 12 years of age and older. Of these 48 leaders, 11 (23 percent) had leadership positions in the church only and 37 were leaders in nonchurch behavior settings as well as church settings. Forty-two percent of Methodist leaders were men, they led in 46 percent of the church's behavior setting occurrences, and 33 percent of all their leadership positions were within church-related behavior settings. Fifty-eight percent of Methodist leaders were women. They led in 54 percent of the church's setting occurrences, and 40 percent of all their leadership positions were in church behavior settings. These data indicate that church leadership is widely distributed among Methodist Church inhabitants, that most Methodist leaders are also active leaders in the wider community, and that Methodist men and women do not differ greatly in the extent of their leadership in church and community.

There were 121 women who regularly inhabited Methodist Church settings in 1963–1964, and they fell into three categories of power and responsibility with respect to the programs of the church. (a) Sixteen (13 percent) were *attenders* only, going to church school classes and women's meetings and sitting among the congregation at worship services. (b) Thirty-seven (30 percent) of the women, at some time during the year, were responsible performers or leaders in such nonreligious behavior settings as Mother-Daughter Banquet, Youth Trip to Burris University, Ice Cream Social. The success of Methodist social and recreational settings depended on the reliability and competence of these women. None of them served at this level in connection with the next category of behavior settings. (c) Sixty-nine (57 percent) of the Methodist women were performers or leaders in primarily religious behavior settings—teachers of classes, leaders of study groups, members of the Official Board. On their reliability and competence depended the effectiveness of important religious programs of the church. Overall, 87 percent of the women who were active in the Methodist Church of Midwest in 1963–1964 were more than attenders; they held positions of power and responsibility. This would appear to be a very impressive proportion of responsible persons and it carries with it many implications for the life of the institution.

The proportion of the inhabitants of the church-related behavior settings of Midwest who hold responsible positions, as performers or leaders, is undoubtedly higher than it is in larger churches. Other research has shown that institutions whose behavior settings have relatively few inhabitants to carry out the important functions of the settings involve a greater proportion of them in positions of power and responsibility than do institutions with large settings. This is particularly clear in the case of schools (Barker and Gump).[6] More people are important in small schools, and fewer are expendable than in large schools. This is undoubtedly true of churches, too. Some relevant church data are presented in Figure 4. These data show that small churches, whether in cities or in towns, have relatively larger Sunday schools than large churches; and Sunday schools, as we know, require the voluntary, responsible performance of many people. Surprise has sometimes been expressed that large and wealthy churches with extensive educational plants do relatively poorly in attracting and holding voluntary participants, performers, and leaders. The reason would clearly seem to be that there is a dynamism in institutions that have small settings that is not present in those that have large settings, and the great number of responsible participants in the Midwest church-related behavior settings demonstrates this principle in a very striking manner.

THE NATURE OF THE CHURCHES' CONTRIBUTION TO THE TOWNS

Our final question is: What is the nature of the churches' contributions? What do the churches add to Midwest and Yoredale as places to live?

---

[6] Barker, R. G., and P. V. Gump, *Big School, Small School.* Stanford, Calif.: Stanford University Press, 1964.

FIGURE 4

CHURCH MEMBERSHIP AND SUNDAY SCHOOL ENROLLMENT

Churches of Topeka, Highland, Wichita, and Soloman Presbyteries in Kansas, and Kansas City, Missouri

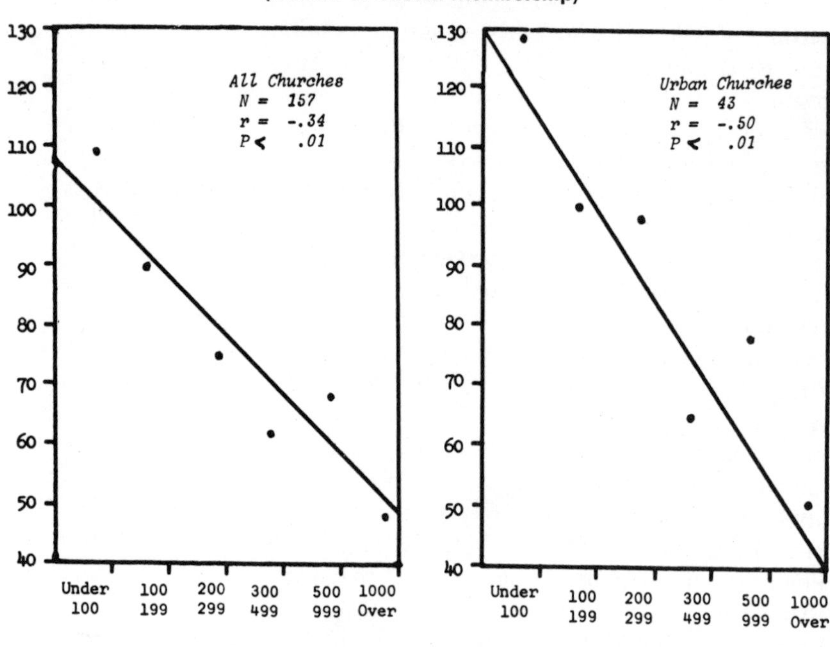

Source: Barker, R. G., "Ecology and Motivation," in M. R. Jones (ed.), *Nebraska Symposium on Motivation*. Lincoln: University of Nebraska Press, 1960, p. 40.

BEHAVIOR SETTING GENOTYPES OF CHURCH-RELATED SETTINGS

Evidence that the church-related behavior settings of Midwest and Yoredale have a variety of content is found in Tables 3 and 4, where their genotypes are listed. The church-related behavior settings of Midwest were of 27 genotypes in 1954 and 31 in 1963; they range from Worship Services to Hayrack Rides; those of Yoredale were of 18 genotypes in 1954 and 28 in 1963; and they vary from Card Parties to Worship Services. Clearly the church-related behavior settings of Midwest and Yoredale offer a range of programs. The data of Tables 3 and 4 also show, however, that occupancy of the church-related settings is concentrated in a few genotypes: Religion Classes, Religion Study Groups, Religious Prayer and Meditation Services, and Religious Worship Services, all of which have a high religious content. The occupancy times of the behavior settings in these genotypes are represented in Figure 5 as percentages of the occupancy time of all church-related settings. More than 70 percent of the occupancy times of the church-related behavior settings of Midwest and Yoredale occur in these genotypes. In terms of person-hours of occupancy, the church-related settings of Midwest and Yoredale are devoted primarily to religion.

ACTION PATTERNS OF MIDWEST AND YOREDALE AND THEIR CHURCHES

We have approached the question of what, rather than how much, the churches contribute to Midwest and Yoredale in another way. We have rated the behavior settings of Midwest and Yoredale on 11 attributes called *action patterns*. The program of a behavior setting receives a high rating on any action pattern (Recreation, Religion, Education) if the setting is primarily devoted to that action pattern. A behavior setting that receives a high rating on the action pattern religion, for example, is one in which religious behavior predominates as indicated by worship, prayer, preaching, teaching about religious matters, use of religious objects (hymnals, the Bible, the cross). A church Worship Service is such a setting. A behavior setting with a high rating on the action pattern Aesthetics is one in which aesthetic creation (painting, singing), and/or aesthetic appreciation, and/or aesthetic objects or events (pictures, musical compositions) are essential components, for example, choir practice.

TABLE 3

MIDWEST CHURCH-CONNECTED GENOTYPES, 1954 AND 1963; NUMBER AND OCCUPANCY TIME OF SETTINGS IN EACH GENOTYPE

	1954-1955		1963-1964	
Genotype Name and Number	Number of Settings	OT	Number of Settings	OT
24. Building, Construction, and Repair Services	1	71		
36. Club Officers Training Classes	1	114		
44. Custodial Work Groups			3	104
47. Day Care Homes and Nurseries	*2	412	3	191
50. Dinners and Banquets	1	72	4	559
51. Dinners with Business Meetings	2	775	1	9
53. Dinners with Recreational and Cultural Programs	2	485	1	242
55. Educational Methods Classes			1	114
63. Excursions and Sightseeing Trips	1	21	3	206
73. Food and Rummage Sales	3	103		
76. Funeral Services, Church	*3	796	*3	816
82. Graduation and Promotion Exercises	2	340	2	83
86. Hayrack Rides			*1	71
93. Ice Cream Socials			1	41
96. Installation and Induction Ceremonies	1	114		
117. Meetings, Business	11	877	27	852
119. Meetings, Discussion			1	21
125. Music Classes, Vocal	3	1,599	6	491
135. Parties	3	597	4	163
137. Pastors Studies			*1	1,124
143. Picnics	2	404	3	103
144. Plays and Programs	4	1,077	8	493
148. Programs of Choral Music	3	305	2	62
154. Receptions	*1	72		
157. Religion Classes	*23	11,052	*42	7,657
158. Religion Study Groups	*1	1,943	*25	2,602
159. Religious Fellowship Meetings	*13	5,654	*10	731
160. Religious Prayer and Meditation Services	*1	41	*6	696
161. Religious Worship Services	*12	12,631	*23	12,478
162. Restaurants and Organization Dinners for the Public	3	835	4	555
164. Roller Skating Parties			1	9
179. Sewing Club Meetings	*1	913	1	2,285
186. Solicitation of Funds	1	72	2	50
187. Solicitation of Goods			*1	41
192. Swimming Excursions and Classes			1	41
215. Weddings, Church	*2	775	*2	283
	103	42,150	193	33,173

* Genotypes that were unique to the churches.

TABLE 4

YOREDALE CHURCH-CONNECTED GENOTYPES, 1954 AND 1963: NUMBER AND OCCUPANCY TIME OF SETTINGS IN EACH GENOTYPE

Genotype Name and Number	1954-1955 Number of Settings	1954-1955 OT	1963-1964 Number of Settings	1963-1964 OT
13. Award Ceremonies	1	106		
18. Baptism Services			*2	66
26. Bingo Games			*1	218
35. Card Parties	1	2,080	1	422
36. Carnivals	2	446	1	292
54. Confessions, Roman Catholic Church	*1	224	*1	496
74. Educational Methods Classes			*1	7
84. Excursions and Sightseeing Trips	2	529	7	1,224
91. First Aid Classes and Demonstrations			1	18
93. Food and Rummage (Jumble) Sales			4	242
98. Fund Raising Socials			1	66
99. Funeral Services, Church (Including Graveside Services)	*4	1,244	*3	786
131. Meetings, Business	11	549	10	543
132. Meetings, Cultural			3	758
134. Meetings, Social			2	108
141. Moving Picture Shows	1	200		
143. Music Classes, Vocal	1	705	2	2,371
152. Organ Concerts			1	176
156. Parties	4	291	6	805
160. Plays and Programs	3	632	2	152
166. Programs of Choral Music	3	580	2	375
173. Receptions			3	109
176. Religion Classes	*8	4,817	8	2,854
177. Religion Study Groups			*9	1,263
178. Religious Fellowship Meetings	6	2,436	*2	344
179. Religious Prayer and Meditation Services (Includes Open Church)	*4	648	*3	747
180. Religious Worship Services	18	17,923	11	19,554
201. Solicitations of Funds	4	117	4	144
210. Swimming Classes			1	153
227. Weddings, Church	*4	568	*3	234
	78	34,095	95	34,527

* Genotypes that were unique to the churches.

FIGURE 5

PERCENT OF THE OCCUPANCY TIME OF ALL CHURCH BEHAVIOR SETTINGS THAT OCCURS IN STATED BEHAVIOR SETTING GENOTYPES

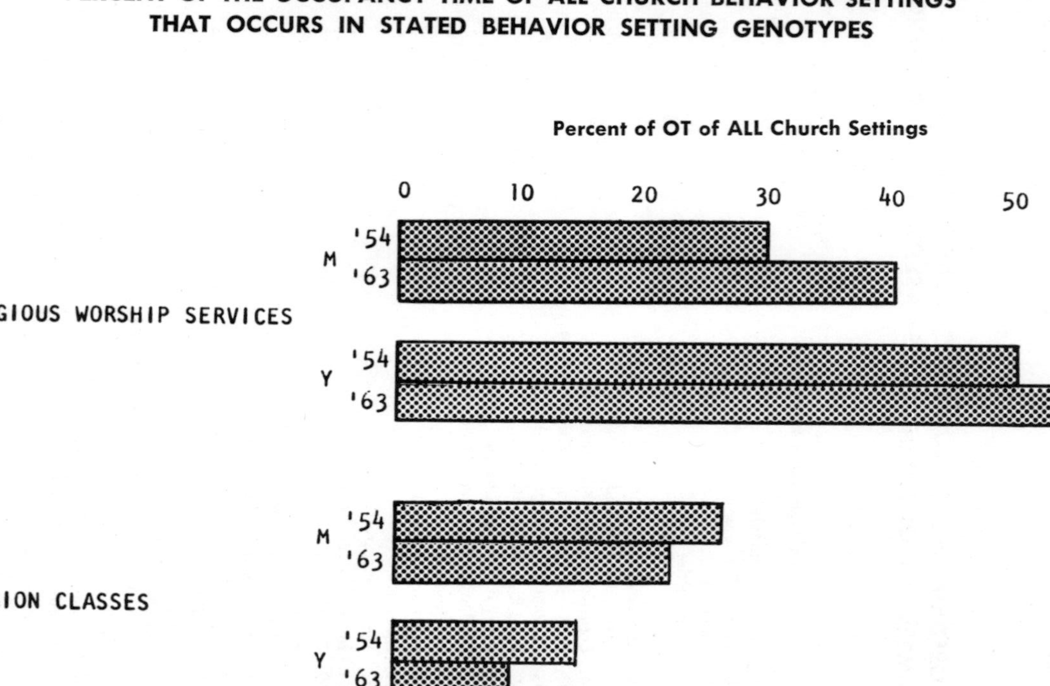

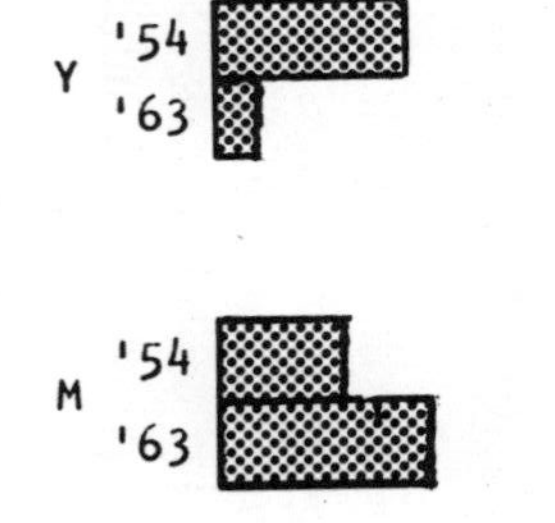

Midwest and Yoredale, 1954 and 1963

Information on the contribution of the churches to action patterns present in the towns is contained in Tables 5 and 6. With respect to the action pattern Aesthetics, for example, the data indicate that in 1954 the occupancy time of Midwest church-related behavior settings with high action pattern ratings for Aesthetics was 13,534 hours. This is 44.1 percent of the occupancy time of all Midwest settings with high aesthetic ratings, and it is 32.1 percent of the occupancy time of all church-related settings. These data mean that the church-related behavior settings of Midwest provided 44.1 percent of the town's total aesthetic environment, measured in terms of person-hours of occupancy of behavior settings with high aesthetic ratings, and that almost one-third of Midwest's church-related behavior settings have high aesthetic content.

The contributions of the churches to the action pattern components of the towns' environments may be summarized briefly as follows:

The churches of Midwest and of Yoredale in both years provided more than 80 percent of the religious environments, more than 30 percent of the aesthetic environments, and more than 4.5 percent of the social environments. The churches contributed very little to the recreational, business, professional, governmental, nutritional, cosmetic (personal appearance), and health aspects of the towns' environments.

The churches of Midwest and Yoredale are surprisingly similar in their action pattern characteristics, but there is one interesting difference. The churches of Midwest clearly dominate its religious environment; but in Yoredale one-fifth of the occupancy of religious behavior settings occurs in nonchurch settings in 1963; these settings are almost exclusively in the schools of the town.

Changes between 1954 and 1963 in Midwest are in the direction of relatively greater contribution by the churches to the town's total religious environment, and relatively smaller contribution to its aesthetic, educational, and social environments. In Yoredale changes are toward relatively smaller contribution by the churches to the religious and aesthetic environments of the town.

Overall, the data show that over 9 years there are changes in the relative contributions of church-related behavior settings to the action pattern composition of the towns, and in the relative mix of

TABLE 5

ACTION PATTERNS OF MIDWEST CHURCHES:

Number and Percent of Hours Spent by Midwest Residents in Church Settings with High Action Pattern Ratings

Rating	Time in hours		Percent of all town settings with each rating		Percent of all church settings	
	1954	1963	1954	1963	1954	1963
Aesthetics	13,534	11,978	44.1	30.9	32.1	36.1
Business	273	0	0.1	0	0.6	0
Professionalism	41	1,431	0	0.1	0.1	4.3
Education	12,863	8,356	11.7	4.2	30.5	25.2
Government	0	0	0	0	0	0
Nutrition	897	844	0.7	0.5	2.1	2.5
Personal Appearance	775	284	2.2	0.8	1.8	0.8
Physical Health	0	0	0	0	0	0
Recreation	2,401	3,355	1.8	2.4	5.7	10.1
Religion	30,942	26,478	95.0	98.3	73.4	79.8
Social	42,150	32,008	7.2	4.5	100.0	96.5
All Church Settings	42,150	33,173	4.5	3.0	100.0	100.0

TABLE 6

ACTION PATTERNS OF YOREDALE CHURCHES:

Number and Percent of Hours Spent by Yoredale Residents in Church Settings with High Action Pattern Ratings

Rating	Time in hours		Percent of all town settings with each rating		Percent of all church settings	
	1954	1963	1954	1963	1954	1963
Aesthetics	20,385	23,039	43.3	36.2	59.9	67.3
Business	412	135	0.1	0.03	1.2	0.4
Professionalism	260	460	0.01	0.03	0.8	1.3
Education	5,372	4,771	3.6	3.4	15.8	13.9
Government	0	41	0	0.04	0	0.1
Nutrition	0	104	0	0.02	0	0.3
Personal Appearance	645	257	1.1	0.4	1.9	0.8
Physical Health	21	21	0.1	0.1	0.1	0.1
Recreation	3,218	3,946	1.2	2.1	9.5	11.5
Religion	28,828	28,270	86.9	80.7	84.7	82.6
Social	34,010	34,186	4.6	4.5	99.9	99.9
All Church Settings	34,028	34,228	2.3	2.4	100.0	100.0

action patterns within church-related settings. Within Midwest, however, these changes are minor in comparison with the 20 percent decrease in the total occupancy of church-related behavior settings. No change in the relative contribution of the churches to action patterns within Midwest compensates for this general, absolute decline in occupancy of church-related behavior settings. It is interesting to know that in 1963–1964 the church-related religious behavior settings of Midwest accommodated 98.3 percent of all person-hours Midwest residents spent in religious settings; an increase over the 9 years, from 95 percent in 1954–1955. Still, the actual hours of occupancy of Midwest's religious settings decreased over this period by 4,464 hours, or 14 percent. In fact, the occupancy of Midwest behavior settings in which religious action patterns are prominent declined from 46 hours per year per inhabitant in 1954–1955 to 32 hours in 1963–1964, a decline of 30 percent.

The changes over the 9-year period in the relative contributions of the church-connected settings of Yoredale are not overshadowed by a general decline in the occupancy of church settings. They are, therefore, of greater significance in themselves; the *relative* increases and decreases reflect actual increases and decreases in the occupancy times of church-connected settings. On the other hand, there is a basic fact about Yoredale that is important in interpreting the findings about the town's church-related settings. The occupancy of these settings is low in both years in comparison with Midwest: 26 hours per year per inhabitant in both 1954–1955 and 1963–1964 (rather than 59 hours for Midwest in 1954 and 40 hours in 1963). The occupancy of all Yoredale settings in which religious action patterns are prominent is 25 hours per inhabitant in 1954 and 27 hours in 1963 (rather than 46 and 32 hours per Midwest resident).

CONCLUDING REMARKS

Churches, today, continually scrutinize their doctrines, purposes, organizational structure, membership, and finances. It would appear desirable, too, for churches to inspect themselves regularly as behavior habitats of their members and visitors, and as contributors to community environments. This study exemplifies concepts and methods for doing so, and it provides data from two widely separated towns as a basis for comparison and evaluation.

It is obvious that only a beginning has been made, and that more problems have been raised than have been solved, a not-infrequent result of scientific investigation. Fortunately, a scientific method does not have to solve immediately all the problems it raises to be useful. Indeed, to state problems in solvable form, and to point the directions where solutions may be found, is in itself valuable. So we shall close this chapter with two solvable problems which have occurred to us in the course of our study of the churches of Midwest and Yoredale. These will exemplify the directions that applications of the methods can profitably take.

It is not surprising, in view of two of the findings, that small communities frequently cling to their "inefficient," "outdated" churches with what may appear to outsiders to be unreasonable stubbornness. These findings are (a) that churches usually provide a substantial proportion of the total behavior resources of small towns; and (b) that in the behavior settings of small churches many inhabitants have responsibility and power, and are important and valued people. The residents of small communities know that the removal of their churches, for example, by amalgamation with "strong" churches in larger towns, destroys perhaps one-quarter of the behavior resources of the town. This loss of behavior potentialities is undoubtedly resisted not only by those who inhabit church settings, but by noninhabitants as well; for they value future behavior alternatives, they value the behavior opportunities the churches provide for those to whom they are close, and they know that such a massive weakening of the community places its other behavior resources in jeopardy. Those who do inhabit small churches know that consolidation with a larger church reduces for them the likelihood of having an important, responsible part in church activities. Most of the deacons, elders, board members, and presidents of small churches can look forward in the larger church to the role of faithful member.

When small churches are destroyed, for whatever reasons, these reasons have to be balanced against the inevitable diminution and weakening of the local community environment and the deprivation of many church inhabitants of the satisfactions of making important contributions to church programs. For some of these persons, church settings provide their only opportunity to be valued within the community at large, and this is one of the strongest motives in our culture. So the question inevitably arises, are there other solutions to the problem of weak local churches than their elimination? Other solutions are possible, and a variety of them can be investigated by the methods that have been used in the research. The kinds of satisfactions occurring in churches of differing sizes and types of organization can also be readily studied by other methods of ecological psychology (see *Big School, Small School*).

The data of the study show that in both Midwest and Yoredale, the behavior setting resources of the churches increased, but that there was no accompanying increase in the use of these resources by the residents of Yoredale, and that there was actually a decrease in their use by the residents of Midwest. In the case of Midwest, it is as if a museum director almost doubled the number of the museum's exhibit galleries and more than doubled the days and hours they were open to the public, but found that the person-hours of viewing actually decreased by one-fifth. The director would undoubtedly ask, "What is wrong?" and the church people of Midwest ask this, too. Further investigation along the lines of the study could find an answer, but with the data now available we can only raise some possibilities. Much of the increase in the number of behavior settings was instigated by the larger church organizations—by regional and national assemblies, by curriculum committees. One can wonder if the behavior setting structure that is appropriate for large suburban churches, which are often strongly represented in the larger church organization, is suitable for a small church. On the other hand, it may be that settings which were irrelevant to the churches' mission (like a museum's poor art collections) have been eliminated, and a greater number of more relevant, small settings added, making the fewer hours of religious experiences more meaningful. These are questions that can be investigated and answered.

SUGGESTIONS FOR FURTHER READING

Allport, F. H., *Theories of Perception and the Concept of Structure*. New York: John Wiley and Sons, 1955.

Asch, S. E., *Social Psychology*. Englewood Cliffs, N. J.: Prentice-Hall, 1952.

Bales, R. F., "The Equilibrium Problem in Small Groups," in Parson, Bales, and Shils (eds.), *Working Papers in the Theory of Action*. New York: The Free Press, 1953.

Bales, R. F. and E. F. Borgatta, "Size of Group as a Factor in the Interaction Profile," in Hare, Borgatta, and Bales (eds.), *Small Groups: Studies in Social Interaction*. New York: Alfred A. Knopf, 1955.

Barker, R. G. and H. F. Wright, *Midwest and Its Children*. New York: Harper and Row, 1955.
Barker, R. G. and Louise S. Barker, "Behavior Units for the Comparative Study of Cultures," in B. Kaplan (ed.), *Studying Personality Cross-Culturally*. New York: Harper and Row, 1961.
Barker, R. G., "Exploration in Ecological Psychology," *American Psychologist*, Vol. 20, No. 1, 1965.
Barker, R. G. and P. V. Gump, *Big School, Small School*. Stanford, Calif.: Stanford University Press, 1964.
Cleland, S., *Influence of Plant Size on Industrial Relations*. Princeton: Princeton University Press, 1955.
Coleman, J. S., *The Adolescent Society*. New York: The Free Press, 1961.
Haire, M., "Size, Shape and Function in Industrial Organizations," *Human Organizations*, Vol. 14, 1955.
Hare, A. P., "A Study of Interaction and Consensus in Different Size Groups," *American Sociological Review*, Vol. 17, 1952.
Kelley, H. H. and J. W. Thibaut, "Experimental Studies of Group Problem Solving and Process," in G. Lindzey (ed.), *Handbook of Social Psychology*. Cambridge, Mass.: Addison-Wesley, 1954.
Marriot, R., "Size of Working Group and Output," *Occupational Psychology*, Volume 23, 1949.
Tallachi, S., "Organization Size, Individual Attitudes and Behavior: An Empirical Study," *Administrative Science Quarterly*, Volume 5, 1960.
Thibaut, John W. and H. H. Kelley, *The Social Psychology of Groups*. New York: John Wiley and Sons, 1959.
Thomas, E. J., "Role Conceptions and Organization Size," *American Sociological Review*, Vol. 24, 1959.
Thomas, E. J. and C. F. Fink, "The Effects of Group Size," *Psychological Bulletin*, Vol. 60, 1963.
Worthy, J. C., "Organizational Structure and Employee Morale," *American Sociological Review*, Vol. 15, 1950.

CHAPTER 7

PARTNERSHIP BETWEEN THE SOCIAL SCIENCES AND THEOLOGY

COLIN WILLIAMS

Why should representatives of the churches explore the findings of the various social sciences about the nature and sources of change in small communities? For insights the church can use as it seeks to break down resistance to what it considers essential changes? If so, the social sciences are useful instruments for the church. Or for additional insights into what these changes should be and how they should be handled? If so, social sciences can be seen as partners with theology in making value decisions about the nature and direction of social change.

Previous chapters of this book have brought into the open value questions such as:

What losses and gains occur when urbanization brings about the gradual elimination of the dispersed institutions that have traditionally characterized small communities?

What do the people who go to churches expect from religious experience? What functions do they expect churches to fulfill?

SOME QUESTIONS OF MUTUAL INTEREST

These questions can be approached empirically. The social sciences can explore various aspects of them; but what is the source of ultimate decisions on the value questions the social scientists can explore? Social scientists can empirically explore the dimensions of such

---

The Reverend Colin Williams is Associate Secretary, Division of Christian Life and Mission, National Council of the Churches of Christ in the United States of America.

questions: how people feel about problems such as the loss of small schools, hospitals, and other institutions; and the effects of these problems on the psychological, social, and economic structures of their existence. But, it is not the task of the social scientists (at least as scientists) to make value judgments about what *ought* to be done about such changes—whether to use social science insights to expedite the changes or to stand out against some of these changes.

Who then is responsible for judgments about what ought to be done? They are political judgments; but are there behind these decisions some ultimate religious or theological sanctions? Social scientists ask, "What do the churches think their role ought to be? Do they believe they can offer these value judgments?"

Behind such questions is a fairly strong tradition about the relation between the social sciences and theology. It has often been assumed that whereas the social sciences begin from entirely within the human situation, operating empirically, "from below," theology starts from the other side and brings to the human situation beliefs about how things ought to be, "from above."[1] The social sciences are inductive disciplines, theology a deductive discipline, and dialogue between them is a meeting between two completely different entities.

This traditional picture must be abandoned. The changes that have led to the rise of the modern social sciences are also leading to similar changes in the field of theology; with the result that the dialogue between them must be seen as a dialogue between complementary disciplines, all operating "from below."

THREADS OF CONVERGENCE

We need to go back to the history of the rise of the social sciences. In the Middle Ages, theology was called "the queen of the sciences." It was assumed that all knowledge must begin "from above"—starting from first principles that came from the metaphysical world. The world of theology was the world of revealed truth, revealed from the world beyond the temporal (meta-physics=beyond substance). Theology therefore was the queen, because her rules gave the starting point from which the sciences operated.

---

[1] I have explored this traditional position, and the radical change now occurring in theology, in *Faith in a Secular Age*. New York: Harper and Row, 1966.

The collapse of Christendom, however, is associated with the revolt against the authority of theology (or metaphysics) over our understanding of the world. The famous Enlightenment slogan *Sapere Aude* (Dare to be Wise) mirrors this revolt. Man is encouraged to think for himself without benefit of clergy—without beginning from metaphysical first principles.

At first it was assumed that there was a difference between various areas of human existence. The empirical approach—starting entirely from below—was accepted as right for the "natural sciences," for the physical world had been created with its own inherent structures that can be explored by direct observation. But many still assumed that in the area of immediate human existence—where man is concerned with purpose, moral truth, and ultimate reality—science ended. There knowledge of truth still had to come to us from beyond the realm of direct observation. This kind of division of realms was in fact the basis for much of the (uneasy) settlement between science and religion.

The trouble was that science kept pushing its boundaries closer and closer to the very citadel of human inwardness. When finally psychology staked out even religious experience as its ground, the question was inevitably asked: Where does theology operate? Is there really any realm beyond the empirical approach of exploration from below?

We now are in the position where (finally) theology joins the parade. It too must now approach its subject "from below"; and many theologians today are approaching their task in precisely that fashion. They see their field as the exploration, *from within the historical process*, of the questions of historical purpose, ultimate values, human meaning. They see the collapse of the "sacral," metaphysically enclosed view of life, and the developing process of "secularization" with the rise of the open, empirical, functional attitude, as not only acceptable to the Christian faith but (at least in part) as the outcome of the Christian faith.

The German sociologist von Oppen speaks of the change from a world of "order," in which it was assumed that life here below is meant to reflect the order of the eternal world, to a world of "organization," in which it is taken for granted that man is free to organize his world as he chooses, to achieve ends he is free to change according to the new possibilities his explorations uncover. And von

Oppen sees this change as fully consonant with the biblical view of history.

What is involved? The claim is that Christian theology must now see itself as dealing with historical (empirical) phenomena, and that these phenomena ask to be approached empirically. When the Old Testament speaks of Yahweh as the God of Abraham, Isaac, and Jacob, it speaks of a God who is known in historical events. The New Testament claims that in the life of a man—Jesus of Nazareth—we are given, in an event of history, the essential clue to the meaning of history. In other words, the meaning of history does not come "from above"; it comes "from below." The discipline of theology does not deal with outside principles. Rather, it explores the claim that we can discover, in certain historical situations, clues that enable us to decide questions of meaning in other situations.[2]

Clearly the empirical task here is quite different from the tasks undertaken by economics, sociology, psychology, anthropology; although cultural anthropology soon finds itself delving into such norm-producing phenomena, and psychology and sociology approach the questions from their particular angles. The question is: What is the proper relation between the various empirical disciplines, with their varied subject matter?

R. G. Collingwood has suggested some clues here,[3] which I want to expand into a suggested approach to this problem. Think of human reality on a *continuum*—"exact sciences," through the social sciences, to the "peculiarly human" including art, history, and religion.

←——————————————————————————→

Objectivity Subjectivity

We could speak here of a "law of diminishing scientific returns." As we move along the continuum from left to right, the nearer we approach the specifically human the less becomes our scientific "control." The method of exploration has to be answerable to the nature of the phenomena; thus, as we come closer to the human,

---

[2] I have explored this question in *Faith in A Secular Age* in the chapter entitled "Is the Secular Society Viable?"

[3] See particularly his *An Autobiography*. New York: Oxford University Press, 1939.

scientific "predictability" decreases. The "decreasing scientific returns" are in the area of objective control and predictability, which occur as the human factor increasingly enters the field of observation. It could be argued (with some justification) that to speak of decreasing *scientific* returns means that we have defined science from only one end of the continuum of the reality science must explore—the physical end where "objectivity" is greatest. If we allow science to be defined instead by the subject matter to be explored, then as we move toward the human end we have decreasing "objective" returns but increasing returns in some insights into the more "subjective" phenomena that characterize the specifically human areas of existence.

This is not an unimportant point. Because many social scientists have carried over the methods and expectations of the physical sciences into the social sciences, they have arbitrarily argued that only what can be objectively measured is the proper field of science. In this way they have removed questions of value, purpose, and commitment from the proper concern of the scientist. I would argue that they should be responsible for exploring these questions from the particular angle on reality represented by their science. Science does need to be "disinterested," in the sense that it seeks to see everything in the field it is exploring, regardless of the consequences for particular personal interests. But this statement must not be taken to mean that science need not explore the value judgments, the purposes, the commitment systems that lie behind such personal interests. In fact, only as the social sciences combine with the disciplines of history, philosophy, theology, so that each throws whatever light it can on the question of how these values, purposes, and commitments arise, will we be able to move toward the more satisfactory social ethic needed to help us with complicated decisions and actions in contemporary society.

Perhaps, then, we should speak of a law of decreasing objective returns rather than decreasing scientific returns. By so doing, we draw attention to the decreasing predictability and control, and to the increasing emergence of questions of value and purpose and of the need for the scientist to accept responsibility for these phenomena as he encounters them in the field of his exploration.

The point is that the human questions can be explored from various angles by the varied disciplines. The *value questions* (for example, what should be our attitude to the changes occurring in small communities, and to the levels of acceptance and resistance to it?) are raised by each of the disciplines from their specific subject matter areas.

The *economist* reveals the changing structures of human association and human commitment in the way men continue their search for wealth.

The *psychologist* reveals the responses of persons and groups to such changes—including the deep sense of loss of their traditional personal values as the pursuit of greater wealth leads to radical changes in institutions.

The *anthropologist* explores questions such as the varied cultural responses by which communities have sought to guard cherished values and to handle social changes.

The *sociologist* can explore the springs of social change in various communities—the open and hidden sources of power and the nature of resistances to change (how it is accepted in one place, rejected in another).

From every one of the disciplines the problems of value, of judgment as to what ought to be, are illuminated and explored. Each discipline explores those questions from within its proper subject matter, but none is responsible for giving normative answers to the various questions raised.

AN EMERGING COMPLEMENTARITY OF FUNCTIONS

I suggest that the answer to such value questions cannot be given by the separate disciplines, but should not be given without them. Direct responsibility for dealing with such questions is approached in the fields of history and philosophy, and in the field of theology. *History* explores how such value judgments have been made; *philosophy* accepts the critical task of exploring the significance of the various attempts to express ultimate human wisdom; and *theology* directs us to the commitment faith communities have made to the particular claims to final meaning that have appeared in historical events, such as those recorded in the Bible.

What I am saying, as a Christian theologian, is this. The church is made up of those committed to the decision that in Jesus of Nazareth the essential meaning clues have been given to us. But when we explore those meaning clues, we are necessarily driven to make judgments about how we should act. We must act according to the effect of our actions on the texture of human life. Our theology gives us clues as to *what* we should work for—what human values we should struggle to protect and promote. It even tells us something of *how* we should work for those values (servant love, and so on). But we still have to make vital judgments as to whether certain courses of action—for example, in the civil rights struggle—offer the best hope of achieving the ends we believe in, by the best methods demanded of us. And more and more, in our complicated society, only through a pooling of all the best insights from our respective disciplines can we together as *human beings* make the political judgments that are needed in the midst of social change.

At a conference recently a psychiatrist severely criticized the church for leaving "the seat of moral authority" in our community vacant. Too often, he said, when ultimate ethical decisions are to be made (for example, on sexual morality), clergy expect the social scientists to accept responsibility.

I would answer that we must all accept responsibility, as human beings, for the seat of moral authority. Scientists, artists, theologians, all explore value questions from different angles. Full understanding requires all possible contributions. The value decisions then are to be made together—not as scientists or theologians, but in the light of the insights provided by our scientists, our artists, our theologians.

In his recent book, *Elements for a Social Ethic,*[4] Gibson Winter makes an important attempt to explore how the social sciences can work in partnership with theology and philosophy to develop a social ethic that will provide the guidance now needed for public policy. He insists that social scientists, no less than historians, philosophers, and theologians, work at particular dimensions of the ethical question. A social ethic is needed, to draw together the insights from all these fields.

For this to happen we need greater freedom among various members of the potential partnership. We need to overcome the resistance of some social scientists to direct concern for questions of value and purpose—a resistance deriving from a model of science adopted from the physical sciences. With some, this resistance can reach the point of insisting that value and meaning questions are simply epi-

[4] New York: The Macmillan Company, 1966.

phenomenal—products of deeper forces. True science limits itself to the disinterested exploration of these underlying forces. With others, the resistance simply tries to insist that these questions are outside the field of science, and that philosophy or religion must accept responsibility for them. But if questions of value and meaning arise as genuine human questions reflecting man's capacity to accept responsibility for existence, we should insist that human sciences accept responsibility for these questions as they present themselves within the particular field of their inquiry. To exclude the specifically human is not only to impoverish; it is to distort the "understanding" that scientific exploration of the whole range of phenomena seeks to provide.

AN ULTIMATE INTERDEPENDENCE

But if some social scientists resist their responsibility for questions of value, meaning, and commitment, many theologians resist any attempt to develop a social ethic in a way that seems to draw equally (even indiscriminately) from theological insights and empirical socio-science insights. Such an ethic seems to them to threaten the integrity of theology and its need to take its starting point solely from revelation. For Gibson Winter this "neo-orthodox" attitude, though understandable and in large measure fruitful, has now run into a cul-de-sac. Now we must see the full consequences of the fact that Christian revelation occurs in history. This fact opens theology to partnership with social science disciplines, which are finding skillful methods for exploring particular segments of the total texture of human relationships. So long as these skilled ways of seeing are freed from ideological pretensions (or better, so long as the value assumptions they are using are brought to the surface), they can throw considerable light on the nature of the value decisions that constantly confront us, in the midst of which the claims of faith come to us.

What is the contribution of theology to this partnership? I speak here as a Christian theologian. The Christian faith claims that in Jesus of Nazareth there emerged in history a picture of the true shape of human existence. In the New Testament that picture is expressed in the language of the time—and first century language and ideas were largely "mythical" and "metaphysical." Theology, therefore, has a task of translation. It has to bring this vision of the true shape of human life and human community out of the first century language (or languages) and translate it into today's language (or languages). This, by the way, is already a partnership task. The help of the *human sciences* is needed to make the translation,[5] for we must seek to bring the picture to life in the midst of the present-day problems of human living.

For example, the New Testament picture of Jesus gives us a picture of man participating in the *shalom* (peace-wholeness-completeness) of God. So Jesus is pictured as working to make man healthy in every aspect of his life: in body, in psyche, and in relation to nature. The New Testament puts that in the language of its day. Jesus is seen as a miracle worker, giving man the fullness of life: healing his body, casting out the demons from his psyche, restoring human mastery over nature (for example, walking on the water).

Theology now has the task of translating this vision into contemporary understanding; and to do it theology must work with the physical and social sciences. For example, the vision of man free from *the demons of prejudice* can be constructed best by cooperative work with the sciences not only on the nature of prejudice but on the possible ways for overcoming it (exorcizing the demons!).

Or take another New Testament picture of the vision of human existence. Jesus is pictured as "the man for others," taking constant risks to reach out to the outcasts. The community of that day (like ours) had constructed limiting boundaries to try to keep the community safe from disruption: health boundaries (lepers relegated to the desert); moral boundaries (harlots, publicans—and thieves out in the suburbs, with the morally acceptable in the city!); spiritual boundaries (those not observing the common religious practices excluded from the good community as sources of possible infection).

Jesus broke through the health, moral, spiritual, class, and ethnic safety boundaries, saying that God's love knew no such safety lines, and that the aim of community must be openness of opportunity for all. Hence the vision of Paul follows what they saw empirically in Jesus. "[In Christ] there is neither Jew nor Greek [race barrier],

---

[5] For example, Harvey Cox in his *The Secular City* (New York: The Macmillan Company, 1965) speaks of politics being the language of today in the sense that metaphysics was the language of the first century. So he tries to translate the normative picture of life given in Jesus of Nazareth into the language of politics.

there is neither slave nor free [class], there is neither male nor female [discrimination on the basis of sex]."[6]

The vision has obvious and powerful consequences for the change from our traditional small communities to the more open (in principle) urban communities. It clearly has a lot to say about the fears that are apparent in the contemporary change processes (after all, Jesus went to a cross because of the fears exposed by his crossing all the accepted safety boundaries). But when we try to translate this vision into a program for dealing with social change, we have to deal with complicated social questions. What is the best way to move toward the goal of an open community without unnecessary destruction of the values of personal freedom? What is the best way to push on to the goal of equal access for all, without unnecessarily arousing destructive hatreds?

Here we see how we require a partnership of all the skills and insights of the local science disciplines. The partnership made possible by the pooling of our skills should make possible, then, a co-operation by us, as human beings, in suggesting strategies for change that will best preserve and foster the human values and goals that have emerged in history for our guidance.

SUGGESTIONS FOR FURTHER READING

Bennett, John C. (ed.), *Christian Social Ethics in a Changing World.* New York: Association Press, 1966.

Clark, Henry B., *The Church and Residential Desegregation.* New Haven: College and University Press, 1965.

Glock, Charles Y. and Rodney Stark, *Religion and Society in Tension.* Chicago: Rand McNally, 1966.

Loen, A. E., *Secularization.* London: SCM Press, 1967.

Mathews, Z. K. (ed.), *Responsible Government in a Revolutionary Age.* New York: Association Press, 1966.

Marty, Martin E. and Dean G. Peerman (eds.), *New Theology, No. 4.* New York: The Macmillan Company, 1967.

Munby, D. L. (ed.), *Economic Growth in World Perspective.* New York: Association Press, 1966.

Underwood, Kenneth, *Protestant and Catholic.* Boston: Beacon Press, 1957.

de Vries, E. (ed.), *Man in Community.* New York: Association Press, 1966.

---

[6] Galatians 3:28.

Change in the Small Community

Winter, Gibson, *Elements for a Social Ethic*. New York: The Macmillan Company, 1966.

Winter, Gibson, *The New Creation as Metropolis*. New York: The Macmillan Company, 1963.

World Council of Churches, *The Church for Others*. Geneva and New York: 1967.

CHAPTER 8

THE NEXT STEP

LEROY C. HODAPP

In his Introduction, Professor Gore viewed the exchange between science and theology from the standpoint of a research scientist. In this concluding chapter, I propose to comment on it from the viewpoint of an institutional churchman.

THE IMMENSE JOURNEY

Any piece of research in any field is only part of an immense journey.[1] This journey encompasses the total existence of life on this planet and is currently advancing into the uncharted paths of space. This is not simply a geographic pilgrimage but one that also embraces social, economic, political, and religious components.

Leroy C. Hodapp is the Superintendent, Bloomington District, Indiana Conference, The Methodist Church. He is involved in several collaborative relationships with Indiana University.

[1] The phrase is used as the title of a book by an extremely creative anthropologist who incarnates the blending of poet and scientist. See Loren Eiseley, *The Immense Journey*. New York: Random House, 1957. The image is also appropriate for contemporary theology. The introduction to the published volume of papers from the World Council of Churches' study on "The Missionary Structure of the Congregation," includes the following statement: "It may also be helpful for an understanding of the documents of this volume and the study as a whole, to point out that while they do not represent a particular type of theology, they reflect a common concern for a certain stance of *theologizing*. This stance is perhaps best captured by the image of the pilgrim or the wandering people of God." Thomas Wieser (ed.), *Planning for Mission*. New York: U. S. Conference for the World Council of Churches, 1966, p. 13.

For purposes of discussion, we might consider this journey analogous to an African safari or an early American wagon train into the West. The theologian on such a safari, in traditional thought, is concerned with its purpose and goal. He asks questions about the original initiative in organizing the group, the current motivation of the travelers, and the distant end toward which they are moving. When his interest moves from the dim haze of the horizon to the immediate problems of the journeying community, it centers on the relationships among the travelers, especially as they reflect an understanding of the larger meaning of the caravan. The theologian is guided in such endeavors by a faith commitment, involving an understanding of One who sustains and ultimately governs the affairs of the entire journey—a transcendent power working within the obvious human processes. The more defined this faith becomes, however, the more it apparently conflicts with the legitimate contributions of other people in the pilgrim community, especially the scientist.

The scientist, in traditional thought, has a primary concern for immediate problems. He desires to choose the best path through the underbrush just ahead. On the basis of past experience, both mistakes and successes, he attempts to plot a route that avoids impassable rivers, uncrossable deserts, and dangerous quicksand. Therefore, he is constantly engaged in a process of self-correction and evaluation of data. The scientist also has a contribution to make regarding the relationships among the travelers, again based on experiment and observation rather than a religious faith commitment. Ultimately, the scientist hopes to plot charts and maps that will provide a comprehensive understanding of the journey, and also to create models for improved human relationships along the way; but for the moment he is still seeking more immediate and partial knowledge.

There are at least two serious difficulties in this traditional form of analogy. It is obviously an overdrawn and oversimplified caricature. First, the journey it envisions is far too circumscribed and easily defined. The American West or the African continent have limits. The immense journey of which we are writing is gloriously open-ended. Anthropologist Eiseley helps our imagination to understand this by describing his expedition down into a narrow slit of sandstone and clay. As he descended through the layers the centuries had formed, one on top of another, he suddenly came upon a skull embedded in the solid sandstone.

It was not, of course, human. I was deep, deep below the time of man in a remote age near the beginning of the reign of mammals. I squatted on my heels in the narrow ravine, and we stared a little blankly at each other, the skull and I. There were marks of generalized primitiveness in that low, pinched brain case and grinning jaw that marked it as lying far back along those converging roads where, as I shall have occasion to establish elsewhere, cat and man and weasel must leap into a single shape.

It was the face of a creature who had spent his days following his nose, who was led by instinct rather than memory, and whose power of choice was very small. Though he was not a man, nor a direct human ancestor, there was yet about him, even in the bone, some trace of that low, snuffling world out of which our forebears had so recently emerged. The skull lay tilted in such a manner that it stared, sightless, up at me as though I, too, were already caught a few feet above him in the strata and, in my turn, were staring upward at that strip of sky which the ages were carrying farther away from me beneath the tumbling debris of falling mountains. The creature had never lived to see a man, and I, what was it I was never going to see?[2]

A second limited aspect of the analogy is its tendency to polarize the scientist and the theologian, when actually they share common concerns and purposes. It is probable that the scientist concentrates his professional interest on charting and mapping, while the theologian has a vocational concern for the direction of the journey; but both, as human beings, are journeyers together and are therefore interrelated.

Hans Schmidt offers an interpretation of one current predicament on our journey:

We find ourselves caught in a dangerous discrepancy between human abilities directed toward means and instruments and human will directed toward goals. We live in a "time of perfect means and confused motives" (Einstein). "Thus far, humanity has survived because it did not have the knowledge to realize its goals, however unwise they may have been. Now, as we are in the process of acquiring this knowledge, we need more wisdom than ever, in view of the goal of life. But where, in our confused age, can we find such wisdom?" (B. Russell).[3]

It will not do, in such a time, to suggest that the scientist has done his work and now the theologian must function. The problems we face are human problems. What is needed, under such circum-

---

[2] Eiseley, *op. cit.*, pp. 4–5.

[3] Wieser (ed.), *op. cit.*, p. 105.

stances, is more exposure to one another by open-minded scientists and theologians. Those from each discipline who reject any absoluteness in methodology, and also recognize the fallacy of narrow assumptions about the nature of reality, must begin to meet and explore mutual concerns about their common journey. Such an exchange, if it really happens, will make scientists better scientists and theologians better theologians.

It cannot be emphasized strongly enough, however, that such an exchange will demand much of the participants. Because of reasons that will be stated later, it will be especially demanding on those representing theology. The spirit advocated by Alexander Vidler in his introduction to *Soundings*, a publication containing essays by British scholars on new directions in the church, will have to prevail.

> It is a time for ploughing, not reaping . . . it is a time for making soundings, not charts or maps. If this be so, we do not have to apologize for our inability to do what we hope will be possible in a future generation. We can best serve the cause of truth and of the Church by candidly confessing where our perplexities lie, and not by making claims which, so far as we can see, theologians are not at present in a position to justify.[4]

Neither science nor theology has charts and maps at the present point of progress. Within the last thirty or forty years, our journey has taken us into new and uncharted territory. We are in the midst of what Kenneth Boulding defines as "the second great transition in the history of mankind,"[5] moving from civilized to post-civilized society. In such a day, everyone is seeking new data.

This book includes some of the research of social science, primarily concerning the attempt to understand the change that is taking place in the small community in America. Thus, Fox offers insight into the small community in its larger economic setting—the functional trade area within a one-hour commuting distance. Gallaher suggests understanding of the two opposite social systems operating in the small community—the "insideness" and "outsideness" types of behavior. Lowry and Mitchell outline a method of determining and understanding community power structures. Swanson

---

[4] A. R. Vidler (ed.), *Soundings*. New York: Cambridge University Press, 1964, p. ix.

[5] Kenneth Boulding, *The Meaning of the 20th Century*. New York: Harper and Row, 1964, p. 1.

delineates a political evaluation of factors that encourage change in the small community. Barker investigates the significance of behavior settings in the small community. Each of these research findings is important. Each assists in identifying dangerous deposits of quicksand along the human path, or points to a safer route. But they are not yet located on a comprehensive map.

Philip M. Hauser, Professor of Sociology at the University of Chicago, makes this point quite clear in an address delivered to the Public Affairs Committee in March 1966.

> Since the social sciences are still relatively young, we have not begun to get a proliferation of social engineers to translate the findings of science into action, comparable to what has happened on the engineering front in relation to the physical sciences and to the biological sciences. Of course, we don't call them engineers in the biological sciences—we call them physicians, or surgeons, or doctors.
>
> Social engineering professions are still emergent. We have some. What else is the social worker? What else is the educationist? What else is the public management expert? The businessman is increasingly a graduate of the School of Business and is becoming a form of social engineer, utilizing the findings of science to conduct his business.
>
> The social sciences are still emergent and are still meeting tremendous resistance. This is partly because every man is a member of society, every man has attitudes, values, and behaviorisms which the social sciences are trying to understand.[6]

As the maps and charts gradually come into being, they must represent the totality of human experience and wisdom, not just one particular approach to life. Mathematician J. Bronowski expresses this concern, on behalf of science, when he writes:

> A civilization cannot hold its activities apart, or put on science like a suit of clothes—a workday suit which is not good enough for Sundays. . . . A civilization is bound up with one way of experiencing life. And ours can no more keep its concepts than its wars apart in pigeonholes.[7]

The same concern is voiced, on behalf of theology, by Nathan A. Scott, Jr., Professor of Theology at the Divinity School of the University of Chicago, in an article on "Faith and Art in a World Awry."

---

[6] Philip M. Hauser, "On the Gap Between Public Policy and Action and the Social Sciences," *Information Service*, National Council of Churches, New York, 1966, Vol. XLV, No. 15, p. 2.

[7] Reprinted with permission of Julian Messner, Division of Simon & Schuster, Inc., from *Science and Human Values* by J. Bronowski, Copyright © 1956, by J. Bronowski.

It would seem to behoove the Christian in his intellectual existence not to segregate himself from anyone and not to suppose that he has been given exclusive charge of the truth about any segment of human reality. In other words, he had better not come prancing into the forums of our cultural life with a Christian system of aesthetics or with a Christian system of psychology or with a Christian system of anything else. For the world is one, the same for the Christian as for all other men of whatever persuasion: if Christ is truly the *Logos*, then He is witnessed to in all apprehensions of truth, whether they occur within a framework of Christian concern or not. And, this being the case, the Christian theologian will not be in a hurry to sponsor any particular system as necessarily *the* Christian way of ordering the data in a given field of inquiry.[8]

This emphasis upon the unity of human knowledge has a broad geographical base in contemporary theology. German theologian Wolfhart Pannenberg, Professor at the University of Mainz, is currently emphasizing that all truth is one. "What is learned from science and philosophy, as well as world history, must be integrated with what is learned from Scripture and the Christ-event."[9] In England, David Jenkins, Fellow and Chaplain at Queen's College, Oxford, points to the same concern by suggesting that we must begin to work our way toward a post-Copernician natural theology. This he describes as

. . . an account of revealed truth which is always sensitive to origins on the one hand and practical relevance on the other, and the development of a spiritual discipline and discipleship which is clearly an experimental attempt to make sense of our modern life in the light of our theistic understanding and to make sense of our theistic understanding in the light of our modern life. In other words, there is no way forward in the doctrine of God save on the broadest of fronts and by combining a number of enterprises.[10]

Among these enterprises, Jenkins goes on to list psychology, sociology, and other social sciences. Thus, the theological basis for our proposed exchange is well established.

---

[8] Nathan A. Scott, Jr., *The Broken Center*. New Haven: Yale University Press, 1966, p. 200.

[9] John B. Cobb, Jr., "A New Trio Arises in Europe," *New Theology No. 2*, Martin E. Marty and Dean G. Peerman (eds.). New York: The Macmillan Company, 1966, p. 263.

[10] David Jenkins, "Whither the Doctrine of God Now?," in *ibid.*, p. 71.

Another word of advice about serious exchange between science and theology needs to be heard. It comes from Dean Walter G. Muelder of the Boston University School of Theology.

> The unity of selfhood, the unity of God and the unity of truth support the idea of an ultimate unity between faith as response to disclosure and knowledge as verified discovery. Yet no easy schemes of continuity should blur the autonomy, the different methods, the contrasting modes of verification and the distinct functions, of science and theology.[11]

The scientist and the theologian both have a contribution to make to our immense journey. It is equally unfortunate either to allow them to remain in isolation or to attempt, at the other extreme, to fuse them into a single individual, losing the distinct contribution each has to offer. The exchange we envision cannot enrich the human community unless divergent viewpoints are honestly communicated by both disciplines, then discussed with a common commitment to truth.

From the standpoint of the institutional churchman, therefore, let us now consider certain aptitudes and inaptitudes that theology brings to this proposed exchange, and then anticipate some of the values that the theologian may acquire from the scientist in such a dialogue.

One final point of clarification should be made before we continue. The theological position assumed in this chapter is based on the biblical, Judeo-Christian understanding of God and man, and any mention of theology or the theologian should be read in this context. This statement is not to propose that Christian theology is superior to Buddhist, or any other, theology, but simply to identify the faith commitment of the author.

THE CONTRIBUTION OF THEOLOGY

Let us begin by admitting one great difficulty the theologian must overcome, a propensity growing out of the tradition of his discipline. This is the inclination toward ideological thinking and closed-mindedness in the face of new and fresh data. Probably it is simply a human fault, but the emphasis on divine revelation compounds the handicap in the theologically oriented mind.

---

[11] Walter G. Muelder, "Theology and Social Science," *Christian Social Ethics in a Changing World,* John C. Bennett (ed.). New York: Association Press, 1966, p. 346.

Thus, the theologian on the safari of life may be inclined to be so enraptured by his comprehensive vision of the ultimate goal that either he is not interested in the scientific concern for the next best step, or he is actually antagonized by the possibility that his vision must be adjusted and adapted to conform to certain scientifically established facts. Any open and honest exchange must obviously admit the possibility of compromise and growth by all who participate. The theologian, depending on how much detail he ascribes to revelation, discovers himself at times unable to submit his views to arbitration.

If the content of his revealed truth merely points in a general direction, he is more free to meet the scientist than if his revelation encompasses such details as the next path or the next step. For instance, if theology insists on bringing a dogmatic understanding of the Virgin Birth to an exchange with biology, the meeting—to say the least—is burdened with obstacles. Or if theology brings an orthodox and traditional doctrine of original sin to an exchange with psychology, and there is no willingness to compromise, similar obstacles appear.

The same difficulties arise when theology approaches anthropology or geology with a literal understanding of the Genesis creation myths; when theology meets sociology with a dogmatic Pauline interpretation of marriage; or when theology meets political science with an insistence that the New Testament attitude toward the state is a divinely ordained pattern for all societies.

Fortunately, most contemporary theology does not take such a dogmatic approach. Today's theologian conceives the revealed aspect of truth in general and broad terms. But nonetheless, the very fact that revelation is inherent to the discipline of theology establishes a certain inaptitude for the theologian when he enters into dialogue with the scientist. This can never be forgotten, nor can we dismiss it as an insignificant factor in the exchange.

On the other hand, the qualified theologian brings certain other aptitudes to the meeting, which should more than compensate for the presence of revealed truth in his discipline. At least four such aptitudes are evident in contemporary theological thought.

1. *Theology brings to an exchange with science a high and responsible regard for the earth and for all natural phenomena.* Of all the great world religions, the Christian faith is the most earthy. The

biblical doctrines of Creation and the Incarnation both assume a positive understanding of the physical order.

Harvey Cox points to the biblical doctrine of creation as one of the most significant contributing factors in the development of modern science.

> The Genesis account of Creation is really a form of "atheistic propaganda." It is designed to teach the Hebrews that the magical vision, by which nature is seen as a semi-divine force, has no basis in fact. Yahweh, the Creator, whose being is centered outside the natural process, who calls it into existence and names its parts, allows man to perceive nature itself in a matter-of-fact way. . . . For the Bible, neither man nor God is defined by his relationship to nature. This not only frees both of them for history, it also makes nature itself available for man's use.
>
> Max Weber has called this freeing of nature from its religious overtones "disenchantment." The word is intended to connote not disillusionment but matter-of-factness. Man becomes in effect a subject facing nature. He can still enjoy it and delight in it, perhaps even more so since its terrors have been reduced for him. But man is not a mere expression of nature, and nature is not a divine entity.
>
> This disenchantment of the natural world provides an absolute precondition for the development of natural science. . . . No real scientific breakthrough is possible until man can face the natural world unafraid.[12]

Equally significant is the Christian doctrine of the Incarnation—the faith that God was in Christ. Here, Paul M. Van Buren speaks for the fundamental attitude of the theological community when he writes:

> The traditional doctrine of the Incarnation says that God entered the realm of history in the person of Jesus Christ. This is a statement of faith; it will no longer function as an empirical proposition, if indeed it could ever have been said to have done so. The doctrine is frequently cited as the "reason" for taking a positive attitude toward material things, or history, or people. Because, as he says, the Christian believes in the Incarnation, he is therefore impelled to take this world, men, and history seriously. Precisely. His attitude verifies, and therefore gives the meaning of, his faith. The doctrine of the incarnation of the Logos in the realm of human activity points toward history. It expresses the believer's deep concern with history, the world of men, and the world which man investigates; it indicates that his attitude toward men and their activities is related to his attitude toward a particular piece of history. The Christian's perspective is not determined by an idea or an ideal; not by an

---

12 Harvey Cox, *The Secular City*. New York: The Macmillan Company, 1965, pp. 23–24.

ideology or a theory; but by the "fact" that a piece of human history has become a situation of disclosure for him.[13]

The Christian theologian, then, brings to an exchange with science a faith that permits him to appropriate the scientific method and the highest concerns of science. The theologian, despite certain heretical traditions in the church which have attempted to divert his attention to other-worldly interests, shares the scientist's regard for the "things of earth." Though he may speculate about what lies "beyond the horizon" on man's immense journey, the true theologian refuses to allow such speculation to divest him of concern for temporal matters.

In fact, as the Apostle Paul admonished the Galatian church, the Christian faith not only demands concern for the earth, but it requires *responsible* concern. ". . . we were slaves to the elemental spirits of the universe. But when the time had fully come, God sent forth his Son, born of woman, born under the law, to redeem those who were under the law, so that we might receive adoption as sons. . . . So through God you are no longer a slave but a son, and if a son then an heir."[14] Commenting on this passage, Bishop J. E. Lesslie Newbigin writes:

> The adult status which, according to Paul, is offered to men in Christ is on the one hand a deliverance from bondage to elemental powers. On the other hand it is an invitation to responsible sonship of the Father in whose hands all created things, all so-called powers and forces, and all history lie. It is therefore an invitation to deal boldly and confidently with the created world and all its powers. It is a deliverance from pagan fear of the mysterious powers of the cosmos. It is a desacralizing of the natural world which sets man free to investigate, and to experiment and to control. There are no more gods, demi-gods or demons presiding over the various aspects of the natural world. All belongs to God, serves his will, is plastic in his hands. And man is invited, if he will, to become God's son and heir and to have the freedom of the whole estate subject only to his obedience to the Father.[15]

Bishop Newbigin's concluding phrase needs to be heard as our

---

[13] Paul M. Van Buren, *The Secular Meaning of the Gospel*. New York: The Macmillan Company, 1963, p. 160.

[14] Galatians 4:3–7.

[15] From *Honest Religion for Secular Man*, by Lesslie Newbigin. Published in the U.S.A. by The Westminster Press, 1966. © SCM Press Limited, 1966. Used by permission.

immense journey leads us into phases of technical progress where it becomes increasingly dangerous for any members of the human community to pronounce ultimate claims of authority. The discoveries of science, physical and social, can be used for both divine and demonic purposes. Perhaps this is the point where theologians and scientists should seek an exchange with leaders of the political establishments of the world, in whose hands rest primary decisions about the use to which the "things of earth" shall be directed. Not only such sophisticated "things" as computers and nuclear energy, but also such common "things" as grain and pure water, must be used in "obedience to the Father," or they may become the means by which some lesser god attempts to dominate and enslave the pilgrim community of man.

2. *Theology brings to an exchange with science a sincere desire to discover the meaning of human existence.* Whatever else we may conclude about the current radical "death-of-God" theology, surely we must admit that it is a revolutionary seeking after meaning. It is a questioning by theology of the most basic assumption on which the life of the discipline is founded. However appalled many church men have been with this rigorous inquiry, it has been received with openness and seriousness by the academic theological community. Thus, although the present "God is dead" emphasis may pass, the spirit that has motivated this new school of theologians will increasingly make possible an open exchange between theology and many other spheres.

Professor Langdon Gilkey of the University of Chicago Divinity School has isolated five major emphases of the new radical theology:

> (1) the problematic character of God and of man's relation to him today, (2) the acceptance of the secular world as normative intellectually and ethically good, (3) the restriction of theological statements to what one can actually affirm oneself, and with this the rejection of certain traditional ideas of tradition and authority, (4) the centrality of Jesus as one who calls us into the world to serve him there, (5) uneasiness with mythological, super-historical, eschatological, supernatural entities or categories.[16]

Each of these emphases establishes new possibilities of dialogue

---

[16] From *Radical Theology and the Death of God*, copyright © 1966, by Thomas J. J. Altizer and William Hamilton, reprinted by permission of the publishers, The Bobbs-Merrill Company, Inc., p. 46.

with the "secular" academic disciplines. The major thread running through all of them is disillusionment with a dogmatic or absolutist theological stance. In our vast human journey, the theologian has arrived at the point where he believes that answers to problems of the everyday progress of the community of man must come from within that community. William Hamilton states this conviction clearly:

> Religion is to be defined as the assumption in theology, preaching, apologetics, evangelism, counselling, that man needs God, and that there are certain things that God alone can do for him. I am denying that religion is necessary and saying that the movement from the church to the world that we have taken as definitive of Protestantism not only permits but requires this denial. To assert that we are men moving from cloister to world, church to world, to say that we are secular men, is to say that we do not ask God to do for us what the world is qualified to do. Really to travel along this road means that we trust the world, not God, to be our need fulfiller and problem solver, and God, if he is to be for us at all, must come in some other role.[17]

Most contemporary theologians would identify this "other role" in terms similar, if not identical, to Paul Tillich's "ultimate Ground of Being." God is the transcendent within the secular, known in the "depth" of human relationship. His existence denies the validity or the authenticity of any other lesser gods. Such a theological understanding not only invites dialogue within the human community, it actually makes such exchange an opportunity for the experience of the divine presence.

If the spirit of the new radical theology prevails, the theologian will do more listening than talking in any exchange with science. "Before contemporary theology can become itself, it must first exist in silence."[18] The concept of the church as a "presence" in the world listening before attempting to speak, which is prevalent in campus and inner-city ministry today, provides an excellent model for the theologian in dialogue with other academic disciplines. Certainly he must "listen" long enough to appropriate the vocabulary and concepts of those with whom he wishes to converse. Can this ultimately mean anything less than certain theologically equipped young men also seeking Ph.D. training in various scientific fields? In

---

[17] *Ibid.*, p. 40.
[18] *Ibid.*, p. 15.

this manner, theology can demonstrate its serious intent and concern for the exchange with science.

3. *Theology brings to an exchange with science a sincere desire to serve the human community.* Again in the words of Hamilton, "Even when he [the theologian] knows so little about what to believe—he does know where to be. Today, for example, he is with the Negro community in its struggle, . . . working and watching, not yet evangelizing. He is also with all sorts of other groups: poets and critics, psychiatrists and physicists and philosophers."[19]

Biblically, the image of Jesus as the "suffering servant" of his people provides the model for this concern. Theologically, the exposition of this image in the life and writings of the German martyr-theologian Dietrich Bonhoeffer witnesses to the contemporary significance of the Christian as the "man for others." Writing in 1944 to a friend, from his cell in a Nazi prison, Bonhoeffer scribbled words which ever since have excited the imaginations of theologians the world over.

> Man is challenged to participate in the sufferings of God at the hands of a godless world. He must therefore plunge himself into the life of a godless world, without attempting to gloss over its ungodliness with a veneer of religion or trying to transfigure it. He must live a "Worldly" life and so participate in the suffering of God. He *may* live a worldly life as one emancipated from all false religions and obligations. To be a Christian does not mean to be religious in a particular way, to cultivate some particular form of asceticism (as a sinner, a penitent or a saint), but to be a man. It is not some religious act which makes a Christian what he is, but participation in the suffering of God in the life of the world. This is *metanoia*. It is not in the first instance bothering about one's own needs, problems, sins, and fears, but allowing oneself to be caught up in the way of Christ, into the Messianic event, and thus fulfilling Isaiah 53.[20]

A second passage from Bonhoeffer is contained in an outline for a book, also envisioned during his imprisonment, which because of his death on a Nazi scaffold was never written. The sentences and thoughts, only notes to himself, are not complete, but the meaning is evident.

---

19 Altizer and Hamilton, *op. cit.*, p. 92.

20 Dietrich Bonhoeffer, *Letters and Papers from Prison.* New York: The Macmillan Company, 1960, pp. 122–123.

> What do we mean by God? . . . Encounter with Jesus Christ, implying a complete orientation of human being in the experience of Jesus as one whose only concern is for others. This concern of Jesus for others the experience of transcendence. . . . Faith is participation in this Being of Jesus (incarnation, cross and resurrection). Our relation to God not a religious relationship to a supreme Being, absolute in power and goodness, which is a spurious conception of transcendence, but a new life for others, through participation in the Being of God.[21]

If the theologian remains true to this biblical and theological insight, he will never be inclined to use the findings of science for selfish, manipulative, or destructive purposes, but will always insist that they serve the needs of the total community. Writing these words on the 25th anniversary of December 7, 1941 (a date that brings to mind not only Pearl Harbor but also Hiroshima and Nagasaki), the author is acutely conscious of the necessity for modern man to live "for others," rather than for nation, class, race, cult, or self. If the theologian brings only this one contribution, and it is accepted, his presence in any dialogue is justified.

4. *Theology brings to an exchange with science a faith that any specific human predicament can be transcended, and any obstacle surmounted.* This faith is grounded in the historical experience of the people of God. Two events, primarily, provide the substance of such a hope: (1) the Exodus, when God enabled his people of the Old Covenant, Israel, to transcend their bondage in Egypt, and (2) the Resurrection, when God in Christ revealed to his people of the New Covenant, the church, the power of life over death. This prior activity of God in the immense journey of human history is the basis for the observation, first voiced by Martin Luther, that Christians are merry men of God who are merry when there is nothing to be merry about.

We are not suggesting that the theologian is just a rosy-eyed optimist, who refuses to confront the evil in life. The symbol of the cross does not permit such cheerful megalomania. The theologian is rather quite conscious that the Exodus meant forty years in the wilderness for Moses and his people before they reached the promised land, and that the Resurrection was preceded by crucifixion and death for Jesus. J. C. Hoekendijk reminds us that the same rhythm of life exists today.

---

[21] *Ibid.*, pp. 164–165.

> Let us not have any illusions, the way toward the world of tomorrow leads into the desert. I believe that the Biblical story of the exodus will, in a very special way, become our story—even if the outcome is different. Disappointment and setbacks await us, but they are surrounded by a host of signs and miracles. In the drought we shall find an oasis, indeed also Mara, bitter water. And when we dare not expect anything further, suddenly we are surprised by Elim: wells and palm trees, and in the barren land, manna every day anew. Where now we only vaguely and uncertainly detect a track, there will be a path clearly shown to us. What happens along the way will not be so conspicuous. Nothing for the newspapers. Here and there a sign of shalom: reconciliation, peace, joy, freedom. A pennyworth of hope for people who have given up hope. A parcel of desert made inhabitable, a bit of life made human by that incorrigible Humanist, who is well pleased with mankind.[22]

This, then, is the undying hope which the theologian brings to an exchange. "A sign of shalom—a pennyworth of hope—a parcel of desert made inhabitable—a bit of life made human." Where else is the meaning of the immense journey? And where, at our current point of progress, is man without need of such hope—the inner-city ghetto, the economically affluent (but culturally deprived) metropolitan suburb, the diminishing small open-country town, the static and half-dead county seat community? Our pilgrim caravan must advance. We are already in the desert, with some among us longing to return to the flesh pots of Egypt. The theologian, however, constantly recalls the words of Moses: "The Lord your God is bringing you into a good land, a land of brooks of water, of fountains and springs, flowing forth in valleys and hills, a land of wheat and barley, of vines and fig trees and pomegranates, a land of olive trees and honey, a land in which you will eat bread without scarcity. . . ."[23] With that hope, theology always dares to venture and to explore.

WHAT THEOLOGY CAN LEARN

We turn now to what the theologian can learn from an exchange with the scientist. In one of the study papers prepared for the World Conference on the Church in the Modern World, sponsored by the

---

22 From *The Church Inside Out*, by J. C. Hoekendijk, translated by Isaac C. Rottenberg. The Westminster Press. Copyright © by J. C. Hoekendijk, 1967. English translation copyright © 1966, by W. L. Jenkins. Used by permission.

23 Deuteronomy 8:7–9.

World Council of Churches in Geneva during the summer of 1966, Dr. Richard Shaull, Professor of Ecumenics at Princeton Theological Seminary, writes of the fact that our human journey has taken us into a thoroughly secular landscape:

> . . . the real test of any theological and ethical perspective will be its ability to recognize fully the importance of the insights of the expert and to contribute something in the dialogue with him. . . . We live in a world in which there is no longer any image that reflects generally accepted common ideals. If we want to get anywhere in solving our problems, we must study the diverse aspects of reality with the tools provided by the various scientific disciplines.[24]

It is evident that theology can learn much from science about methods and techniques of dealing with specific human problems. But any attempt to list these learning possibilities here would literally be endless. Therefore, let us concern ourselves instead with three of the more universal values inherent in the scientific community, from which the theologian or churchman can gain wisdom.

1. *In an exchange with science, theology can learn the worth of the scientific process.* To be introduced to these values, let us listen to J. Bronowski.

> The dizzy progress of science, theoretical and practical, has depended on the existence of a fellowship of scientists which is free, uninhibited and communicative. . . . The men and women who practice the sciences make a company of scholars which has been more lasting than any modern state, yet which has changed and evolved as no Church has. What power holds them together?
>
> In an obvious sense, theirs is the power of virtue. By the worldly standards of public life, all scholars in their work are of course oddly virtuous. They do not make wild claims, they do not cheat, they do not try to persuade at any cost, they appeal neither to prejudice nor to authority, they are often frank about their ignorance, their disputes are fairly decorous, they do not confuse what is being argued with race, politics, sex or age, they listen patiently to the young and to the old who both know everything. These are the general virtues of scholarship, and they are peculiarly the virtues of science.[25]

Bronowski then discusses how these virtues are neither the product of any personal goodness in scientists nor of science as a pro-

---

[24] Richard Shaull, "Revolutionary Change in Theological Perspective," Bennett (ed.), *op. cit.*, p. 42.

[25] J. Bronowski, *op. cit.*, pp. 58–59.

fession. Rather, they are the inescapable conditions for the practice of science. "Truth is the drive at the center of science; it must have the habit of truth, not as a dogma but as a process."[26] In order for such a process to function, the values of independence, originality, and freedom to dissent must also be present within the scientific community.

> These values are so familiar to us, yawning our way through political perorations, that they seem self-evident. But they are self-evident, that is, they are logical needs, only where men are committed to explore the truth: in a scientific society. These freedoms of tolerance have never been notable in a dogmatic society, even when the dogma was Christian. . . . If these values did not exist, then the society of scientists would have to invent them to make the practice of science possible. In societies where these values did not exist, science has had to create them.[27]

The values Bronowski describes are not unique to the scientific community. We have already spoken of how the theologian brings a similar commitment for the discovery of truth, which obviously demands the same processes. But too often the theologian, in his isolation, assumes that he is alone in this concern. As he recognizes his common commitment with science, a firm basis for exchange will be established. The theologian must at all times remember, however, that when truth has been based on revelation, the past history of the church has not always demonstrated tolerance. Therefore, the scientist is rightly suspicious of theological openness. This is not to say that dogmatic scientists have not existed, and do not exist today, but only that in the exchange that we envision, dogmatic attitudes—scientific or theological—must be absent. Such an exchange is in itself a scientific process, and as such must be "free, uninhibited, and communicative."

2. *In an exchange with science, theology can learn the ability to exist in an atmosphere of intellectual pluralism.* Pluralism is not an end in itself, but it is the only valid stance in a learning process. We can hope that, eventually, intellectual pluralism will by mutual consent be transcended as men approach a common understanding of meaning and significance.

Currently, however, the contemporary scientist realizes that the

---

[26] *Ibid.*, p. 60.
[27] *Ibid.*, pp. 62–63.

human community has no complete understanding of ultimate reality. We are simply creating models and then testing them to see whether or not they prove to be realistic. In our original analogy, we are making maps and charts in uncharted territory, and no one has yet discovered whether these tentative maps correctly describe the actual terrain we are traveling. Under such conditions. one man's map or model may be just as accurate as that of his colleague.

An example from the past will illustrate the point. Anyone who has seen maps of the North American continent made by the early explorers recognizes how distorted were many of their geographical understandings of the land into which they were moving. The distance between Maine and New York City quite often appears on these maps as far greater than that between New York and the Mississippi River. Almost invariably, north-south distances were overestimated and east-west distances were underestimated, primarily because the former had been traveled and the latter were still in the imaginative stage. Also, early methods and implements of measurement were primitive and not totally accurate.

If they had possessed either the technical skill and equipment, or a modern spacecraft from which to gain an adequate perspective on the whole area, our fathers would have moved on their journey westward with much more precision. In actuality, they groped and at times wandered aimlessly, often learning through bitter experience, until gradually the landscape became clear and precise.

Today, although physical science has provided us with some very sophisticated maps and charts of our earth, and is presently turning toward a similar charting of the universe, the social sciences are still in their infancy. We have just landed on many new shores of understanding. The charts and maps are just now being made or projected, and the details are still to be determined.

In such a setting, the scientist must operate without absolutes or preconceived dogma. Anyone who discovers a basis for creating a new model must be given an open hearing, and his model must be tested against the best actual experience available. Thus, the explorers in the forefront of man's immense journey are pragmatic and empirically oriented people. At any given moment, two or three maps may appear to possess equal merit, even though they differ in some specific details. Thus, the research scientist learns of necessity how to live within an intellectual pluralism, sometimes granting opposing theories equal value, at least until enough data can be unearthed to prove one better than the other.

This is not the traditional *modus operandi* of theology. Therefore, it becomes difficult for the idealistic theologian to engage in dialogue with the research scientist. Fortunately, theology is beginning to face this dilemma honestly. Pointing to the biblical admonition of Jesus that truth is to be *done*, rather than talked about, Harvey Cox concludes:

> Authentic secularity demands that no world-view, no tradition, no ideology be allowed to become *the* officially enforced world-view beside which no others are tolerated. This in turn requires pluralistic social and political institutions.
>
> We should not be dismayed by the fact that fewer and fewer people are pressing what we have normally called "religious" questions. The fact that urban-secular man is incurably and irreversibly pragmatic, that he is less and less concerned with religious questions, is in no sense a disaster. It means that he is shedding the lifeless cuticles of the mythical and ontological periods and stepping into the functional age. He is leaving behind the styles of the tribe and the town and is becoming a technopolitan man. As such he may now be in a position to hear certain notes in the Biblical message that he missed before. He may be ready, in some respects, to "do the truth" in a way his superstitious and religious forerunners were not.[28]

As the exchange between science and theology is enlarged, we will discover how adequately theologians can adapt to this new secular setting. Perhaps, however subtly, they may insist on seeking to take a few "scalps for the Lord," thus transforming the proposed exchange into a conspiracy.

3. *In an exchange with science, theology can learn a commitment to partial wisdom.* In his concern with metaphysical systems, the theologian has traditionally assumed that all wisdom, to be of value, must immediately fit into some larger picture. Here again, Cox questions our traditional theological stance.

> That the pragmatist works at his problems one at a time testifies to his belief in the order of things. Conversely, it is a mark of unbelief in the ontologist that he must always scurry about to relate every snippet to the whole fabric. One suspects that he fears the universe will fall into pieces unless his conceptualization constantly fixes everything in place.[29]

---

[28] Cox, *op. cit.*, pp. 69–70.

[29] *Ibid.*, p. 66.

Cox then cites an article by Harry O. Morton, which suggests that operating in this fashion is really to believe Paul's word to the Colossians, that it is God in Christ who holds the world together, so that the cohesion of the universe is not in any sense of the word dependent upon us.

> . . . the fact that we approach life today without feeling the need for a big key that fits everything together as one great whole, and are able to concentrate instead on isolating particular issues and dealing with them as they come up, shows that we have a basic confidence that the world is held together, is strong, is self-consistent, has regularity in it and can be put to the test without everything in life going to pieces.[30]

Thus, by unifying truth around a particular human problem rather than some metaphysical system, we are much more likely to *do* the truth, not simply to think about it.

Here again, we are in the process of gaining some theological clarity, which will permit an open exchange with science. But merely to state this faith theologically is not to *do* it. It remains to be demonstrated that a theologian can hear and appreciate the data of a research scientist who has spent his whole creative lifetime patiently and meticulously isolating a few new facts to contribute to the pool of human knowledge. This data may appear to be unrelated to the vastness of the human journey and, in fact, it may eventually prove worthless. But on the other hand, it may be the key to the whole map.

The process is somewhat like the scout, on our mythical journey, who discovers a few animal tracks in an apparently isolated canyon. His colleagues may admonish him that there is not time to track stray animals, for everyone's energy must be directed toward finding a route over the mountain range ahead. The scout, however, by pursuing his investigation, finds that the animals tracks lead to the very mountain pass for which the whole group has been searching. Of course, they might have led up a blind canyon, but the research scientist accepts such a risk. He is willing to give his life in devotion to a few minor facts, trusting that some day they may fit into the total map of human progress.

There is a dedication here that should speak to any theologian, if he has eyes to see and ears to hear. If nothing else, the lesson in per-

---

[30] Quoted by Cox, *ibid.*, p. 66.

sonal humility is worth any time invested in the exchange with science.

THE LIFE OF THE JOURNEYERS

We have considered the possibility that better maps may be created by an exchange between the scientist and the theologian. Maps and charts are not our only concern, however, nor even the primary one. Because man's viewpoint will always be the relativity of our human situation, our maps will never be perfect. They will constantly be in a stage of revision and refinement. But maps and charts are *things*. They are important only as they improve the condition of *people*. The most significant component of any journey is the journeyer.

The scientist and the theologian need each other, not alone to create better charts, but simply to live together as human beings. In the words of the popular song, "People who need people are the luckiest people in the world." The scientist who is in dialogue with the theologian is a better scientist, because he is a more whole human being. And the theologian who is in dialogue with the scientist is a better theologian for the same reason. Our immense journey has no foreseeable end. It derives significance, therefore, from what happens to the lives of the journeyers along the way.

In the May 1965 issue of *Fortune*, Vannevar Bush, honorary board chairman of the Massachusetts Institute of Technology and formerly Dean of its School of Engineering, published an article on the relationship between science and theology. For the sake of any who may still have reservations about our proposed exchange, Mr. Bush's concluding paragraphs offer a word of hope.

> [Philosophy] can return to its mission in its day of glory. It can dream and it can guide the dreams of men. To do so it will need to present its visions humbly, and in the concepts of the universe that science offers. There are a few who labor to do just this. Their task is difficult, for the universe that science presents as probable is continuously altering, and depends for its grasp upon mathematics that requires deep study for many years. Nevertheless, the opportunity is there to present widesweeping thought that will sway the minds of men.
>
> And the theologian. He can accept the aid of science, which draws for him a wide universe in all its majesty, with life in all its awe-inspiring complexity. He can accept this knowing that on the central mysteries science cannot speak. And he can then step beyond to lead men in paths of righteousness and in paths of peace.

And the young man. As always he will build his own concepts, and his own loyalties. He will follow science where it leads, but will not attempt to follow where it cannot lead. And, with a pause, he will admit a faith.[31]

SUGGESTIONS FOR FURTHER READING

Bennett, John C. (ed.), *Christian Social Ethics in a Changing World.* New York: Association Press, 1966.

Bonhoeffer, Dietrich, *Letters and Papers from Prison.* New York: The Macmillan Company, 1960.

Bronowski, J., *Science and Human Values.* New York: Harper and Row, 1965.

Cox, Harvey, *The Secular City.* New York: The Macmillan Company, 1965.

Hoekendijk, J. C. *The Church Inside Out.* Philadelphia: The Westminster Press, 1966.

---

[31] Vannevar Bush, "Science Pauses," *Fortune,* May 1965, p. 172.

ABOUT THE FORMAT

The text of this book is set in Linotype Electra, 10 point leaded 3 points. Designed by the late artist and illustrator, W. A. Dwiggins, this is an original type face, not based on any traditional model.

Typographic design by Margery W. Smith

HIEBERT LIBRARY
3 6877 00048 4526